DATE DUE			
Mar 4 '70			
Sep 27 73			
Oct 21 '74			
GAYLORD M-2			PRINTED IN U.S.A.

THE FRENCH RACE:

THEORIES OF ITS ORIGINS AND THEIR SOCIAL AND POLITICAL IMPLICATIONS

PRIOR TO THE REVOLUTION

THE FRENCH RACE:

THEORIES OF ITS ORIGINS
AND THEIR
SOCIAL AND POLITICAL IMPLICATIONS

PRIOR TO THE REVOLUTION

BY

JACQUES BARZUN

KENNIKAT PRESS, INC./PORT WASHINGTON, N. Y.

THE FRENCH RACE

TO
ANNA MARY SWOPE
TRUE TEACHER
AND
PERFECT FRIEND

FOREWORD

An essay upon a phase of Montesquieu's work, written for the seminar of Professor Carlton J. H. Hayes in 1927-28, led the writer to examine in detail the political and social ideas historically connected with the racial and national origins of France. In the eighteenth century, the outstanding writers who dealt with this topic were the Comte Henri de Boulainvilliers and the Abbés Dubos and Mably; but as their works appeared harvests of theories rather than first shoots, the field of inquiry was extended to include previous writings by the most significant authors who had touched upon race-conflict and its socio-political ramifications in France to the Revolution. The result of these researches is embodied in the following pages.

To be sure, the brilliant erudition of Augustin Thierry (1795-1856) was from the start at the writer's disposal and indicated the general lines to be followed. It is likely that if Thierry had filled out the brief outline of his *Considérations sur l'Histoire de France* (1840), the present neglected subject would long ago have been exhaustively treated by scholars. As it is, many of the source-ideas gathered here are nowhere available in English, and their coordination into a critical and chronological narrative has not, it is believed, been attempted in any language. Necessarily, many minor publicists and historians had to be omitted from this survey to avoid meaningless repetition of theories; it is nevertheless thought that no major race-doctrine or historical " system " evolved in France during the specified period has been overlooked. A brief postscript has been added to show the persistence of the Nordic-Latin struggle in modern France.

Needless to say, such an attempt at tracing the history of many subtle and changing ideas in their interrelations could not have been brought to something like completion had not the bulk of the introductory material (chs. I and II) been found available in secondary sources from the pens of recognized authorities; and had not the author taken advantage of the help and advice generously extended to him in the course of his work. Professor Hayes was kind enough to read the several drafts of the essay and offered notable improvements in organization. Professors Lynn Thorndike, Austin P. Evans and David S. Muzzey, as well as Dr. C. W. Cole likewise contributed exceedingly valuable suggestions. The Bar Association Library in the person of Mr. A. S. McDaniel extended with every courtesy the use of its resources, as did M. Cadet de Gassicourt of the *Bibliothèque Nationale* and the Librarians of Princeton and Columbia Universities.

J. B.

Columbia University,
May 1, 1932.

TABLE OF CONTENTS

INTRODUCTION

IF the phenomenon of nationalism is the most significant factor in contemporary public life,[1] it is equally true that one of the most deeply rooted and persistent convictions upon which nationalism rests is the belief in race. The notion that there exists in the world a number of races, ancient, distinct and variously gifted, is, in Europe, at least as old as Herodotus;[2] and the fact that modern scientists have come to doubt the very meaning and validity of the concept, race,[3] has had but little influence upon the active and even the reflective part of mankind. The feelings which accompany national loyalty find it still convenient to attach themselves to the " facts " of *racial homogeneity, racial purity, racial ability,* and in any event *racial superiority.*

In that nationalistic sense, " race " means any group which the speaker chooses to adorn by joining it. The Negro is a unit in a separate race, as well as the " Aryan ", the " Nordic ", the " Teuton ", the " Anglo-Saxon " or the " Italian ". Not only publicists but also scientific men, in their search for more stable criteria have found " races " and " sub-races " in plentiful numbers,[4] without coming

---

[1] Hayes, C. J. H., *Essays on Nationalism*, New York, 1926, p. 8.

[2] *History*, Everyman Edition, bk. i, p. 1; bk. ii, p. 110.

[3] Boas, F., *Anthropology and Modern Life*, New York, 1928, pp. 20, 23-4, 35. " The inference that various populations are composed of individuals belonging to various races is ... objectively unproved," p. 35.

[4] *Cf.* Ripley, W. Z., *The Races of Europe*, London, 1899, p. 597 *et seq.*

to any agreement except that racial divisions cut across national boundaries.[5] It may be for that reason that the most current racial division today, the most widely accepted, by intellectuals and masses alike, is that which finds in Europe three distinct races, the Teutonic (Nordic, Germanic), the Alpine (Celtic), and the Mediterranean (Iberian, Southern or Latin). And of these distinctions, that between the second and third is often slurred, to contrast the two halves of Europe as Nordic and Latin. It is with some aspects of this venerable and continuing distinction that the present essay has to do.

It is commonly supposed that the Nordic idea is a product of scientific research in philology and anthropology carried on chiefly by nations with " Teutonic " origins. Impartial investigation reveals, however, that the Nordic idea existed in more than embryonic form in Rome of the second century A. D. Further research shows that the opposition of Nordic to Latin (Gaul or Roman) has run through French history from the sixteenth century onwards. Lastly, an examination of influential writers leads to the noteworthy paradox that the various concepts of Nordic superiority have in every case been originated in " Latin " countries by " Latin " writers.

In the present essay, which deals ultimately with the progress of the Nordic race idea in France to the time of the Revolution, the foregoing assertions will be demonstrated. Meantime it may be profitable to locate this historic idea in the present-day world and also justify extended research into its beginnings.

Various reasons make the history of the Nordic idea of general importance. Foremost is the undeniable fact that

[5] Hayes, *op. cit.*, p. 8; *cf.* Deniker's racial map of Europe showing five races in Italy, four in Norway, etc., in Ripley, *The Races of Europe*, Appendix D, p. 599.

some of the nations which believe themselves most assuredly Nordic, including naturally the "Anglo-Saxon" group, have played in the nineteenth century and are still playing an important role in the world's destinies. As a result, ardent nationalism and self-importance have made these nations increasingly aware of their early German ancestors— Teutons, Angles, Saxons. They have moreover frequently ascribed to these progenitors the peculiar racial virtues that have produced those modern achievements which are worthy of national pride.

On the other hand, the fact that "Teutonic unity" suffered a severe strain in the War of Nations, has brought about a further, more intimate regrouping of the "Anglo-Saxon" nations, principally directed at the exclusion of Germany and the inclusion of the United States and the British dominions.

These may be unconscious factors in the minds of many, conscious in those of a few; but to show their presence everywhere, a few examples must be adduced. At the outset it should be noted that the feeling of race division between Latin and Saxon has passed into common speech as well as into the formal utterances of thoughtful men. It is no vulgar fallacy, and its success is largely due to its convenience. The Lord Bishop of Ripon may base upon Anglo-Saxon racial character a conservative appeal to self-reliance;[6] a philosophical poet of England may bemoan the breach made by the war between "sister" nations:

> I walked in loamy Wessex lanes, afar
> From rail-track and from highway, and I heard
> In field and farmstead many an ancient word
> Of local lineage like ' Thu bist ', ' Er war ',
> .   .   .   .

[6] *Parliamentary Debates*, July 20, 1908, 4th ser., vol. 192, pp. 1393-5.

> Then seemed a heart crying: ' Whosoever they be
> At root and bottom of this, who flung this flame
> Between kin folk kin tongued even as are we. . .'[7]

A newspaper may enlighten its readers by printing: " U. S. Urges Latins to Naval Truce ";[8] meaning France and Italy, and implying that the U. S. is the opposite of a Latin country. A scholar, to capture the imagination and fix the memory, may entitle a section of his " Atlas of American History ", " Latin or Saxon? The Hundred Years' War ",[9] referring to the Colonial conflict between France and England in the eighteenth century. The distinction in all these senses is useful. Yet it is easy to see how exaggerated and dangerous applications of the idea to the lives and policies of nations have occurred.

That in the nineteenth century England became the foremost industrial and colonizing nation in the world; that Germany achieved national unity, and by rapid industrialization began to rival her " sister " nation; that towards the last quarter of the century, the United States and the British dominions began to participate prominently in world affairs, no one will deny. But that these accomplishments coincided with intensified Nordic racial self-consciousness seems equally apparent. " Until recently ", says a careful student of English literature, " the English looked upon Chaucer as the father of their poetry. They discovered the earliest source of their literature in that fourteenth century in which, on British soil, the fusion of the Anglo-Saxons and the Franco-Normans was consummated. Today they trace their literary origins back to the seventh century. They give out that Caedmon and the unknown author of Beowulf were

[7] Thomas Hardy, " The Pity of It," April, 1915. *Collected Poems,* New York, 1926, pp. 509-10.

[8] *New York World,* Nov. 1, 1930.

[9] Fox, D. R., *Atlas of American History,* New York, 1920, pp. 134-9.

their first poets. . . . To the question ' When does English literature begin?' they answer unhesitatingly that it begins with the first verse sung, the first line written in a Germanic tongue in the country now called England." [10] The writer goes on to point out that it was during the last hundred years or so that the Anglo-Saxons in their life and literature have been regarded by the English as their literary or spiritual forefathers. And this, as a result of Germany's rise to power and the mutual recognition of kinship by the two countries.[11]

Similarly, it may have been a fresh matter of boast in the nineteenth century for an English critic to say of Shakespeare, " he uses 15,000 words, and he wrote pure English: out of every five verbs, adverbs, and nouns four are Teutonic; and he is more Teutonic in comedy than in tragedy "; [12]—but this late discovery came nearly two hundred years after the Frenchman Rivarol had written from exactly opposite motives: " The Saxons having conquered it (England) they settled there, and it is of their former jargon that the English language, called Anglo-Saxon, was formed. This tongue was forgotten by the people, . . . but finally national jealousy having been aroused, the rival language (French) which the English genius long since rebelled against, was exiled." [13] In a word, the feeling of Nordic brotherhood is a recent growth among the Nordics

[10] Legouis, Emile, *A History of English Literature*, New York, 1929, p. 3. *Cf.* also the influence of Taine's notion of " race, time, and environment," *History of English Literature*, London, 1906, 4 vols., Introd., p. 17.

[11] Legouis, *op. cit.*, p. 4. For confirmation from a different angle by an American scholar, see Emery Neff, *Carlyle and Mill*, New York, 1926, pp. 187-8, 198 *et seq.*; and by an English writer, J. Oakesmith, *Race and Nationality*, New York, 1919, p. 136.

[12] Brooke, Stopford, *English Literature*, New York, 1894, p. 97n.

[13] Rivarol, A., *De l'Universalité de la Langue française, 1783*, New York, 1919, p. 31.

themselves, though the awareness of it among the Latins is not. Indeed, it goes back, as we shall see, to Roman times.

In strictly historical writing, what has variously been called Myth *Teutonicus, furor Teutonicus,* and *Teutonismus,* was probably first embodied in the England of the nineteenth century by J. M. Kemble in his book *The Saxons in England* (1849) which obtained notable success there and in Germany.[14] Freeman in his *History of the Norman Conquest* carried the idea even further, and by finding the real sources of English political liberties in the German folkmoot, influenced such scholars as Bishop Stubbs, Maitland and the ultra-democratic John Richard Green.[15] But, again, before Kemble and Freeman, and Stubbs and Green, a French officer, Paul de Rapin-Thoyras (1661-1725), having been stranded in England after disappointment in his own country, proceeded to write a *History of England* setting forth that very theory of political liberty inherited from the Anglo-Saxons.[16] And the same idea was given wider currency in the middle of the same century by the celebrated name of Montesquieu.

Stimulated in England by the contact of English literary men [17] with the Germans who admired Shakespeare and Milton as contributors to the Teutonic heritage, the idea of kinship and superiority of the Germanic races rebounded to Germany proper where the nationalistic historians, Sybel and Treitschke, promulgated these views to an avid public indifferent to historical impartiality.[18]

[14] *Cf. Encyclopedia Americana,* ed., 1920, vol. xiv, p. 237.

[15] *Cf.* Green's *Short History of the English People,* New York, 1916, pp. 1-5.

[16] See below ch. viii.

[17] *Cf.* again Carlyle's being aroused by the book of the famous Mme. de Stael, *De l'Allemagne,* pub. in 1810, and his consequent determination to learn German, then a rare accomplishment in England. Neff, *op. cit.,* p. 198.

[18] *Encyclopedia Americana,* vol. xiv, p. 237.

But before their works, as well as before the popular English novelist, Charles Kingsley, had written his best seller *Roman and Teuton* to contrast the " young and virile Teutonic forest-children " with the " Romans of a Dying Empire ", another French writer, the disgruntled nobleman Count Arthur de Gobineau, had promulgated a theory [19] of race superiority that, among other things, " did much to strengthen the cause of Nationalism in Germany." [20]

Neglected in France, where his marked preference [21] for the German Aryans ran counter to a diametrically opposite nationalism, Gobineau was taken up by numerous groups throughout the " Anglo-Saxon world " [22] and especially in Germany, where Ludwig Schemann created for himself a hero of biography [23] and for the *Gobineau Vereinigung* a veritable cult; [24] predilections that were widely shared by the affiliated members of the *Alldeutscher Verband,* or Pan-German League.[25]

The fruit of these nineteenth-century ideas is visible in our contemporary Anglo-Saxon apologists and proselytes. Ranging from the deification of the German people by men like Houston Stewart Chamberlain [26] to the notion enter-

---

[19] *Essai sur l'Inégalité des Races Humaines,* Paris, 1854. Dedicated to the King of Hanover. See 2nd ed., Paris, 1884, 2 vols.

[20] Wertheimer, M., *The Pan-German League,* New York, 1924, p. 17.

[21] Gobineau, *op. cit.,* vol. ii, p. 343 *et seq.*

[22] *Cf.* reverberations in the works of John Fiske, Macaulay, Taine, Roosevelt, *passim.*

[23] Schemann, Ludwig, *Gobineaus Rassewerk, etc.,* 1913-16.

[24] *Cf.* Wertheimer, *op. cit.,* p. 19.

[25] *Ibid.*

[26] *Die Grundlagen des 19ten Jahrhunderts,* München, 1899. *Cf.* Trans. by John Lees, London, 1911: " the awakening of the Teutonic peoples to the consciousness of their all-important vocation and culture forms the turning-point . . . " (in the history of Europe), Introd., p. xv.

tained by such as Homer Lea [27] and Madison Grant [28] that modern history is essentially the history of the conflict between the Anglo-Saxon race and the inferior races of the world, the Nordic cult thrives in the energetics of Theodore Roosevelt,[29] the metrical sermons of Rudyard Kipling, and the numberless publications in every language which either contest or defend the Nordic myth.[30] For, a denunciation like Mr. Hilaire Belloc's based on the contrary system of the survival of Roman civilization,[31] attests no less than L. F. Clauss' *Rasse und Seele, Eine einführung in die Gegenwart,* the tenacious life of the idea.

Every important phase or revival of it, it can be shown, has followed some impulse given by a disillusioned member of the race one would think least likely to single out the Anglo-Saxon for merit. It is noticeable, however, that in almost every case the " point " was made *against* the Latin, rather than on behalf of the Nordic. At the same time, the element of major interest for the purpose of this essay should not be forgotten, namely that the controversy between Latin and Celt on the one hand and Nordic on the other has raged not alone in Europe and the world as between nations, but in France itself, as between social

---

[27] *The Valor of Ignorance* and *The Day of the Saxon* are pessimistic with regard to the Saxon who "... has given down to this neglected race a world such as mankind has never known before—an empire over which the sun and stars shine together; where night never falls nor dawn begins." *Day of the Saxon*, London, 1912, p. 4.

[28] *Cf. The Passing of the Great Race*, New York, 1916.

[29] *Cf.* the introduction to *The Winning of the West*, New York, 1904, p. 4 where the American frontiersmen are seen as continuators of the German peoples' expansion.

[30] *Cf.* A. Gehring, A. L. Guérard, H. Hauser, F. H. Hankins, F. Hertz, D. A. Hawkins, A. Casanova, B. L. P. Weale, M. Barrès, C. Spiese, J. Persijn, and such periodicals as *Det Nye Nord*, Copenhagen. (I am indebted for this last reference to Dr. J. H. Wuorinen.)

[31] *History of England*, New York, 1925, p. 3 *et seq.*

classes and political parties.[32] In order to set the stage for
this race conflict in France, the present study will treat first
of the origins of the French " race " as seen by the classic
historians Caesar and Tacitus; then of the actual mixture
of peoples that occurred in France in the first four centuries
A. D. as that mixture appears to modern scholars; thirdly,
of the political forces that ushered in and perpetuated race-
theorizing from the sixteenth century on. From that century to the Revolution many issues arose out of the problems
of origins and many others were added to the original ground
of difference, only to be supplanted by still others, equally
relevant. Within the period embraced, every generation of
historians and publicists studied early French history with
a different ulterior motive in mind. In every instance, the
rival contentions of superiority made by the pro-Nordics
and the pro-Gauls or Latins have been made the vehicle of
some other partisan question of more immediate concern.
From the Count of Boulainvilliers, championing the cause
of his noble order, to Mlle. de Lézardière, devoting her
younger years to a democratic ideal, every investigation of
the Germans and their invasions, of the Frankish monarchy,
of the Estates-General, has provided an arsenal of arguments
for the " systematic " historian. The work of Gobineau
and his followers in the nineteenth century did but reopen
a controversy deeply rooted in the national and constitutional development of France, and seemingly settled by force,
as will be shown, in the French Revolution itself.[33]

But before the specifically French theories and their side-

[32] In Spain also, the nobility has always claimed descent from the
Goths—whence the general use of the phrase "blue blood", i. e. that of
a fair-haired person, to indicate noble birth. (See Havelock Ellis, *A
Study of British Genius*, p. 242 *et seq.*). The Portuguese, however, have
not usually entertained this belief in Nordic nobility. (See H. M.
Stephens, *The Story of Portugal*, pp. 11, 40, 45.)

[33] See below Sieyès, ch. xiv, p. 248.

issues, came the source of many of the facts and much of the mischief, in an historian of scope and merit, of whom it has truly been said that he ". . . painted the Germans as Montaigne and Rousseau the savages, in a fit of ill-humor against his country." [34] That historian, Tacitus, was in effect the first writer of "Latin" race to deal with the Nordic question, as he is also the only one of the apostolic succession to deserve the racial epithet of "Latin". It is in his thirty-page essay on *Germany, its Geography, Manners, Customs, and Tribes* that we find the combined elements of history and moralization which form the fruitful germ of the Nordic idea.[35]

While we examine the *Germania* in the next chapter, it should be kept in mind that no attempt has been made to discuss, and even less to decide, the many points of interpretation, raised by our author. Indeed, the two chapters following are intended merely as a summary of facts and opinions, such as may be obtained from easily accessible secondary sources, to establish a background of information before approaching the earliest theories of race in France. As is well-known, the field here briefly surveyed teems with controversial problems well-nigh insoluble for lack of evidence, and has given rise to an abundant literature which it would be irrelevant even to indicate.

For the so-called Barbarian invasions, the views of recognized modern French scholars have for obvious reasons been selected and adhered to; and equally accessible texts have been used to gather the testimony, often to be re-cited, of Caesar, Tacitus, and Gregory of Tours.

[34] From Guizot, quoted in Oakesmith, *op. cit.*, p. 103.

[35] Tacitus' ". . . tickling of national vanity through praise of German virtues . . . has conspired to exalt it as the synoptical gospel of German politics and of German economics." Hayes, C. H., *An Introduction to the Sources relating to the Germanic Invasions*, New York, 1909, p. 48.

CHAPTER I

Tacitus—Caesar—The Barbarians

Of the scholars, philosophers and pamphleteers whom we
shall see taking part in the great continuous battle of *Frank*
versus *Gaul, German* versus *French* in the history of France,
not one fails to mention the " last great Roman historian ",[1]
Tacitus, to find in him whatever their contention requires.
A member of the high senatorial class and an opponent of
the upstart rulers and the parvenu mob of his day,[2] Cor-
nelius Tacitus finds in the Germans and their modes of life
abundant material for pointing the lesson of sobriety and
old-fashioned virtue at his Roman contemporaries. Thus,
at the very outset of what might be termed their " literary
career ", the Germans are used for propaganda purposes,
against some existing state of affairs. The ammunition that
Tacitus provides to all future controversialists is compact
but explosive. He begins by asserting that the Germans are
a native and unmixed race,[3] a fact which he deduces from
the originality of their mythology, mentioning their god
Tuisto (whence our Teuton) as the legendary father of the
race. By this purity of race, Tacitus explains the " marks
of a distinct national character " visible among its members.[4] The anthropological " sign of the Nordic " is pat-

[1] Rostovtzeff, M., *A History of the Ancient World*, New York, 1927,
vol. ii, p. 213.

[2] *Ibid.*, p. 225.

[3] *Germania*, Arthur Murphy trans., in Tacitus, *Works*, vol. ii, p. 312.
Checked with Teubner ed., *Cornelii Taciti Libri qui Supersunt . . .* ,
Leipzig, 1907, pp. 220-44.

[4] Tacitus, *op. cit.*, p. 314.

ented: " The same form and feature, stern blue eyes, ruddy hair, their bodies large and robust ", constitutes the first and to this day unchanged picture of the " blonde beast ", highest exemplification of Nature's nobleman in the eyes of the Anglo-Saxon fanatic.[5]

Moral simplicity—which was the chief teaching Tacitus intended for his Roman readers,[6]—the chivalric ideal,[7] love of freedom and a marked individualism are likewise characteristics of the Germans. Their government is both free and simple, as well as democratic. " The king of the tribes is elected by reason of his noble birth; the general is chosen for his valor." [8] But the power of the former is strictly limited, and important questions are reserved for the decision of the whole community.[9] Sixteen centuries after this brief description of the German tribal government, it seems indisputable to a great mind and many of his readers that the English parliamentary system emerged from the Schwarzwald.[10]

In contrast with the softness and luxury that he fustigated in Rome,[11] the author of the *Germania* stresses these barbarians' valor.[12] All business is carried on by men fully armed, the right to bear arms being a matter of state jurisdiction indicative of fitness and manhood. A spirit of emulation prevails in war, which is in keeping with the fierce

[5] Tacitus, *op. cit.*, p. 314.

[6] *Ibid.*, p. 315.

[7] " There is in their opinion something sacred in the female sex." Tacitus, *op. cit.*, p. 317.

[8] *Ibid.*, p. 315.

[9] *Ibid.*, p. 318.

[10] Montesquieu, *Esprit des Lois*, ed. Garnier, Paris, 1922, vol. i, p. 162. Also Gibbon, *Decline and Fall of the Roman Empire*, ed. Milman, Philadelphia, 1867, 6 vols., vol. iii, p. 611.

[11] Rostovtzeff, *op. cit.*, p. 225.

[12] Tacitus, *op. cit.*, p. 315.

individualism already observed.[13] The modern semi-detached bungalow, for example, would by no means have been tolerated by the present Anglo-Saxon's ancestor. " Every tenement stands apart with a vacant piece of ground round it." [14] No cities could flourish, as in fact even a " continuity of houses was forbidden." [15] It is, according to Tacitus, the combination of a simple life with a warlike spirit that makes for the greatness of the Germans. Simple foods, simple entertainments—including dice—and simple domestic arrangements, promote a healthy and satisfying existence concluded by simple rites in death.[16] In this connection masculine emotion is self-controlled; only the women weep. This characteristic repression does not connote coldness in social relations. Although the Roman observer is again struck by the individualism of sitting upright and alone at meals, he recognizes that the Germans can justly boast of their generosity and frankness.[17]

In this robust but humane society, justice is rendered by the priests interpreting the will of God, distinction being drawn between public and private crimes. The former " cannot be too soon buried in oblivion ". [18] The latter give the family of the injured man a right of revenge which is customarily bought off by the doer of the injury.[19] This system of insuring the peace of the community is the *wergeld* of Anglo-Saxon times in Britain and the " composition " of the Salian Franks which has caused more ink to flow than the crimes it compensated did blood.

[13] Tacitus, p. 320.
[14] *Ibid.,* p. 321.
[15] *Ibid.*
[16] *Ibid.,* p. 327.
[17] *Ibid.,* p. 325.
[18] *Ibid.,* p. 319.
[19] *Ibid.*

Nor is the brief but thorough historian silent upon the pregnant subject of the relations between Germans and Latins, and more specifically Gauls. He admits the one-time superiority of Gaul over German. He concedes also the probability of early Gallic colonies in Germany—a concession upon which rest so many of the theories we shall later examine. The Rhine, Tacitus unerringly points out, is not an obstacle but a help to intercourse, and he considers it obvious that the Helvetians and Boians (Swiss and Bohemians) were originally Gallic nations.[20] At the same time, whatever the origin of the German tribes, it must have been forgotten by the peoples themselves, for he records the strong pride in purely German nationality evinced by numerous groups, such as the Ubians.[21]

Although in the case of the Chaucians freedom seemed to Tacitus compatible with love of justice and peaceful habits,[22] " warlike spirit is the bulwark of the German tribes ". From this warlike spirit Rome herself suffered defeat, not once but repeatedly. " Not the Samnite, nor the republic of Carthage, nor Spain, nor Gaul, nor even the Parthian, has given such frequent lessons to the Roman people. The power of the Arsacidae was not so formidable as German liberty. . . . The Germans can recount their triumphs over Curbo, Cassius, Scaurus Aurelius, Servitius Caepio, and Cneius Manlius. . . ." Since then, there have been Roman victories, it is true, yet " we have triumphed and Germany is still unconquered." [23] The destiny of the Nordic seemed as manifest to the pessimistic first-century Roman as it did to a twentieth-century optimist like Roosevelt. This is not to say that Tacitus painted a picture that was out of draw-

---

[20] Tacitus, *op. cit.*, p. 329.

[21] *Ibid.*

[22] *Ibid.*, p. 333.

[23] *Ibid.*, p. 335.

ing. Scholars are agreed that he used the best materials available judiciously.[24] But the slight bias of the man with something to prove has given a foothold to every subsequent system-builder, even though the object of proof was something neither Tacitus nor his contemporary Germans could dream of.

To be kept in mind for our purpose are the facts relating to the freedom and individuality of the Germans, their method of electing a king and holding assemblies; the purity of their race and of their morals; the family loyalty they evince and its result on their criminal law; their historical relation to Gauls and Romans, and lastly the implicit and all-important assumption that what Tacitus says of the Germans generally holds true of every tribe or man of them individually.

Since the object of this study is to make clear the origins and development of the French " race " in fact and theory, the work of Tacitus has been analyzed in order to furnish at the outset the ultimate source of numerous " points " in the dogma of Nordic supremacy in France. But we obviously must equip ourselves as well from the ultimate source of information used by French historiographers regarding the " inferior " or conquered race, namely the Gauls to whom reference has been made out of the pages of Tacitus.

Less detailed and more matter-of-fact, Caesar is nonetheless the outstanding Roman authority on the Gauls. A consideration of the Fourth and Sixth Books of his " *Commentaries* " takes us back chronologically a century and a half and geographically across the Rhine into the territory extending between it, the English channel, the Pyrenees and

[24] *Cf.* J. Oakesmith, *Race and Nationality,* p. 103 *et seq.*

the Alps. Throughout this region, says Caesar, " there are two orders of those men who are of any rank and dignity: for the commonalty is held almost in the condition of slaves and dares to undertake nothing of itself and is admitted to no deliberation." [25] When in debt, or unable to pay their taxes, or oppressed by the higher nobles, the Gauls give themselves up in subjection to the former, who possess over them the " same rights, without exception, as masters over slaves ". [26] Of the upper orders, one consists of the Druids or priests, the other of Knights. The Druids are held in highest respect and besides exemption from military service decide matters of state as well as of law.[27] The Knights assume all the obligations of war, which occurs very frequently in the defense of Gaul against enemies from without or in Gallic aggression into German territories. Those Knights most distinguished by birth and wealth have the greatest number of dependents about them.[28]

A general assembly is held in the central part of Gaul and appears to be chiefly devoted to settling disputes, though decrees are issued to which all must submit—an institution thought to have been devised in Britain.[29] Thus, Caesar's description of Gaul not only contrasts sharply with Tacitus' later account of German democracy but indicates a status of persons which is held by many of the later French historians to have been a result of the Germanic invasions, four and a half centuries after Caesar's time!

Caesar himself having come in contact with the German tribes that pressed upon the inelastic right bank of the

[25] Caesar, *de Bello Gallico,* E. Brooks, trans., Philadelphia, 1895, bk. vi, ch. xiii, p. 199.

[26] *Ibid.,* p. 200.

[27] *Ibid.*

[28] *Ibid.,* ch. xv, p. 202.

[29] *Ibid.,* 201 (i.e. Celtic Britain).

Rhine, could not fail to observe the contrast we have noted, and he sets down a number of the points Tacitus made after him,[30] stressing more strongly, however, the Germans' fierce individualism and sense of tribal possession.[31]

Military ardor he sees as the Germans' great national character, and finds it enhanced by a life of hunting and fishing rather than agriculture—

lest they may be anxious to acquire extensive estates and the more powerful drive the weaker from their possessions; lest they construct their houses with too great a desire to avoid cold and heat; lest the desire for wealth spring up, from which cause divisions and discords arise; and that they may keep the common people in a contented state of mind, when each sees his own means placed on an equality with those of the most powerful.[32]

By reason of this difference between the Gauls' and the Germans' way of life, the latter are now the more powerful, though there was a time " when the Gauls excelled the Germans in prowess." [33]   At that time the Gauls called Volcae Tectosages seized the most fertile parts of Germany around the Hercynian forest (Schwarzwald) and settled there. They adopted and retained the same indigent, hardy, militaristic habits as the Germans about them, whereas the remaining Gauls have been overmatched both by luxury and by foreign assailants.[34]

The fickle character of the Gauls—possibly the source of Napoleon's later disparagement of the French—occurs also in Caesar.   The Gauls, he says,

[30] Caesar, *op. cit.,* bk. iv, chs. i, ii, and iii on their courage, nomadic life, and freedom from luxury.

[31] *Ibid.,* bk. vi, ch. 23, p. 207.

[32] *Ibid.*

[33] *Ibid.*

[34] *Ibid.,* p. 209.

are easily prompted to take up resolutions and much addicted to change. . . . They yield to mere unauthorized reports . . . often engage in resolutions concerning the most important matters, induced by these reports and stories alone; of which they must necessarily instantly repent . . . since most people give to their questions answers framed agreeably to their wishes.[35]

As a corrective to this oft-quoted paragraph, Caesar's own preliminary statement should be recalled, that the Gauls are divided among the Belgae, the Aquitanians, and the Celts. " All these differ from each other in language, customs and laws." [36] The Belgae are the bravest, he goes on to show, " because they are farthest from the civilization and refinement of (our) province, merchants resorting to them least frequently to bring things which tend to effeminate the mind; likewise because they are nearest to the Germans, who dwell beyond the Rhine and with whom they are continually waging war." [37] This warlike relation of a part of the Gauls with the Germans is of course the historical starting point of the conflict of races underlying some of the theories that form the subject of this study. It is evident that already in Caesar's time there was sufficient diversity of character and interest between Gauls and Germans to furnish a basis for group-consciousness, and we have it on Tacitus' authority that this consciousness was highly developed among certain German tribes.

Now it is expedient to review cursorily the sequence of events in the so-called Barbarian invasions as they have been reconstructed by modern scholarship. From the third century onward " The Gauls " — which is to say, not the

[35] Caesar, *op. cit.*, bk. iv, ch. v, p. 112.

[36] *Ibid.*, bk. i, ch. i, p. 2.

[37] *Ibid.*

peoples of that name but the regions embraced in Caesar's famous opening sentence, " *Gallia omnis est divisa in partes tres* ",[38]—were largely unfortified and exposed to the Barbarians [39] who were attracted into the country by reason of its great fertility.[40] The historian of the Franks, Gregory, recounts that by about 388 the Franks, led by their dukes, pillaged the (Roman) province of Germany as far as Colonia Agrippina (Cologne).[41] Their base of operations was "*Francia*", that part of Germany occupied by the Franks, the name of which moves southwest with their migrations and settlements.[42] For, although the modern historian recognizes the long-established fact of predatory raids by the Barbarians, he must admit into his account of the fusion of the Nordic and Latin civilizations the powerful influence of Gallo-Roman culture on the conquering Germans.[43] Not only were intermarriages frequent despite the laws against them, but barbarian modes, names and fashions were taken up in Rome, and even more completely in the Rhenish provinces where the pressure of numbers was greatest.[44]

As a result, the Germans became part of the Empire's organization as soldiers; their women, as concubines; and at the very time when the Franks were pillaging north-eastern Gaul,[45] some of their fellow Germans were being

[38] Caesar, *op. cit.*, bk. i, ch. i, p. 1.

[39] Lavisse, E., ed. *Histoire de France depuis les origines jusqu'à la révolution*, Paris, 1900-1911, vol. ii, part i, p. 55. The authors of this volume are: C. Bayet, C. Pfister, and A. Kleinclausz.

[40] *Ibid.*, p. 62.

[41] Gregory of Tours, *Histoire Ecclésiastique des Francs par Saint Grégoire*, ed. Bordier, Paris, 1859, bk. ii, ch. ix, p. 61.

[42] *Ibid.*

[43] Lavisse, *loc. cit.*, p. 58 *et seq.*

[44] Lavisse, *loc. cit.*, p. 59; Lot, F., *La Fin du Monde Antique et le Début du Moyen-Age*, Paris, 1927, pp. 249, 272.

[45] Lavisse, *loc. cit.*, p. 69.

employed to defend and cultivate it.[46]   On vast, untilled
estates, the Barbarians had long been *coloni,* or serfs.
Others had competed for high posts — as personal guards
of the Emperor,[47] as consuls, would-be emperors, emperors,[48]
and mothers of emperors.[49]   Such names as Arbogast,
Stilicho, Bauto, Richomer, Merobaudus, Odoacer reveal the
Frankish, Vandal, Goth or Rugian origin of these barbarian
official masters of Rome.   The conclusion for modern
scholars is that there was in this process of mutual adjust-
ment no racial hatred.[50]   For the Barbarians the Roman
Empire was a land of promise, attractive by its opulence,
while a continued sentimental patriotism held the provinces
and Rome together.[51]

By the second half of the fourth century, the Huns were
pushing the German peoples westward, and Gaul, overrun by
the latter, faced the necessity of defending itself at the same
time as it was trying to establish local independence from
Rome and Rome's frequently corrupt, incompetent officers.[52]
The result of this double and confused movement in Gaul—
which is the factual basis of the controversy treated in this
book — was the settlement of the Visigoths in Aquitania
under Athaulf (*circa* 414 A. D.); of the Burgundians in
the Rhone valley; of the Alamans in Rhenish Gaul; of the
Riparian or River-Franks in and about Trier; and of the
related but more aggressive Salian Franks along the lower
Rhone.[53]   The two last-named tribes, destined to hegemony,

---

[46] Lavisse, *loc. cit.,* p. 62; *cf.* Lot, *op. cit.,* pp. 228, 269, 362.

[47] Lot, *op. cit.,* p. 269.

[48] Lavisse, *loc. cit.,* p. 63, but disputed by Lot, *op. cit.,* pp. 229-31.

[49] Lavisse, *loc. cit.,* p. 63; Lot, *op. cit.,* p. 272.

[50] Lavisse, *loc. cit.,* pp. 44, 64.

[51] *Ibid.,* pp. 64-5.

[52] *Ibid.,* pp. 70, 87-8.

[53] *Ibid.,* pp. 72-3; Lot, *op. cit.,* p. 362.

occupied together the left bank of the Rhine to the Meuse and
Sambre Rivers, the region of the southern Scheldt and the
Ardennes—a territory sparsely settled by the Romans, and
the almost exclusive possession of which by these " Nordic "
invaders explains the Flemish enclave in modern France.[54]
The Franks were temporarily pushed back by Aetius, Roman
commander (431-54 A. D.), who later managed to form a
coalition of Romans and Germans to repel the Huns. But
after his death (454) which may be taken as the end of the
Western Roman Empire's effective control,[55] the Franks
once more extended their domain in Gaul.

A valid conception of the Barbarian invasions cannot
therefore be simplified into any general mode of conquest
or peaceful penetration. The Barbarians did occupy parts
of Gaul by violence. A contemporary in a poem on the
Providence of God, deplores the destruction of wealth and
civilization at their hands. He even feels a patriotic despair
at the devastation of the fatherland.[56] But the dispossession
of the Gallo-Romans was, in many instances, juridical, if
not legal.[57] " No invasion nor conquest, perhaps, but an
evil greatly resembling those usually produced by invasion
and conquest." [58]

To modify the picture yet further, it should be remembered that public and vacant lands were first distributed to
these conquerors who did not conquer. Thereafter, landowners may have suffered spoliation, but they were those
who could best withstand it, the large landowners. A few
resisted, but the majority submitted.[59] In the south and

[54] Lavisse, *loc. cit.*, p. 73; Clough, S., *A History of the Flemish Movement in Belgium,* New York, 1930, pp. 3-4.

[55] Lavisse, *loc. cit.,* p. 77.

[56] Quoted, Lavisse, *loc. cit.,* p. 78.

[57] *Ibid.,* p. 79.

[58] *Ibid.*   [59] *Ibid.*

east, the division of public and private lands was fairly
regular.   The Barbarians were often given one-third of the
slaves, land, etc. when they made treaties with the Romans.[60]

The attitude of the contemporaries must therefore have
varied according to the region, the social position, and the
particular temper of the individual.   In the north there was
consternation at the violent anti-Christian advance of the
Franks.[61]   But friendliness and understanding soon grew
up.[62]   Many of the Christian Romans from the outset did
not despair of converting the Barbarians; later this sentiment changed to the hope that the barbarian virtues already
discerned by Tacitus would lead to Christianity, by reaction
against Roman vices.[63]   Christianity likewise induced a religious resignation to conquest and loss of goods which led
in turn to political resignation.[64]   In the fourth century, the
Christians in Gaul were still loyal to the Empire.   In the
fifth century, on the testimony of the historian Orosius
(*circa* 417 A. D.) the establishment of the Barbarians was
accounted a blessing.[65]   To others still, the Barbarians were
the scourge of God on a corrupt and dissolute people.   According to Salvian, priest of Marseille, writing about the
year 439, " The Romans wish to be never more constrained
to being subjects of Rome.   They pray God to let them live
as they now do with the Barbarians." [66]   Still, whatever con-

[60] Lavisse, *loc. cit.*   The Franks did not share in this manner, see below,
this chapter.

[61] *Ibid.*, p. 80.

[62] *Ibid.*

[63] *Ibid.*, p. 66.   *Cf.* Salvianus, *De Gubernatione Dei*, bk. iv, ch. 14; bk.
v, ch. 8; bk. vi, chs. 12-13; bk. vii, chs. 6, 18, and Orosius, *Historiarum
Adversum Paganos Libri VII*, bk. vii, the latter an important source for
the eighteenth century pro-Romans; see below Dubos, ch. ix.

[64] Lavisse, *loc. cit.*, p. 81.

[65] *Ibid.*, p. 82.

[66] *Ibid.*

sciousness the masses may have had of the revolution in progress, there was left in Roman Gaul a small class, of which Sidonius Apollinaris, bishop of Clermont, is representative, whose aristocratic culture naturally attached to the past glories of Rome.[67]

Now, the Franks, who were the last of the Barbarians to settle in the richer portions of Gaul but who were ultimately to dominate it and give it their name, were real Barbarians in the modern sense of the word: crude and pagan, destroyers of Gallo-Romans and Christian civilization as it existed in the plains of northern Gaul.[68] Their leaders, who were often their kings, despite Gregory of Tours' belief that they did not develop a kingship before the end of the fourth century,[69] were in the beginning incapable of statesmanship in the manner of Athaulf, Euric, or Gundobald.[70] Childeric, reputed by some to have been the first Frankish king settled in France, because his tomb, complete with horse and weapons, was discovered at Tournai in 1653, was first an ally of the Romans.[71] As such he was no more to be distinguished than his ancestors who fought under Aetius against the Huns. But his son Clovis, who acceded to the throne of a single tribe in 481, came at a time very propitious to kingly ambition. No emperor reigned in Italy; no one knew exactly who was master. In Gaul, but little more certainty existed regarding Syagrius, Master of the Militia.

Clovis prepared by alliance and carried to a successful issue the defeat of Syagrius.[72] His Franks pillaged the

[67] *Ibid.*, p. 84.

[68] *Ibid.*, p. 94; Lot, *op. cit.*, p. 365.

[69] Lavisse, *loc. cit.*, p. 56.

[70] *Ibid.*, p. 94. The Riparian Franks were even inferior to the Salian in political sense.

[71] *Ibid.*, pp. 94-5; Lot, *op. cit.*, p. 363.

[72] Lavisse, *loc. cit.*, p. 97.

country, even to its churches, though Clovis, first statesman
among the Franks, was careful to conciliate the bishops.[73]
The famous admonitory and yet diplomatic letter of Bishop
Remi to Clovis is held by Bayet to be dubious in origin.[74]
But before nineteenth-century scholarship attacked its authenticity, it formed the basis of the most fertile speculations
concerning the character of the Frankish state.

Among those who joined in the resistance to the Franks
were the *Arborychans* mentioned by Procopius,[75] and concerning whom there exists a lively controversy among
French historians. Some would read, instead of *Arborychans, Armoricans*, that is to say inhabitants of Armorica,
five provinces of northwest Gaul of which more will be
said later for upon it depends the antiquity of the Bretons'
alliance with or defiance of the embryonic French kingdom.[76]

After Clovis' defeat of the Roman troops in Gaul, that

[73] Lavisse, p. 97; Lot, *op. cit.*, p. 367.

[74] Lavisse, *loc. cit.*, p. 96.

[75] *De Bello Gothico*, bk. i, ch. xii.

[76] The modern peasants of Brittany, lineal descendants of these ancient
Armoricans, still remain tenaciously attached to their customs, language
and traditions. (Hayes, *Essays*, pp. 15, 47.) Like Roman Britain and
Scotland, the Armoricans suffered in the fourth century from the raids
of Picts and Saxons—to such an extent that the west coast down to the
Loire was included in the Saxon shore (*Litus Saxonicum*). (Lot, p. 249,
Lavisse, *loc. cit.*, p. 74). In the fifth century began an immigration into
that region from the British Isles, the history of which is obscure. The
tradition survived, however, until the ninth century when the abbot of
Landevenec, Wrdisten, claimed the island of Britain as the "cradle of his
race". (Lavisse, *loc. cit.*, p. 91; Lot, *ibid.*) This tradition taken with
that of the patriotic "Armorican Republic", of which more hereafter,
definitely establishes a cross-cut in the conflict of racial consciousness in
France that serves to explain the modern movement of "Breiz Atao".
(*Cf. Breiz Atao*, newspaper of the autonomist Breton Party, Guin-
gamp, Côtes du Nord, France.)

politic [77] ruler certainly effected a rapprochement—indefinite in nature—with the Armoricans.[78] Gregory says: "Since Clovis' death the Bretons have always been under the dominion of the Franks and their rulers have been called counts, not kings." [79] Clovis made himself acceptable also to the Gallo-Roman soldiers by leaving them their insignia; [80] to the Christians by marrying Clothilde, niece of Gundobald and a Catholic; by having his children baptized into that faith; [81] and by his own conversion with that of his followers after the victory of Tolbiac against the Alamans.[82] Catholic Gaul and all its bishops were thenceforth his allies against the older-established but heretical (Arian) kings of Burgundy and Aquitaine. With the support of the Roman population, therefore, Clovis conquered the Burgundians and humbled the Goths.[83] Paradoxically enough, the hatred of heresy overcame here for the first time in Gaul the attachment of the Romans to their culture which the Burgundians and Goths were seeking to preserve far more than Clovis.[84]

Seeing as they did in this "religious" war against the Goths a vindication of the true doctrine of the Trinity, Clovis' contemporaries were gratified when the Eastern emperor Anastasius conferred upon him the dignity of consul in

[77] Lot, *op. cit.,* p. 367.

[78] Lavisse, *loc. cit.,* p. 97.

[79] Gregory, *op. cit.,* bk. iv, ch. iv, p. 149; *cf.* also Lot, *op. cit.,* p. 249.

[80] Lavisse, *loc. cit.,* p. 97.

[81] *Ibid.,* p. 98.

[82] *Ibid.,* pp. 98-9. This connection of the victory with Clovis' conversion, though traditional, is descredited by Lot, *op. cit.,* p. 367 following Léon Levillain, Le Baptême de Clovis, *Bibl. de l'Ecole des Chartes,* 1906.

[83] Lavisse, *loc. cit.,* pp. 100-1 ; Lot, *op. cit.,* p. 368.

[84] Lavisse, *loc. cit.,* pp. 101-2.

legitimation of his conquest.[85]   It remains to be seen how
that accepted fact, disputed in its interpretation, will change
in the minds of historians from the sixteenth century onwards the whole character of the Frankish invasion.[86]

The remainder of Clovis' reign (481-511) is characterized by a series of judicious dynastic and family murders,
which the episcopate interpreted as a heavenly vindication
of Clovis' purpose in extending his rule over other Frankish
tribes.[87]   Clovis continued his favors to the bishops,[88] of
which the famous story of the Soissons vase gives a trivial
but vivid example made much of by speculative historiographers.   Again, Clovis spread Catholicism in the north,[89]
and obtained not only popular support for his zeal, but what
might be considered the basic charter of Gallicanism and
royal supremacy: the right to control ecclesiastic benefices,[90]
" none but sons, grandsons, and great-grandsons of priests
can be ordained clerics ".   Bishops submit to " their lord,
son of the Catholic Church, the most mighty king Clovis ".

Despite his concessions to the Gallo-Roman bishops,
Clovis was still to his people the long-haired warrior of a
royal race.   He followed and encouraged Frankish tastes
and customs by example, and embodied them in laws.[91]   There
thus subsisted in France " a true barbarian law far into the
middle ages ", the Salic law.[92]   Similarly, although Clovis

[85] Lavisse, *loc. cit.*, pp. 103, 103n.

[86] See below ch. ix.

[87] Lavisse, *loc. cit.*, p. 105.   Gregory said later: " God struck down
each day his enemies . . . and increased his kingdom because he walked
straight before Him with a pure heart and carried out His Will."   Bk.
ii, ch. 37, p. 100.

[88] Lavisse, *loc. cit.*, p. 105.

[89] *Ibid.*

[90] By the Council of Orleans, 511 A.D. Lavisse, *loc. cit.*, p. 106.

[91] Lavisse, *loc. cit.*, p. 106.

[92] *Ibid.*, p. 114.

remained at heart a barbarian, violent and cunning, to the older population he was the representative of the Emperor in Gaul, a magistrate, befriended by the bishops; and to both his peoples, an absolute and sacred monarch.[93]

Yet, in accord with the perpetual contradiction that seems to qualify the whole history of the German settlement among the Gallo-Romans, the latter continued to be tried and judged according to Roman law,[94] and thus were able to preserve almost unimpaired a legal system which was to play its part in French history at the critical time when the fate of absolute monarchy was in the balance.[95]

The Salic law, on the other hand, reflects Frankish society at the end of the fifth century. It deals in the main with the terms of composition or the buying off of revenge.[96] Composition, in Salic terms, *faidus,* is the stated legal price paid in effect to atone for a crime committed. Much was later made by celebrated scholars including Montesquieu, of the difference in composition established by the Salic law between a Roman and simply a "man". The Roman is worth 100 *sous* to the Frank's 200.[97] Yet, there is no mention in the Salic law of any distinction between victor and vanquished.[98]

Nowhere either is any division of lands between Franks and Romans referred to. "Contrary to what happened in territories occupied by Visigoths and Burgundians, the former inhabitants of regions where Clovis settled were not affected in their property rights."[99] In northern Gaul, it is

---

[93] Lavisse, *loc. cit.*, pp. 103, 106.

[94] *Ibid.*, p. 113.

[95] See below ch. iii.

[96] Lavisse, *loc. cit.*, p. 108.

[97] Lavisse, *loc. cit.*, p. 114. A *sou* was a gold coin weighing 85.3 grains or a silver coin weighing 252 grains.

[98] *Ibid.*, p. 113.   [99] *Ibid.*, p. 114.

true, the original sparse population had at first been dis-possessed by marauding Franks. But as Clovis' sway spread, the bulk of the Franks were provided for, and became shep-herds and farmers, though retaining a passion for the hunt.[100] Such Franks as remained in the region as soldiers conquered public lands and seldom touched private property, with the exception of inevitable isolated acts of spoliation. There was probably among the Franks no *legal* partitioning of land.[101]

Now, in view of these relevant facts, an explanation can be found for the difference in *pretium hominis,* or *wergeld.* It is not necessarily a discrimination against the individual, but more likely a safeguard for the lives of the Frankish minority.[102] That the discrepancy in numbers was great is attested by the rapid adoption of the Roman tongue by the Barbarians, and the fact that in some regions no German cemeteries can be found.[103]

In social organization the Franks greatly resemble those of their fellow Germans who settled in the British Isles. Their law protects individual property; inheritance, called *alleu,* or *alod,*[104] occurring equally among the sons; lacking sons, the mother, then the brother, sister, maternal aunt, inherit.[105] Such is the original significance of the Salic law.

[100] Lavisse, *loc. cit.,* pp. 114, 112: Game and fishing laws were of course extremely severe.

[101] *Ibid.,* p. 114.

[102] *Ibid.,* p. 113; *cf.* Guizot, F., *Essais sur l'Histoire de France . . . ,* Paris, 1847, pp. 172-3. *Cf.* also an ingenious modern explanation by H. Brunner, "Sippe und Wergeld," *Zeitschrift der Savigny-Stiftung,* vol. xvi, 1882, p. 14.

[103] Lavisse, *loc. cit.,* p. 114. In the valley of the Moselle, where the Romans were least numerous, the Frankish conquerors did not even impose their tongue. Lot, *op. cit.,* p. 248.

[104] The meaning of the term later changed radically.

[105] Lavisse, *loc. cit.,* pp. 110-1.

As misapplied later to the right of royal succession, it finds no basis in any of the drafts extant.[106]

As the Frankish kingship, supported by the bishops, the conquests, and the military organization of the state, grew in power, the aristocracy fell behind in the competition of merit, the nobility crumbled. In the fourth and fifth centuries, it had in fact been mentioned only in connection with the election of the king,[107] all of which conclusions it is important to bear in mind until the theory that the French nobles are all Franks and the commoners all Gauls reaches maturity and gains credence in the seventeenth century.[108]

To conclude the description of what most probably happened in Gaul of the sixth century, it may be said that beyond a few well-defined legal distinctions the tenor of the evidence is that the Romanization of the Franks was accompanied by a reciprocal Germanization of the Gallo-Romans.[109] The German army not only changed Roman arms, Roman tactics, the Roman custom of proclaiming the Emperor, but even Roman vices.[110] These changes were not exerted merely on the lowest orders of society. By the time of Julian, the emperor had discarded the toga for animal skins; and at the same time Sidonius Apollinaris compliments the Roman commander Syagrius on the excellence of his German; and certain Romans—men and women—conceal their origin under Frankish names which have a tremendous vogue.[111]

---

[106] Lavisse, *loc. cit.*, pp. 109n., 205. *De terra nulla ad mulierem hereditas perveniat* was corrected when women were admitted to inheritance to read: *De terra salica*, etc. . . . meaning the ground surrounding the house or *sale*.

[107] *Ibid.*, pp. 58, 57.

[108] See below Boulainvilliers, ch. vii.

[109] Lot, *op. cit.*, p. 272.

[110] Kurth, G., *Histoire Poétique des Mérovingiens*, Paris, 1893, p. 492.

[111] Lot, *op. cit.*, p. 273. The bearers of these names are nonetheless

As regards literature it has been stated that " the Gallo-
Romans had popular folksongs and poems, but it was the
Franks who taught them to combine the tune with imagination," to create as a result the French epic cycle.[112]
The rhythmic beat, the sonorous words, the military cele-
brations and the long hours for idle repetition were the
Barbarians' contribution to the national literature, already
prized at the Frankish sovereign's court.[113] By the time
of Gregory of Tours that mixed heritage had become
one of the literary influences which he felt and unconsciously
reproduced in those passages distinguished by ease and
clarity.[114] Elsewhere, though his grammar defies analysis,
the vocabulary of the sixth-century bishop is rich with the
addition of a moderate number of Celtic, Germanic and
Hunnish words.[115]

The assimilation of German manners took place, in the
opinion of one authority, with " a facility that the French
race never again showed to the same degree ";[116] from
which we may infer some measure of its permanent character. A concurrent conclusion, by another scholar, based
on this same intermingling of cultures, is that the Roman
population would hardly have noticed the difference between
their old Roman masters and the new German ones, had not
the latter been pagan infidels or Arian heretics.[117]

"Roman citizens ", as are the Franks who aspire to honors and conceal
their origin under Roman names. *Ibid.*, p. 271 ; Kurth, *op. cit.*, pp. 524-5.

[112] Kurth, *op. cit.*, pp. 490-2.

[113] *Ibid.*, p. 493.

[114] Brehaut, E., *The History of the Franks* (of Gregory of Tours)
Selections, trans. with notes, New York, 1916, Introd., p. xiv. In
1783, Rivarol will posit the oft quoted axiom " Ce qui n'est pas clair n'est
pas français ", *De l'Universalité de la Langue Française*, p. 44.

[115] Brehaut, *loc. cit.*

[116] Kurth, *op. cit.*, p. 492.

[117] Lot, *op. cit.*, p. 275.

The relevance of these facts and inductions to the subject under treatment is obvious. They suggest not only the items of later discussions but the reason why modern scholarship cannot declare categorically for the theory that the French are all Germans any more than for its rival that the French are all Gallo-Romans who, in casting off the shackles imposed through centuries by a few German conquerors and their descendants, regained in the French Revolution their original liberties. But still a greater significance of these modern findings lies in their having destroyed the old notion of a Gallo-German racial hatred, in having put back to the fourth, fifth and sixth centuries the process of amalgamation which historians until the time of Michelet [118] and Thierry [119] ascribed to long struggles and gradual oblivion.

Before this view, even now far from current, had reached the circles interested in the problem, French historiography presented the endless spectacle of a battleground for the two rival systems.[120] And those two systems with their variants threw into dispute the facts relating not merely to the invasions, the Salic law, the kingship, and the early historians; but also to the fiefs, the three orders, the Church, the Estates General and the syntax of the French language. In the controversy were involved the capitularies of Charlemagne as well as the charters of the Communes, the history of Gregory of Tours equally with the legends of Mérovée. It was, as we shall see, the foundations of the French nation that were being perpetually tested and criticized by scholarship, nascent and full-fledged.

[118] *Histoire de France*, Paris, 1819, vol. i, p. 184.

[119] Thierry, Aug., *Récits des Temps Mérovingiens*, Paris, 1846, p. 16.

[120] *Ibid.*, pp. 17-18; Leber, C., ed., *Collection de Pièces* . . . Paris, 1838, vol. i, Pref., pp. xiv-xv.

CHAPTER II

Gregory of Tours—The Trojan Myth

Before we can judge critically the theories built on this multifarious evidence, however, it is necessary to acquire some slight notion of the opinions held by the " French " concerning their race after the invasions had become an accomplished fact, and from that time through the Middle Ages to the Renaissance. Of the former period, the churchman Gregory is at once a product and a witness.

Georgius Florentius Gregorius, Bishop of Tours (538-594 A. D.), author of some twenty books of Histories, Miracles, Lives, Psalms, and Astronomy, wrote his *History of the Franks* during the last quarter of the sixth century. His Roman ancestry and clerical training certainly contributed to making him cultured and skeptical, says Kurth (p. 482); superstitious as a savage, says Brehaut (xi, xx-xxi). He was in reality skeptical of the Frankish traditions and credulous about the Christian-Roman, superior to the people whose history he wrote and whom he regularly calls Barbarians.[1] Nonetheless, Gregory furnishes not only valuable direct evidence, but takes as scientific an attitude toward the question of the Franks' origin and customs as might be expected in his time and position. In fact, for fourteen hundred years,[2] the fundamental dynastic and military events of early French history were gathered by scholars from the pages of Gregory, and even today the primary-school child

---

[1] Gregory, *op. cit.*, bk. iii, ch. 15, p. 127; bk. vii, ch. 31, p. 155.

[2] If we except the scholarly and limited researches of Duchesne, A. de Valois, le Père Lecointe, etc.

42

in France is still made to learn, painfully but painstakingly, the bloody anecdotes of Clovis' reign and of Brunehilde's.[3]

On the grave subject of origins, Gregory alone among early historians reports that many people think the Franks originated in Pannonia (Hungary); that they first settled thereafter on the banks of the Rhine; then having crossed this river, they invaded Thuringia, where they established in command over them *reges-crinitos*—"long-haired kings taken from their best families".[4] But this fashion of wearing their blond hair long and loose on the shoulders, is the distinguishing mark not only of the Merovingian Kings, but also of the barbarian warrior invaders.[5] In point of fact, according to Gregory, many persons are in ignorance regarding who was the first King of the Franks—a riddle of the last importance in determining for future Frenchmen the "race" of the whole people. Sulpicius Alexander, an historian known to us only through Gregory, speaks at great length of the Franks in his history, yet never tells us who was their first king: he says only that they had dukes.[6] By this term the earlier chronicler obviously means the *duces* or leaders of which Tacitus speaks. Sulpicius in his Fourth Book calls certain leaders "royal", though Gregory does not know whether they were kings or simply exercised the functions of kingship.[7] On this problematic report hinges in turn the entire controversy of later French historians regarding the democratic or autocratic character of what they are pleased to call the "French Monarchy".

---

[3] See for instance the small one-volume *Histoire de France* written by Lavisse for elementary schools, or even the recent American guide, *Old France* by J. Coulter, New York, 1931.

[4] Gregory, *op. cit.*, bk. ii, ch. 9, p. 67; *cf.* bk. iii, ch. 18. His mistake in geography will be discussed below.

[5] Lavisse, vol. ii, pt. 1, p. 73.

[6] Gregory, *op. cit.*, bk. ii, ch. 9, p. 61.

[7] *Ibid.*, bk. ii, ch. 9, p. 64.

From the *History of the Franks* we gather nonetheless the elements of that genealogy of Merovingian kings which was still held to be historical by some of the writers of the eighteenth century. According to it, Clogio (or Clodio, or modern: Chloio) was the first king of the Franks, Merovech succeeded him and gave his name to the royal line. Childeric was the next in order, characterized by immoral depredations which led to his exile by the Franks for eight years, returning under romantic circumstances with his host's wife. Childeric died in 481 and his son Clovis ascended the throne at the age of fifteen.[8]

It was not long after the death of Childeric, according to Gregory, that "the redoubtable name of the Franks resounded in the country [Gaul], and as everyone passionately desired the establishment of their dominion", St. Aprunculus became suspect to the Burgundians.

From then on [the historian continues] many people in Gaul ardently desired to live under the domination of the Franks. Whence it happened that the bishop of Rodez, Quintian, hated on this score, was harried out of the town. He was told: ' It is because thy desire is that the Franks should seize this country.' The Goths tried to kill him, but the man of God was warned and escaped.[9]

It is clear from these two significant passages that there were sympathizers of the Franks among the Gallo-Romans, but equally clear that at least among the earlier barbarian invaders of the towns there was widespread opposition to Frankish rule. Therefore, all subsequent historical systems based on either half of the complete statement are alike fallacious.

Of the governmental customs of the Franks, Gregory, as

[8] Gregory, *op. cit.*, bk. ii, ch. 12, p. 72.
[9] *Ibid.*, bk. ii, ch. 36, p. 99.

an Arvernian noble and an ecclesiastic who hated them,[10] says very little. One important item he mentions, however, is the Franks' freedom from tribute (i. e. taxation) on the ground that they were freemen. This seems to have been the case under Childebert the Elder (son of Clovis) though many had been subjected to it by that time.[11] Such a submission, according to some, was held to degrade them to the level of a conquered Gallo-Roman.[12]

It was apparently the custom of the Frankish king on his accession to make a circuit of his kingdom and receive the allegiance of his people.[13] Though it is not known just in what manner or from whom the allegiance was actually received, yet this reported fact suggests a first element of the feudal ritual in Gaul. A second, rife with political and social consequences, may be seen in the order of Chilperic (grandson of Clovis) that " fines be paid by the poor and the younger clergy of the Church because they had not served in the army ", although " there was no custom for these to perform any state service ". [14] The King's order requiring the service of all inhabitants is the Nordic *ban* or *bannus*.[15]

The Franks also brought in the custom—afterwards an oppressive and wasteful privilege of the noble class—of hunting with hawks and dogs.[16] The Franks to whom the

---

[10] Notes to Bordier's *History of the Franks,* vol. ii, p. 406; Kurth, *op. cit.,* p. 482.

[11] Gregory, *op. cit.,* bk. vii, ch. 15, p. 85.

[12] *Ibid.,* bk. iii, ch. 36, p. 144; and also bk. ix, ch. 30, pp. 210-212.

[13] *Ibid.,* bk. iv, ch. 14, p. 160; bk. vii, ch. 8, p. 78; bk. ix, ch. 30, pp. 210-212.

[14] *Ibid.,* bk. v, ch. 27, p. 254. These two provisions suggest Norman improvement of French feudal customs in England; notably William's Salisbury Oath and Henry II's scutage.

[15] Brunner, H., *Deutsche Rechtsgeschichte*, Leipzig, 1887, vol. ii, p. 34.

[16] Gregory, *op. cit.,* bk. x, ch. 10, pp. 258, 259.

practice of bequeathing property was unknown,[17] followed
the general " Nordic " custom [18] of choosing their kings
from the royal family but regardless of primogeniture. Indeed all of Clovis' sons ruled, and all of Clotaire's who
survived.

Despite Gregory's lack of sympathy and his preoccupation with churchly and dynastic affairs, he does depict accurately the conflicts, tragedies and persons in this period of
racial amalgamation which covers the second half of the
sixth century. It is for this reason and because he embodied in his work the testimony of two previous historians
unknown to us, the researches of at least seven earlier
writers,[19] and finally, his own observations of twenty years,
that the Bishop of Tours was for so long [20] and has remained the chief source of information on the early Frankish Monarchy. His immediate successors do but repeat his
words, often inaccurately—as does Pseudo-Fredegarius—or
else invent. It is a combination of these two methods that
gave rise to the extraordinary legends concerning the origins
of the French people current in the Middle Ages and of
which cognizance must be taken as constituting a hiatus between the Frankish invasions themselves and the Gallo-Frank
disputes of the Renaissance.

In the preface to his *History,* written the year of his
death, Gregory tells us that already in his day the liberal

[17] *Ibid.,* bk. vi, ch. 45, pp. 63-4. The Gallo-Romans were accustomed to
wills.

[18] See *Beowulf,* lines 5-10 (Duncan Spaeth translation).

[19] Namely Orosius, Eusebius, Jerome, Victor, Sulpicius Severus,
Sidonius Apollinaris, Avitus plus some local annals. (*Opera Gregorii
Tur., Mon. Ger. Hist.,* Pref.)

[20] *Cf.* the Preface by Dom Ruinart to his edition of Gregory, Paris,
1699, in which he calls him " the founder of our history ".

arts " were on the decline, or rather perishing completely in
the cities of Gaul "; and that consequently no " grammarian
able enough in dialectic " has been found to relate contemporary events in prose or verse.[21]   A century later, his continuator, Fredegarius, reasserts the decadence of the world
and the " dulling of wisdom ". [22]   The Merovingian kings
were indifferent to public education, and although the monasteries and churches remained centers of traditional education, the latter were insufficient.   The monasteries likewise
suffered from Charles Martel's extensive confiscation
in the middle of the eighth century.[23]   Charlemagne's interest in the poetic traditions of the Franks did cause numerous epic songs to be written, but these manuscripts did not
survive [24] any more than the interest, which disappeared
with the disintegration of Charlemagne's empire.   By the
twelfth century, as a result of this lack of accurate traditions, the population of ancient Gaul had no remembrance
of its two-fold racial origin, nor of any local distinctions,
if any had existed, between conquerors and dispossessed
landowners.[25]   Instead, the majority of the literary records
indicate a common belief in an entirely Frankish origin,
traced back, not to the swamps of northern Germany, but to
the ancient city of Troy.[26]

The Trojan origin of the Franks is ascribed by some to
early racial recollections of an Asiatic birthplace, modified
to fit Virgil's poem.[27]   By others, notably Godefroid

---

[21] Pref., p. 1.

[22] In his prologue to bk. iv, as before him, Gregory, Prologue, bk. v.

[23] Lot, *op. cit.*, p. 439.

[24] *Ibid.*

[25] Thierry, *Récits,* p. 17.

[26] *Ibid.;* Kurth, *op. cit.,* p. 504 *et seq.*

[27] Such is the hypothesis of Thierry, Pétigny, Ozanam, and Roth,
though the *Aeneid* does not contain a word of the Franco-Trojan story.

Kurth,[28] the descent of the Franks from Aeneas or some other Trojan fugitive is not a national fiction but a scholarly one. In the sixth century, says Kurth, the Franks thought they were descended from Mannus,[29] himself son of Tuisto,[30] progenitor of the whole race. This belief naturally excludes a Trojan origin. But this last was characteristic of the western nations' effort to link themselves to a classical people. The Romans were not exempt from that infirmity [31] and Tacitus mentions that Asciburgium on the Rhine is said to have been founded by Ulysses.[32] It is worth noting that these Germans would be descended from the conquerors of Troy, instead of the Trojans; whereas, if the Franks were descended from the Trojans, as were the Romans themselves, both progenitors of the French race would be conquered peoples in addition to being cousins!

But this erudite story, according to our authority, never strayed outside the monastic manuscripts to penetrate the masses. The very name Frank aroused speculation to explain at once its etymology and the origin of the people. In early writers is found the oft-repeated: *"Franci, quibus familiare est fidem frangere."* "The Franks who commonly break their word." [33] Another parallel etymology endows the Franks with special ferocity and savagery.[34]

Now, at the same time there existed a hero, Francus or Francio, independent of these etymologies and of the Trojan story. The fusion was bound to occur but was not imme-

[28] Kurth, *op. cit.*

[29] *Ibid.*, p. 506.

[30] Lavisse, *loc. cit.*, vol. ii, pt. 1, p. 45.

[31] Kurth, *op. cit.*, p. 505; *cf.* Virgil, *Aeneid.*

[32] Tacitus, *op. cit.*, ch. iii, p. 313.

[33] Kurth, *op. cit.*, p. 506.

[34] Isidore of Seville, *Etymol.*, bk. ix, ch. 11, p. 101; also in *Isidori Originum*, Dom Bouquet, vol. i, p. 818a.

diate. The Trojan origin is first found alone in Fredegarius (*circa* 615): " The Franks had for their first king
Priam, the ravisher of Helen, who had obtained the beauty
prize from a shepherd." The Franks had subsequently
split into three groups — the Macedonians, Frigians, and
Turks.[35] Francus or Francio is as yet only an early king
of the " Franks who are so called because they elected him
king." [36] The next step of course was to make Francio a
Trojan.[37] The author of this legend appears as a very
patriotic Frank, anxious to prove that he belonged to a
never-conquered nation.[38] To bolster up his racial myth,
he perverts the chronicle of St. Jerome and geography both.
He reads " Franci " for " Frigi " and improves " Primus
rex " into " Priamus rex ". [39] The Trojan origin is " a
blunder turned into a fiction ". [40]

It grew as it went: analogies, puns, ignorance, everything
helped it along. For example, in Roman times a Colonia
Trajana, named in honor of Trajan, existed near Xanten,
on the Rhine. Corrupted by popular speech to *Trojana,*
this town name, for the second copyist of Fredegarius, becomes the Troja that the Franks founded in memory of their
native land. Throughout the Middle Ages, its accepted
name was *Troja Minor, Klein Trojen,* etc. at the same time
as it was thought to be the birthplace of the German hero
Siegfried! [41]

[35] Fredegarius, *op. cit.*, bk. ii, pp. 4-6.

[36] Dom Bouquet, *op. cit.*, vol. i, p. 394c. Likewise, the Frigians from
Friga, the Turks from Turcus.

[37] *Cf.* the completed and accepted story in the Chronicle of St. Denis,
Bouquet, vol. iii, p. 155.

[38] Fredegarius, *op. cit.*, bk. ii, p. 6.

[39] Kurth, *op. cit.*, pp. 511-2.

[40] *Ibid.*

[41] *Ibid.*

In the *Liber Historiae* of the next century (*circa* 725) Aeneas himself appears as king of the Franks. Later these settle on the Rhine, choosing Faramond as king.[42] This new personage will in modern times figure prominently in learned research, to be later discredited like Francio before him and Mérovée after.

In a juridical compilation of the twelfth century an effort is made to reconcile the terms *Francus* and *Vassus*. The interim of four hundred years had seen an increase in serfdom and vassalage, creating the distinction between freeman and serf. *Francus* and *Vassus* both refer to the free man; but to the compiler they are also the names of two Trojan princes![43] In the twelfth century also, the influence of the French *chansons de geste* in forming the "national character" by providing it with "historical" traditions is not to be underestimated.[44] One significant feature of this influence is that these epics gave originally the same story-background to the Anglo-Saxons, the Franks, and the Lombards,[45] as the German and English local epics.[46] Siegfried has been accounted a scion of Troja Minor, a Frankish town. The combat of Theodoric the Austrasian and Hygelac the Dane forms the basis of numerous popular legends of Scandinavia, and is finally written down towards the end of the seventh century in England as an incident in the poem of Beowulf.[47] The obvious disregard of race or national consciousness reflects the merging of peoples, languages and heroes.

The spread [48] of these same stories by word of mouth

---

[42] Kurth, *op. cit.*, p. 512.   [43] *Ibid.*

[44] Hayes, *Essays on Nationalism*, pp. 16, 17.

[45] Kurth, *op. cit.*, p. 495.

[46] *Ibid.*, p. 478.

[47] *Beowulf*, Riverside ed., p. 79; also Introd., p. viii.

[48] *Cf. Widsith the Wanderer* in R. W. Chambers, *Widsith, a Study,*

was of course greatly furthered in the twelfth century, through the efforts of the ambulant poets, and ultimately reawakened the poetic strain on the other side of the Rhine and caused the renaissance to which we owe the Nibelungenlied.[49]

The divergence of the " German " from the " French " stream of national epic poetry comes with the change in tastes, the softening of manners resulting from Christian morality. New heroes were given the credit for old deeds.[50] Clovis with his crude pagan prowess is replaced by Dagobert, Charles Martel, and Charlemagne.[51] The latter is of primary importance in coming phases of this study, for he appears on the legendary stage no longer as a Frank but as French, the glorious emperor,

> . . . le roi qui tient douce France.
> Il a la barbe blanche et le chef tout fleuri.
> Il a le corps noble et la contenance fière.[52]

The Alamans of Tolbiac retain their mythical Siegfried and historical Dietrich (Theodoric). But before modern times both groups of mixed German descent will yet be joined together and confused—when, in the Crusades, the oriental infidels designate all westerners as Franks.[53]

Concurrently with these popular notions the French held concerning their origin, they entertained views regarding the institutions of the state that were bitterly contradictory.

Cambridge, 1912, who meets not only a host of famous legendary kings but the Hrothgar of Beowulf and the Hagen of the Nibelungen.

[49] Kurth, *op. cit.,* pp. 496-8.

[50] E. g., *Roman d'Alexandre* (XII Century) in Paris and Langlois, *Chrestamathie du Moyen-Age.*

[51] Kurth, *op. cit.,* pp. 486-7.

[52] *Chanson de Roland,* ed. Bédier, v. 116-8, p. 12.

[53] Duruy, V., *Histoire de France,* trans. Cary, New York, 1929, p. 132.

The nobility maintained the theory of a conquest in the past, won over the aborigines of the country and which had established their present possessions as well as the kingship. Instead of seeing in their annals the barbarian infiltration into a Roman provincial society which we have noted, the nobility from the twelfth century onward borrowed the popular traditions of Charlemagne and his knights fighting the infidels. By transposition they used these legends to account, explain and justify the " Frankish conquest of Gaul ". [54]

Before the fourteenth century, the king himself shared this proud nobiliary opinion: " This kingdom of France that our predecessors, with the grace of God, conquered from the Barbarians. . . ." [55] As a matter of fact, the original Frankish nobility which had participated in the so-called " conquest of Gaul " had long ago disappeared [56] and an entirely new social caste had arisen by the end of the Merovingian dynasty, composed indiscriminately of large Frankish landowners and wealthy scions of the Gallo-Roman senatorial class,[57] both distinguished socially from the rest of the people in only one respect—serving the king.[58] The service of the king in turn carried with it the privilege of receiving not only a triple *wergeld* [59] but a benefice, that is, land to be held outright and hereditarily.[60]

This historical process, distorted in the memory of the noble class, led to the nobles' medieval notion of the origin

[54] du Haillan, B. G., *Hist. Générale des rois de France*, 1576, vol. i, p. 229.

[55] Guillaume de Nangis, in *Soc. de l'Hist. de France*, vol. i, p. 315.

[56] See above, p. 39.

[57] Lot, *op. cit.*, pp. 411, 413.

[58] *Ibid.*

[59] *Ibid.*, p. 412.

[60] *Ibid.*, p. 410; though the king could withdraw what he had granted.

of the fiefs, namely that the companions of Charlemagne, having rid France of the barbarian natives, received from the king the estates of which they found themselves possessed.[61] But in spite of this retrospective religious zeal, the barons of France felt no less enmity towards the clergy than did the older " antrustions " or " faithful " of the Merovingian kings.[62] A document of the thirteenth century clearly reflects the feelings and presumptions of the nobility. It is the draft of an oath of federation subscribed to by the high barons of France [63] in 1247, against clerical justice:

The clergy, with their superstition, do not remember that it is by blood and war that under Charlemagne and other kings, the Kingdom of France was converted from pagan error to the Catholic faith. First they [the clergy] deceived us by a certain humility and now they assail us like foxes hiding under the ruins of the castles that we once built; they swallow the secular justice into their jurisdiction, with the result that sons of serfs judge according to their laws free men and sons of free men; whereas, according to the laws of former days—the laws of victors— they should be judged by us . . . Wherefore, we assembled, nobles of the Kingdom, considering that this Kingdom has been acquired not by written laws nor by the arrogance of clerks, but by dint of sweat and combats, in virtue of these presents and our common oath, do decree and ordain that henceforth no clerk nor layman shall bring anyone to justice before an ordinary or delegated ecclesiastical judge, unless for heresy, marriage, or blasphemy, on pain of loss of all his goods and mutilation of a limb.

Further, we delegate certain persons entrusted with the execution of this ordinance, that our revived jurisdiction may thrive once again; that those who hitherto have become rich from our

---

[61] du Haillan, *op. cit.,* vol. i, p. 229.

[62] Lot, *op. cit.,* p. 414; Thierry, *Récits,* p. 19.

[63] The Duke of Burgundy, the Counts of Bretagne, Angoulême and Saint Pol signed this declaration drawn up in their names.

impoverishment may be brought back to the state of the primitive church; and that by living in contemplation while we lead the active life as is fitting, they may show us miracles which have long since forsaken our age.[64]

Though the character of the royalty in Merovingian France had changed profoundly from those customs described by Tacitus as obtaining in Germany, the tradition of an elective king, of an assembly of warriors and nobles, persisted into the Renaissance period. The coronation ceremony employed formulas which as early as the eleventh century no longer had any basis in reality: ". . . the soldiers and the people, greater as well as lesser, consenting with one voice exclaimed three times: ' we approve it, we wish it, let it be done ' ". [65] The relations of king and people had become obscured through the great increase in the king's power,[66] at the same time as a slow " revolution " was preparing. The popular assembly which had ceased to meet in Merovingian times,[67] was destined to reappear in the fourteenth century and to vindicate its rights as well as those of the people, on an historical basis. At the Estates General of 1484, Philippe Pot, lord of LaRoche, Grand Sénéchal of Burgundy, was to declare openly: "As histories tell us and as I have learnt it from my fathers, the sovereign people in the beginning created the kings by its suffrage. . . ."[68]

This and other limiting functions of the assembly had been replaced in Neustria by the intermittent pressure upon the king of the ecclesiastics and the nobility, led by the

[64] Matthew Paris, *Hist. Angliae Major,* ed. Luard, vol. ii, p. 720.

[65] *Coronation of Philip I* (1060), in Dom Bouquet, *Recueil des Historiens,* vol. xi, p. 33.

[66] Lot, *op. cit.,* p. 401.

[67] Except in Austrasia, which included the lower Rhine and Moselle provinces, Champagne, Auvergne, Poitou and Touraine.

[68] Masselin, J., *Journal des Etats-Généraux de 1484,* p. 147 *et seq.*

Mayor of the Palace. Their extortion of the famous Charter of 614 from Clotaire II created a precedent tending to restrict the Merovingian monarchy to constitutional limitations that the eighteenth-century political writers did not fail to remember and even to compare to Magna Carta.[69] Whether the parallel is well founded or not, the Charter of 614 did guarantee that trial should be granted to every accused person by judges taken from his peers in the locality; that no new decrees contrary to previous ones should be issued from the palace; that the nominee elected by the chapter should be confirmed in his bishopric by the sovereign.[70]

In yet another respect persistent historical tradition worked against an absolute monarchy. Personal taxes levied on the Franks were stoutly resisted as marks of social degradation. Violent uprisings followed attempts of the king to enforce his will.[71] In the Middle Ages, according to Thierry, this feeling was exclusively shared by the nobility;[72] and it has been seen that the medieval privileged order is a mixture of the two races, believing itself pure Frank from lapse of historical memory. The two convictions partly caused and partly resulted from the notion that *Frank* meant *free*. This tenacious adherence to historical ideas engendered a conservative spirit regarding customs outmoded by a changing morality, such as trial by combat. The practice of compurgation or bringing character witnesses was no less Germanic in origin[73] but the ideal and ritual of chivalry had

[69] *Cf.* Moreau, F., *Discours de l'Histoire de France* (1777).

[70] Lot, *op. cit.*, pp. 414-5; Thierry, *Récits*, p. 21.

[71] Lot, *op. cit.*, p. 405.

[72] *Op. cit.*, p. 21. He adduces, however, an ambiguous testimony—that of the Sénéchal of Burgundy, Philippe Pot, quoted above, but whose ideas, discussed below, are clearly not noble partisanship.

[73] See above.

inthroned combat as the religiously and juridically more certain form, to supersede a system which, as it were, rewarded organized perjury.[74]   But when attempts were made to bring back a modified and more modern procedure by witnesses, the class most jealous of the privilege strenuously objected.[75] The emotions accompanying this refusal are already revealed in a thirteenth-century song that combines all these elements of race-pride, confused history, and class prerogatives:

> People of France, wonder and amaze!
> I say to all who were begotten free:
> That *frank* you are no more to be,
> That franchise has from you been grudged
> For now you are by inquest judged.
>
> Sweet France!   No longer be called thus
> But as a subject land be known to us—
>   A land of slaves.[76]

A second group tradition based on race and distinct from that of the noble, was the bourgeois harking back to pre-barbarian times, to the Gallo-Roman cities which laid claim to municipal existence as Provincial capitals during the palmy days of the Empire.[77]   Reims put back its glorious communal origin to the time of St. Remi, converter of the Franks;[78] Metz pretended, with justice, to have enjoyed civil rights before Lorraine (Lothringen, the kingdom of Lothair II, (855) came into being: " Lorraine is young and

---

[74] Montesquieu, *Esprit des Lois,* vol. ii, p. 184 *et seq.*

[75] Thierry, *op. cit.,* p. 22.

[76] Leroux de Lincy, *Recueil de chants historiques français, 1ère série,* Paris, 1842, p. 218.

[77] Thierry, *op. cit.,* p. 22; Picot, G., *Histoire des Etats-Généraux,* Paris, 1889, 5 vols., vol. i, pp. 45, 184.

[78] Letter of John of Salisbury to John of Poictiers, bishop, twelfth century, Bouquet, vol. xvi, p. 368.

Metz is old ".[79] Other important cities of France—such as Lyon, Bourges, Marseille, Toulouse—maintained a belief in "immemorial rights" of urban liberty, civil and political. Local patriotism and a spirit of jealous independence against the encroachments of the nobility were the outcome of these antiquarian elements in bourgeois opinion [80]—elements destined to form a class-consciousness superior in intensity to that of the nobility seduced and weakened by the royal power; [81] and superior necessarily to the inarticulate resentment of the lowest class—serfs and villains.

As we approach modern times in France, we are confronted with clear social divisions based on feudal practices and aggravated by fantastic traditions which force the middle class to the side of the populace in common cause against the nobility. The king continues his policy of playing one group against another, at the same time as the wealth of the middle class makes it a frequently more valuable ally. Simultaneously, a revived classical and historical interest tends to project antiquarian concepts over the reality of the conflict. It is at this point that the interplay of facts and fancies begins to constitute for the student a subject of infinite complexity, leading directly to that phase of French history which was shown in the Introduction to be a part of the Nordic *versus* Latin race problem.

In the following pages it may often seem as if the race issue were losing itself in secondary controversies. Yet to the student who perceives in their complexity the problems of succeeding periods and the minds of those who grappled with them, the underlying relevance of the race question will be at all times apparent. It should be plain that upon the

[79] Popular saying reported in Calmet, *Histoire de Lorraine*, vol. ii, p. 124; quoted by Thierry, *op. cit.*, p. 23.

[80] Thierry, *op. cit.*, p. 24; Picot, *op. cit.*, vol. i, p. 34.

[81] Picot, *op. cit.*, vol. i, p. 206; see below Boulainvilliers, ch. vii.

question "Are Frenchmen Franks or Gauls?" may depend questions of government, e. g. "If the Frankish State included a deliberative assembly, why not restore the Estates General?—or the Parlements?"

Similarly, questions of religion: "If Clovis appointed the bishops, why do they wish to be independent of Louis XIV?"

Questions of taxation: "We, Franks and nobles, conquered you, Gallo-Romans, and exacted tribute from you. Our sole duty is to bear arms for our king. Your demands for equalizing taxation are therefore unhistorical, unsound."

Questions of justice, of social custom, of ancient liberties, of natural rights obviously follow, and their answers are in direct relation to the *a priori race-belief* of him who frames the question. The seventeenth-century historian Boulainvilliers is only one of many cases in point; but it happens that he reveals quite consciously the natural connection between the two sets of facts:

It is very difficult [he says] to treat of that part of our history on which I am engaged without touching upon a quantity of matters which, though differing in substance, are yet so closely connected therewith by circumstance, custom, and the passage of time that it would be impossible to understand the one without the others.[82]

Three more repercussions of the profound racial division may be here briefly localized. Scholarly research produces data concerning racial origins, migrations, kingships, dates and deductions therefrom. Paid historiography adverts to these same facts in tendencious fashion to exalt the absolute monarchy. Lastly, class-war in all its aspects—inter-opposition of king, nobility, clergy, and Third Estate, employs the ammunition of race-pride to vindicate its aims or destroy its opponents.

[82] *Lettres sur les anciens Parlemens de France*, London, 1753, 3 vols., vol. ii, pp. 1-2.

CHAPTER III

The Estates-General—Pasquier—Bodin

Of the three groups, serfs, nobles, and townsmen, the deciding influence by the middle of the fourteenth century was frequently lodged with the last named [1] — the future Third Estate, though it is not to be called so for another 134 years.[2] The renaissance of this municipal spirit however is not connected exclusively with resistance to oppressive taxes. It has roots in historic beliefs and race opinions — hence its relevance to our subject. As early as the end of the eleventh century, town-spirit arose as a reaction to the decentralization of the country by Feudalism.[3] It increased with the revival of classical studies in Italy, the founding of schools and the awakened interest in Roman Law.[4] From the first and last of these sources it was natural that the notions of monarchy and liberty should gain in definiteness—a result to which the large number of jurists drawn from the middle class chiefly contributed.[5] Steeped in the classics,[6] the new Roman-lawyers tried to link the king of France to the imperial tradition interrupted by the barbarian invasions, and more especially by the feudal system.[7]

[1] Picot, *op. cit.*, vol. i, p. 184 and Appendix, Note A, p. 396.

[2] Picot, *op. cit.*, vol. i, p. 15.

[3] *Ibid.*

[4] *Ibid.*, p. 17.

[5] *Ibid.*, p. 16.

[6] *Cf.* the allusions to Latin authors in the Estates-General of 1484, Masselin, *op. cit.*, p. 145 and elsewhere.

[7] Picot, *op. cit.*, vol. i, p. 17.

" Know ye that the king is Emperor in his realm and can do therein all and as much as belongs to imperial right." [8]

The legalism that supported the crown also rested on a growing sense of patriotism, but whether in imitation of classical feelings or in opposition to foreign interventions it is difficult to pronounce. The center for such expressions of national consciousness on the part of the bourgeoisie is the Estates-General. The first genuine Estates, of 1302, were convoked to answer the coercive bull of Pope Boniface VIII [9] against Philippe IV, who took care to present the matter of the quarrel in a manner to " excite national susceptibilities " ; [10] and at a subsequent meeting of the deputies, his minister spoke to arouse the national pride.[11] During the Hundred Years' War this sentiment was even more lively, the Estates of 1347 authorizing, after the defeat of Crécy and the surrender of Calais, levies for an expedition into England.[12] From a legal point of view, the unborn Third Estate could look back to Saint Louis, who evinced a marked interest in justice, and recognized in his edicts that he had consulted the commoners.[13] The men of his " good towns " were to taste of power fifty years later and by an implicit compact [14] with the crown to assure its establishment together with their own ultimate subordination.[15]

Meanwhile, the lawyers of the Estates-General held in 1317 were pretexting on the ancient law of the Salian Franks an entirely new principle: the exclusion of females,

[8] Bouteiller, Jean, *Somme rurale, ou Grand Coutumier de Pratique Civile,* ed. 1603, p. 646.

[9] Picot, *op. cit.,* vol. i, p. 21.

[10] *Ibid.,* p. 22.

[11] *Ibid.,* p. 25.

[12] *Ibid.,* p. 32; *cf.* also the meeting of the Estates of April 1359, p. 81.

[13] *Ordonnances des Rois,* vol. xi, p. 330.

[14] Picot, *op. cit.,* vol. i, p. 15.

[15] Result of the Estates of 1484, see below.

or descendants through the female line, from the crown of France.[16]   In 1328, this innovation found an application at once monarchical and patriotic in the rejection of the English King Edward III's claim to the French throne,[17] and thenceforth the "Salic Law", promulgated by "Roman lawyers", was part of the unwritten constitution of France. To safeguard their own interests, the Estates of 1356, undoubtedly led by the commoners,[18] insisted on the unanimous consent of the three orders to legislation and taxation, "lest two estates, if they were of one mind, bind the third".[19] The struggle over the right to grant subsidies featured the famous estates of 1468 and 1484, just as it did the conflict between king and Parliament in England 150 years later, but with the opposite result.

Towards the end of the fifteenth century, the tact of Louis XI led the Estates themselves "by accord and consent" to grant him the right of legislation and levy in their place, whenever it was inconvenient to call the deputies of the three orders.[20]   With the regency of Anne following the death of Louis XI, a splendid opportunity offered to the Estates of establishing their rights and powers definitely. The delegates met at Tours, January 5, 1484, each having been elected in common by the nobility, clergy, and bourgeoisie of each district.[21]   They represented for the first time France as an entirety, and included in their number some of the most distinguished and talented men of the times.[22]

---

[16] Picot, *op. cit.*, vol. i, p. 28.

[17] *Ibid.*, pp. 30, 34.

[18] On this point see Picot, *op. cit.*, vol. i, p. 99; and Guizot, *Hist. de France*, vol. ii, p. 32.

[19] Picot, *op. cit.*, vol. i, p. 99n.

[20] *Ibid.*, p. 342.

[21] *Ibid.*, p. 351.

[22] *Ibid.*, p. 353.

Instead of first demanding subsidies, the chancellor, speaking for the young monarch, praised the faithfulness of the people as the outstanding national characteristic, and required of the Estates, for the first time in French history, their intelligent counsel.[23] After some weeks of orderly and successful parliamentary work, intrigues broke out among the nobles for and against the regency. It was in the ensuing debate (February 9) that Phillipe Pot delivered a speech which has been called a " magnificent summary of all the principles and ideas of national sovereignty that were to triumph three centuries later." [24] The words of the remarkable orator [25] on the subject of the king's duties have been quoted before.[26] The remainder of his harangue was a plea for the right of the Estates to hear and legislate upon all matters in the kingdom.[27] " Have you not often heard ", says Pot after quoting Cicero, " that the state is ' the thing of the people ' ? " [28]

No less enthusiastic a defender of the popular rights is Jehan Masselin, a lowly canon at Rouen before the meeting of the Estates, who reveals himself, in the Journal he kept of the proceedings, a statesman in all but power. The use of the word " nation " [29] and the repeated expressions of the people's liberty are characteristic not only of his eloquence but of that of the Estates generally.[30] Certain nobles and

[23] Masselin, *op. cit.*, p. 65 *et seq.*

[24] Picot, *op. cit.*, vol. i, p. 365.

[25] He was surnamed " the mouth of Cicero ", Picot, *op. cit.*, vol. i, p. 364n.

[26] See above, p. 56.

[27] Masselin, *op. cit.*, p. 151.

[28] *Ibid.*, p. 147.

[29] *Respublica*, Masselin, *op. cit.*, pp. 591, 647 (several times) and elsewhere.

[30] Masselin, " *libertatem populi* " *op. cit.*, p. 404; " *populus . . . liberae conditionis est, non servilis . . .*" p. 438.

bishops felt all the danger of a discussion in those terms and replied by minatory accusations of sedition, to which the popular leaders answered that "no one should be surprised or irritated that, having received a mandate from the people, having taken upon themselves the burden of its cause, and having sworn to uphold it, they would defend it with all their strength — especially when the matter under discussion was the *tailles,* odious to the nation. . . . Above all, they were representatives of the people."[31] The nobles retorted that the Estates were bent on diminishing the royal authority. One of them went so far as to exclaim: "I for one know the villains and serfs; they must not get even a glimpse of liberty! They need the yoke!"[32]

If Pot anticipates in his works and deeds the principles of popular sovereignty, Masselin certainly expounds the nature of the future enlightened monarch,[33] while reasserting his colleague's views. "Yes," declares Masselin, "the people under a monarchy is sovereign proprietor of the goods it possesses, and it is wrong to take them away when, as a body, they oppose the action. The people is in its status free, not enslaved, though subject to the monarchy; and if Aristotle's saying is true, the most moderate government is the best."[34]

All these sentiments, unfortunately, were reduced to naught by the weariness and discouragement of the remainder of the deputies, who made the fatal mistake of voting the subsidies before obtaining the redress of their grievances. Their descendants of 1789 sedulously avoided their example and realized the possibility, three centuries old, of limiting

[31] Masselin, *procuratores populi, op. cit.,* p. 416.

[32] *Ibid.,* pp. 419-420.

[33] *Cf.* Frederick the Great's *Essai sur les Formes du gouvernement* (1777) ; *Oeuvres, ed. Berlin,* vol. ix, p. 227.

[34] Masselin, *op. cit.,* p. 438.

the monarchy by a deliberative assembly made necessarily periodic by the right to grant subsidies.[35]

Equally distinctive of the Estates of 1484 is the first appearance [36] of that class-name around which the best talent will rally in the oncoming three-cornered conflict between the king, the nobility, and the bourgeoisie—willing to serve but not subserve the royalty in their capacity of Third Estate —a name that is later still to typify in the mouth of Sieyès the downtrodden Gaul taking his revenge upon the domineering Frank.[37] It is for this connection between the vindication of the middle class and the theory of a Frankish Conquest that the affairs of the Estate find a place in this essay.

Meanwhile the advocates and detractors of the Gaul during the period of the French religious wars require attention; focus it all the more sharply that they express their politico-racial bias in a more modern and more recognizable form than their predecessors. The sixteenth century is the age of the historical pamphlet and the historical memoir par excellence.[38]

Somewhat in advance of the period of controversy, the appearance in 1518 of Claude de Seyssel's *La Grant' Monarchie de France* is to be noted, not so much as a forerunner of the historico-political pamphlets to be dealt with, but rather as a reference-point with which to compare the subsequent works. In them all, the religious, the racial and the constitutional question are inseparable. For de Seyssel the monarchy of France is not an absolute one, nor is it

---

[35] Picot, *op. cit.*, vol. i, p. 390: "From 1355 to 1439, owing to the exercise of this power, the Estates attained practical periodicity."

[36] Masselin, *op. cit.*, pp. 76, 669; Picot, *op. cit.*, vol. i, Appendix A.

[37] See below, ch. xiv.

[38] Flint, R., *Historical Philosophy in France* . . . , New York, 1894, p. 185.

limited by any other enumerated institutions. Neither the Estates-General, nor the King's Council, in his view, exercise specific checks. The mere reasonableness of good policy and the great weight of old laws, customs and traditions together keep the government of France from being absolute or tyrannical.[39] The legalistic stamp of the age is seen in his approval of the growing force of the *Parlements* which he says " were instituted for this reason and this end, that they restrain the absolute power which the kings would fain enjoy." [40]

The three points made by de Seyssel relevant to this study are first, the binding force of immemorial rights, liberties, and franchises; [41] second, the notion of an unwritten constitution providing all wise checks and balances; [42] and lastly his reason for the establishment of the *parlements*. That such were the prevalent ideas concerning the French monarchy in the beginning of the sixteenth century is attested not only by the researches of modern scholars [43] but by the negative testimony of a foreign observer in France some twenty-eight years after the publication of de Seyssel's book (1546). In the famous *Relazzioni* of the Venetian Ambassadors, Marino Cavalli writes:

" The French have entirely given up their liberties and free choice into the hands of the king. He has but to say: ' I want such a sum, I demand, I order '—and the execution is as prompt as if it were the whole nation which had decided of its own volition." [44]

[39] *La Grant' Monarchie*, bk. i, chs. i, ii, iv, viii; bk. ii, ch. iv.

[40] *Ibid.*, bk. i, ch. x.

[41] *La Grant' Monarchie*, bk. i, chs. viii, xi.

[42] *Ibid.*, bk. i, ch. xii.

[43] Allen, J. W., *A History of Political Thought in the 16th Century*, New York, 1928, p. 275; A. Jacquet, *Revue des quest. hist.*, vol. lvii, pp. 400-440; and esp. pp. 424-5.

[44] *Relations des ambass.*, vol. i, p. 273.

It was when these questions of constitutional and immediate political import began to find exponents who searched
history for substantiation of their views that the connection
between the nature of the government and the people's historical traditions became apparent.[45] But before the junc-
tion of reason and history in polemic occurred in the remarkable work of Hotman entitled *Franco-Gallia,* a no less
remarkable man had undertaken, though not completed, a
collection of materials on French history, explicitly to
remedy the indifference which the early Gauls and their
successors felt regarding their deeds and fame.[46]

That man, Estienne Pasquier (1529-1615), was not only
a serious and practical thinker but a critical and philosophical
historian,[47] whose first book of *Recherches* was published in
1560, six years before the *Method of History* of Bodin,
and thirteen years before the *Franco-Gallia* of Hotman.
In his early work, *Le Pourparler du Prince,* Pasquier reveals himself a partisan of royal authority as limited by the
Estates-General. He utters the epigram to be reproduced
verbatim in Hotman's subsequent *Franco-Gallia*: " Kings
are made for the people and not the people for kings." [48]
But in the *Recherches* that partisan spirit is subject to the
critical method and translates itself into a lack of " system "
which has furnished " a mine of information to administra-
tive and political history ". [49]

Pasquier is probably the first historian of France to call

[45] See Hayes, *Essays in Nationalism,* p. 16.

[46] Pasquier, E., *Recherches de la France,* bk. i, ch. i, pp. 3, 6. *Cf.* also
the work of Ramus, *de Moribus veterum Gallorum,* Paris, 1559, trans. by
Castelnau.

[47] Thierry, *Dix Ans d'Etudes Hist.,* p. 369; Baudrillart, H., *J. Bodin
et son temps,* Paris, 1853, pp. 77-8.

[48] Cited in Baudrillart, p. 77.

[49] *Ibid.,* and Flint, p. 189.

the successors of the Romans in Gaul—namely the Franks—
Français,[50] and at the same time, to call the Gauls " our
good old fathers," [51] adding "these '*braves francais*' in time
became naturalized in the country as ' legitimate Gauls '." [52]
A further element of racial patriotism is to be found in Pasquier's attack on the modern Italian historians who call the
French barbarians, and in his proof that such was not the
opinion of Caesar regarding the Gauls.[53]   In the latter's
time, according to Pasquier, it is clearly the Germans who
are barbarians.[54]   The Gauls, lovers of justice,[55] enjoyed
" franchises and liberties " which not even Caesar or Ario-
vistus, the one a Roman, the other a German conqueror,
thought of destroying.[56]   And of the nations of old, it is
indubitable that the first and oldest is that of the Gauls, the
second is the Germans, and the third the Saracens.[57]   The
Gauls conquered all Europe,[58] and in the process established
colonies, among other places, in the Hercinian forest of
Germany, under the leadership of Sigovese.[59]   But Pasquier
does not seem to regard these colonies as the racial source
of the later Frankish invasions.   In fact, he rebukes the
great jurist François Conan for excusing his nation by
means of this last theory that the Gauls " came back " from
Germany; and he challenges foreign authors, especially

---

[50] Pasquier, *op. cit.*, bk. i, ch. i, p. 3.

[51] *Ibid.*

[52] *Ibid.*, p. 4; *cf.* also: " our old French fathers . . . by some called
Germans . . . ," bk. i, ch. ii, p. 8.

[53] *Ibid.*, ch. ii, p. 7.

[54] *Ibid.*

[55] *Cf.* also ch. iv, p. 14.

[56] *Ibid.*

[57] *Op. cit.*, bk. i, ch. iii, p. 10.

[58] *Ibid.*, and bk. i, ch. vii, p. 22.

[59] *Op. cit.*, bk. i, ch. iii, p. 10, and ch. vii, p. 20.

modern Germans who boast of *their* ancestors' conquest of
Gaul.[60]   He not only cites in a number of places the " prowess and magnanimity " and the " high chivalry of the
Gauls " [61] but he states that the Gauls established fiefs in
their conquest as later the Franks did in Gaul,[62] whence
Pasquier, to confute alien writers, derives a theory of provi-
dential compensations in the fate of nations.[63]   Lastly, he
proves that the " French invasion is not to our dishonor "
and neither was the Roman, because Caesar subjected Rome
to a worse slavery than Gaul, and Clovis, after Tolbiac, subjected the "Allemands" to a harsher rule than he did Gaul.[64]
As a matter of fact, it seems clear that Pasquier felt the
" French " had conquered Gaul not from the Gauls but
from the Romans.[65]

On the specific facts and dates of the French establishment in Gaul, Pasquier wisely admits many doubts and
much ignorance.   He gives and attacks the currently received opinion concerning the Trojan origin of the Franks,
and though he is not loath to repeat the etymology of Frank
as " brave, valiant and daring ",[66] he uses a very scholarly
and ingenious comparative method to show the unlikelihood
of the Trojan origin.[67]   In a later chapter where the same
topic is treated exclusively, Pasquier understands the desire
of all nations to endow themselves with antiquity and borrow the glory of older nations.[68]   He reviews the national

[60] Pasquier, *op. cit.*, bk. i, ch. vii, pp. 20-1.

[61] *Op. cit.*, bk. i, ch. ii, p. 7 ; ch. iv, p. 14.

[62] *Op. cit.*, bk. i, ch. iv, p. 11.

[63] *Op. cit.*, bk. i, ch. vii, p. 20.

[64] *Ibid.*

[65] *Op. cit.*, bk. i, ch. vi, p. 18.

[66] Pasquier, *op. cit.*, bk. i, ch. vi, p. 16.

[67] *Ibid.*, p. 17.

[68] In the manner of modern " subject nationalities ".   *Cf.* Hayes, *op. cit.*, pp. 11-14.

and patriotic claims to the blood of Hercules, Francio, Turcus, Brutus and Antenor, but questions the good judgment of those who choose a vanquished Trojan as the progenitor of their race.[69]

In effect, though Pasquier, alleging historical scruples based on lack of sources,[70] pretends neither to contradict nor to support the popular theory of his day, he thoroughly discredits it in a parenthetical manner. He asserts his belief in Vopiscus who placed the cradle of the German race in the marshy region east of the Rhine and south of the Ocean [North Sea].[71] He finds in old historians only the most laudatory accounts of the "French", most feared by the Romans and whose name also means free;[72] he explains, moreover, that the lack of mention of that nation in Tacitus, Caesar, Pliny, Strabo and Ptolemy is due to the common habit the Germans had of "forging themselves a new name".[73] "French" must have been a "*nom de guerre* later made common as that of the nation or region".[74]

The controversy regarding races Pasquier finds carried over into the question of the origin of fiefs. There are three opinions — one, that they are a heritage from the Gauls; two, that they were established by the Romans; three, that they were introduced by the "French". Pasquier sees clearly the motives for the divergent beliefs. "The last opinion is held because certain persons think themselves nobles, the other two because certain persons do not want to admit any element of barbarism in French institutions";

[69] Pasquier, *op. cit.*, bk. i, ch. xiv, pp. 40-1.

[70] *Ibid.*, p. 40; "All our historians lose their bearings in treating of this question", *op. cit.*, bk. i, ch. v, p. 14.

[71] *Op. cit.*, bk. i, ch. vi, p. 17.

[72] *Op. cit.*, bk. i, ch. v, p. 15.

[73] *Op. cit.*, bk. i, ch. xii, p. 33.

[74] *Op. cit.*, bk. i, ch. v, p. 15.

those who are partisans of the Gauls being so to " gratify our mother-country ". [75]

Pasquier himself favors the Gallic origin of fiefs, but with the qualification that the system of patronage and clientele reported by Caesar did not necessarily involve land, though it did imply military service.[76] Land was definitely assigned in the imperial benefices granted to the Roman Emperor's guard.[77] From these two sources the feudal system was evolved, but after its breakdown, when the nobility had to bear the attacks of the commoners, the principle that nobility is based on land and military service disappeared. The distinction began to be assumed apart from fiefs and war, by letters purchased from the king. Other upstarts alleged the antiquity of their line, having possibly changed habitat to make the fact unverifiable. The incentive to joining the new nobility is not only honor but avoidance of the King's *taille*.[78]

Pasquier evidently does not believe that the nobility of his day are lineal descendants of the French conquerors of Gaul, but he does assert that war as the profession and prerogative of the nobility is a principle " religiously adhered to " in France " in recollection of the way in which our first Frenchmen established the basis of their nobility ". [79] The tradition, if not the line, is unbroken.

In the government of France, the nobles have also had a preponderant influence. The modern Estates-General, in which the " lesser people " not only participates but constitutes the " largest and best part ",[80] are by no means an

---

[75] Pasquier, *op. cit.*, bk. ii, ch. xv, p. 120 *et seq.*   Mother-country: *patrie.*
[76] See above, ch. i.
[77] Pasquier, *ibid.,* p. 121.
[78] Pasquier, bk. ii, ch. xv, p. 128.
[79] *Ibid.*
[80] *Op. cit.,* bk. ii, ch. vii, p. 81.

old-established institution.[81] Caesar's account of the Gallic
assemblies being perpetuated under Roman rule is " a piece
of his usual hypocrisy ". The " lesser people " in the
Roman provincial assemblies " did not amount to zero ".[82]
Likewise under the first and second races (i. e. the Merovingian and Carolingian kings) only princes and nobles were
called to those councils which were the sinew of the nation.
Essentially, however, the status of persons in " our France "
is, by natural and original law, free.[83] Conquests by the
aboriginal peoples themselves, and later by the Emperors,
led to slavery and serfdom. Serfdom was of course introduced by Rome and perpetuated. But writing of contemporary times, Pasquier declares : " In France we must affirm
as an undoubted proposition that all persons are born free.
. . .[84] There are only three orders of persons—the Commoners, the Nobles, and the Ecclesiastics." [85] Against this
French tradition Pasquier finds a host of lawyers who are
attempting to impose Roman precedent contradicting French
law. Not only the Salic law, so profitable to the kingship,
but the practices of primogeniture and apanage, are likewise
prudent provisions derived from French (i. e. German) law
—" Things in truth well ordered by our ancestors ". [86]

A patriotism enlightened and kept from racial prejudice
by research, a national pride glorying in " the common
union of our France ",[87] and a preoccupation with the developing strength of the kingship [88]—such are the contribu-

[81] Pasquier, *ibid.*

[82] *Ibid.*

[83] *Op. cit.,* bk. iv, ch. v, p. 361.

[84] *Ibid.* He makes exception for certain provinces.

[85] *Ibid.,* p. 363.

[86] *Op. cit.,* bk. ii, ch. xvii, p. 136.

[87] Pasquier, *op. cit.,* bk. i, ch. ii, p. 8.

[88] Flint, *op. cit.,* p. 189; Baudrillart, *op. cit.,* p. 78.

tions of Etienne Pasquier to the manifold doctrine of nation and race that motivates our study.

Six years after the appearance of Pasquier's first Book of *Recherches,* ten years before his own *Six Books of the Republic,* Jean Bodin published the *Method for the easy understanding of History,*[89] a brief manual suggesting in part the plan of Montesquieu's *Spirit of the Laws,* the eighteenth-century author's theory of climate conditioning history, and including some remarks on the origins of nations, and the influence that such historical traditions exert on a people.[90]

Like Pasquier before him and like Hotman after, the celebrated jurist and leader of the Third Estate begins by denying to Roman law applicability to matters subsumed under universal law, by which Bodin means both the principles of eternal justice and the body of extant legislation.[91] Comparative law is consequently the higher ground from which Bodin is going to judge governments and make history fulfill its "primary utility: serving politics".[92]   He would also introduce into history that order which he finds reason establishing in the field of natural science.[93]   By his insistence on modern history, Bodin suggests in the section "De historicorum delectu" [94] the similar opening chapter of Pasquier deploring the lack of interest in history shown by the early French historians.   This is only preliminary to the major thesis of Bodin's book, that the difference of races and the difference of climates are the two stable and

[89] *Methodus ad facilem historiarum cognitionem,* ed. 1595.

[90] Bodin, *op. cit.,* ch. ix, p. 303.

[91] Praef, p. 9.

[92] *Ibid.*   Politics is to be taken here in the sense of the art of government, not the purposes of parties.   *Cf.* also ch. vi, p. 140.

[93] Ch. ii, *De ordine historiarum,* p. 26.

[94] Bodin, ch. iv, p. 43 *et seq.*

fundamental factors affecting modern history and modern institutions.[95]

Within this quasi-rationalist system it is logical for Bodin to conclude with a survey of the origins of peoples, partly to refute accepted theories that put back the glory and valor of modern nations into the past, partly to sketch the methodology of comparative history when dealing with primitive times.[96] Thus it is that he cites Tacitus and Caesar to combat the current unsubstantiated notion of Trojan descent.[97] Like Pasquier, but in a more dogmatic manner, he assigns to the Franks a German origin,[98] but forces interpretations of Caesar and Tacitus to establish the explanation that the Franks were but descendants of Gallic colonists beyond the Rhine.[99] Though he condemns racial patriotism in history for its setting up of group against group corresponding to the rival beliefs of superior descent,[100] Bodin is enthusiastic enough to rank Charlemagne as equal to Alexander and St. Louis above Marcus Aurelius,[101] which he can do without national disloyalty inasmuch as for him *Franci* is interchangeable with *Germani*.[102]

The burden of Bodin's teachings regarding history no doubt led him, in the ten years that elapsed between the publication of the *Methodus* and the meeting of the Estates at Blois in 1576, to consider more specifically the body of customs existing in France which tended to limit the power of the hereditary monarchy, so highly praised by him in the

[95] Bodin, *op. cit.,* ch. v, p. 80. *Cf.* in the *Republic,* bk. v, ch. iii.

[96] *Op. cit.,* ch. ix, p. 304.

[97] Bodin, *op. cit.,* ch. ix, p. 327.

[98] *Ibid.,* p. 326 *et seq.*

[99] *Op. cit.,* ch. vi, p. 266; ch. ii, p. 28.

[100] *Op. cit.,* ch. ix, p. 303.

[101] *Op. cit.,* ch. vii, p. 272.

[102] *Op. cit.,* ch. v, p. 93.

book of 1566.[103] Consequently, when he became by a concourse of circumstances the eloquent and far-seeing leader of the Third Estate at Blois,[104] he realized the opportunity to put his beliefs into effect. He invoked the old established law of the kingdom against subjecting one Estate to defeat by the union of the other two.[105] Redoubling his efforts against the encroachments of the aristocracy,[106] he incurred the displeasure of both king and nobles.[107] Mézeray said of him: " He remonstrated there (at Blois) with the freedom of an old Gaul. . . ."[108]

Bodin, in effect, demanded for the nation a true representation in the Estates—" all of France speaks through 400 deputies "—to reduce the number to thirty-six would be to court a lack of confidence on the part of the country.[109] He further maintained that " the king's domain belonged to the provinces and that the king had only the use of them"; [110] that the power of monarchs is limited and that they should govern according to the laws.[111]

It was at the risk of his own comfort, and certainly at the expense of his possible official career,[112] that Bodin thus translated into action the historical system of ideas which make of him, in the words of Baudrillart, " the Montes-

---

[103] *Op. cit.*, ch. vi, p. 157 *et seq.*

[104] Picot, *op. cit.*, vol. iii, p. 59.

[105] *Ibid.*, p. 66. *Cf.* also in the *Republic*, bk. iii, p. 48 for the corresponding maxim. The *Republic* appeared the same year as the Estates met, but before the opening session.

[106] Bodin, *Methodus*, ch. ix, p. 303.

[107] Bayle, P., *Dictionnaire Hist.*, Art. Bodin, vol. ii, p. 46.

[108] Quoted in Bayle, vol. ii, p. 46n.

[109] Picot, *op. cit.*, vol. iii, p. 63.

[110] Bayle, *op. cit.*, vol. ii, p. 46n.; *cf.* Letter of Bodin to Pibrac, Pref. to *Republic*, quoted by Bayle, p. 47n.

[111] *Ibid.*, p. 52.

[112] See notes 107 and 108.

quieu of the sixteenth century ".[113] But we must not forget that by 1576, another and perhaps more direct, more thoroughgoing, more passionate application of the historical method had been made to the confused racial and constitutional issues of the sixteenth century in France. That application is contained in the *Franco-Gallia* of the famous French " civilian " François Hotman.[114]

[113] Baudrillart, *J. Bodin et son Temps,* p. 412.

[114] Civilian was a term applied to masters of Roman civil law. Hotman obtained success in the chairs of law at Strasbourg and Bourges.

CHAPTER IV

HOTMAN—LA BOÉTIE—DU HAILLAN

FRANÇOIS HOTMAN,[1] second only to Bodin among the famous jurists of the sixteenth century, was born in Paris in 1524, in a well-to-do family originally from Silesia. He was sent to the University for a degree in Law and soon came under the influence of the Protestant leaders, whose political ideas he absorbed as avidly as their creed. Deeply learned in Roman law, he soon developed a political ideal in which were combined the classical republicanism of the ancients, the independent national spirit of the Protestants, and the anti-despotic fervor of the Old Testament.

It was after a narrow escape from the massacre of the Saint Bartholomew that as an exile in Geneva, possibly in Calvin's own house, Hotman decided to find in French history a solution to the civil strife which had already been raging since twelve years in his native land (*patriam*), destroying its supremacy in letters and learning.[2] A lover of his country, he sought to remedy the evils by looking into its first constitution, under which the nation (*republica nostra*) flourished over a thousand years. To that end he studied "the earliest of our historians of our Frankish Gaul, both the Gauls and the Germans."[3] The brief but highly condensed result of his researches is appropriately

---

[1] These biographical details are based on: *Biographie Universelle*, Art. Hotman; Bayle's *Dictionnaire Hist. et Crit.*, *ibid.*; Flint, *op. cit.*, pp. 187-8; Thierry, *Récits*, pp. 30-1.

[2] *Franco-Gallia*, ed. London, 1711, Pref., pp. 4-5.

[3] *Ibid.* p. 5.

76

entitled *Franco-Gallia,* and as fittingly dedicated to Frederick, duke of Bavaria, " ever a friend of Franco-Gallia ". [4]

It is in this pseudo-historical pamphlet, extremely popular in its day, though disavowed by both Protestants and Catholics, that we find for the first time a thoroughgoing mélange of the facts and institutions of French history to serve the cause of popular liberty. From the German public assemblies reported by Tacitus, to the Estates-General of the Valois kings, the constitutional development of France points clearly, in Hotman's opinion, to the legislative supremacy of a great national council.

" Before the Roman conquest, Gaul was made up of numerous provinces; some with kings, some ruled by the people with the advice of the Nobles, and these were called free. . . . [5] There was a common council for all Gallia, though not inclusive of the Armoricans in Brittany who were independent. . . . [6] These kingdoms were not hereditary nor arbitrary but conferred by the People upon Just Men, whose authority was circumscribed by Laws. . . . [7] The Constitution created a balance of equal powers between the king and the people." [8]

The author interrupts his principles, based in this regard chiefly upon Caesar, to inquire into the original language of the Gauls. He considers it important as a factor in national life [9] and concludes that it was " British " and

---

[4] Hotman, *op. cit.,* p. 6.

[5] *Ibid.,* p. 2.

[6] *Ibid.,* p. 5.

[7] *Ibid.,* pp. 5-6.

[8] *Ibid.,* p. 7.

[9] Though *Franco-Gallia* was written in Latin, a contemporary translation, under the title of *Gaule française,* appeared in 1574, reprinted in *Mém. de l'Etat de France sous Charles IX,* 1576, t. ii, attributed to Simon Goulart.

still remains as the patois of lower Brittany.[10]   The present
language of France is a compound of the several tongues
of divers nations.   French is one-half Roman; the other
half is one-third ancient Gallic, one-third Greek, one-third
Frank. " Frank, that is to say, German words," explains
the author.[11] It took ten years, he adds boastfully, for this
most valiant and warlike people, the Gauls, to submit to the
Great Beast. The Romans were afraid of the Gauls, who
at one time excelled the Germans in valor and established
colonies beyond the Rhine.[12]

Obviously Hotman is an early, if not the first partisan of
the theory that the Gallic element in the French race contributed most to the formation of the French nationality
which he loves " like a parent, but a greater parent." [13]
Patriotism not only animates him in his task but is to him
the *sine qua non* of a well-born soul: " In Gentle Disposi-
tions, there is a certain inbred Love of their country which
they can no more divest themselves of than of humanity
itself." [14]

To show the unbroken tradition of liberty in Gaul, Hotman points to the cities which were left free under Roman
rule, and to the frequent revolts of the Gauls; which in turn
led to their importation of German auxiliaries.[15]   Thus the
theory of an original invitation to the Frankish invaders is
launched on its career. Beaten or bought off by the Romans,
the Franks were allowed to settle on the borders of Gallia;
from which facts it is to be inferred that the Gauls resented
the " cruel, inhuman, wicked domination of the Romans in

10 Hotman, *op. cit.*, p. 12.

11 *Ibid.*, p. 13.

12 *Ibid.*, p. 14.

13 *Ibid.*, pp. 2, 15.

14 *Ibid.*, p. 2.

15 *Ibid.*, pp. 16-18.

Gaul and multitudes of Franks poured into it." [16]   Despite his proof that the Franks were a group of the Germanic nations, Hotman, like Pasquier, makes the point that they are not mentioned by Ptolemy, Strabo or even by Tacitus. Later historians quietly assume the identity of all German peoples and derive the bulk of their information regarding the Franks from Tacitus who perhaps never heard of them. The Franks, Hotman admits, enjoyed great reputation and power, especially under Charlemagne when they were masters of a great part of Europe, by which time they had assimilated the Roman tongue.[17]

The great jurist is not credulous enough to believe in the Trojan origin of the Franks.   He scouts it as false, and likewise expresses his surprise that Gregory of Tours should not know that the Germans came from the marshes between the Elbe and the Rhine.[18]

But how to account for the absence of the name Frank in early histories?   Either that people must at first have been obscure, or the name arose when those that set up as leaders in the recovery of public liberty called themselves Franks, " by which name the Germans understood such as were free and under no servitude." [19]   Like Montesquieu later, but with better excuse, Hotman thinks the " ferocious Franks " to have been the originators of liberty—whence their fame.   But certain difficulties attend this subsequently popular belief, which the lawyer proceeds to explain : " To obey a king is not servitude ; but to submit to the unfounded Will of a Tyrant, a Thief, an Executioner is to resign oneself to the Knife of the Butcher." [20]   The kings of the

[16] Hotman, *op. cit.*, p. 19.

[17] *Ibid.*, p. 22.

[18] *Ibid.*, pp. 24-7.

[19] *Ibid.*, p. 29.   *Cf. Francisare,* to restore to liberty.

[20] *Ibid.*, p. 31.

Franks, says Hotman, combining history with law, were their protectors, and the keepers of their liberty; an ideal which led them to deliver not only Germany but also Gaul and Italy from Roman oppression.[21]

With historical acumen our author relegates to a dubious past Pharamond, Chlodio, and even Meroveus. The first king of the Franco-Gauls, after he had been elected in a public council of the associated peoples, was hoisted on a shield amid "great acclamations of joy and universal gratulations."[22] Nothing more wise and fitting[23] can be devised, according to the author, than an elective kingship, in which the sons of the royal house are preferred and enthroned by popular choice. He invokes the last will and testament of Charlemagne to confirm his judgment, and indeed uses chiefly Carolingian sources for his description of the Commonwealth.[24] The right of revolt from a bad king is established in the precedent of Childeric's deposition for profligacy,[25] the most noble and glorious deed of our ancestors, showing that in the infancy of the nation the king was accepted upon recognized terms.[26]

Proceeding from the subject of kingly heirs to that of kingly hair, Hotman makes the significant parallel that among the Franks only the royal family had the right to wear long hair, parted in the middle, whereas among the Gauls the entire nation had before been admitted to the privilege.[27] But beyond this distinction both nations limited the power of their kings, Caesar bearing witness to the

---

[21] Hotman, *ibid.*

[22] *Ibid.*, p. 37.

[23] *Ibid.*, p. 77.

[24] *Ibid.*, pp. 38-9.

[25] See above, ch. ii, p. 44.

[26] Hotman, *op. cit.*, p. 44.

[27] *Ibid.*, p. 61.

custom in Gaul; Tacitus to that in Germany.[28] Naturally, the supreme administration of the Franco-gallican kingdom was lodged in the " Annual Public Council of the Nation " [29] (*mallus*) which in after ages was called the Convention of the Three Estates—a happy combination of the three kinds of government—royal, noble, and popular.[30] Indeed, nearly two hundred years before *The Spirit of the Laws,* the *Franco-Gallia* exalts the government of England as the best moderated.[31] The author divides his admiration between the equilibrium of powers in the latter and the democratic independence of his nation's Gallic and Frankish ancestors. His terminology is almost demagogically modern: " The people's Right is a sacred right "; [32] at the same time he gives the principle of liberty an historical justification beyond its wisdom and prudence: " in these most profligate times it is a sort of piety to be pleased with the wisdom of our ancestors." [33]

Suggesting the means to save his native land, Hotman calls for the restoration of the ancient rights: annual meetings of the parliament of the Three Estates,[34] empowered to deal with all matters of state, including what he calls " creating or abdicating the king ", declaring war and peace, making all public laws, conferring all honors, and apportioning the deceased king's patrimony among his children.[35]

[28] Hotman, *op. cit.,* p. 63.

[29] This term and " Convention of the People " are to Hotman interchangeable terms. *Cf. Franco-Gallia,* pp. 48, 104-5, 114-8.

[30] *Ibid.,* p. 66.

[31] *Ibid.,* pp. 68-71.

[32] *Ibid.,* p. 71. *Cf.* ch. xi: " Of the Sacred Authority of the Publick Council " (p. 77) " ... The Solemn General Council of the Nation " (p. 92). Also pp. 106-7; and, ". . . Free and Sacred State ", p. 122.

[33] *Ibid.,* p. 72.

[34] *Ibid.,* p. 71.

[35] *Ibid.,* pp. 77-8. The last enumerated power he makes a point of deriving from the old German custom of *Abannagium,* in French, *apanage.*

From Clovis, the German liberator of the Gauls, to the descendants of Pippin the Short, he adds, all successions, all appointments to high office were made by the sovereign people; [36] and further, suggesting the English parliamentary doctrine of the next century, "the very last resort and disposal of all things was lodged not in Pippin or Charles or Louis, but in the Regal majesty, the seat of which is the Annual General Council." [37]   A people can exist without a king, can rule itself or be ruled by its nobility. Hotman quotes the Saxon Law which at its very outset compares a king and his people to a ship with its pilot; the people is not designed for the sake of the kings, but the king is sought out and instituted for the people's sake.[38]

These things being so, how and why does Hotman have to remind his countrymen of the fundamental constitution? Because in the tenth century, at the time of Hugh Capet's accession, the General Council allowed a great part of its authority to be taken away.[39]   The Council, however, retained the rest of its power until the time of Louis XI, as the histories of Froissart, Monstrellet, Gaguin, and Commines demonstrate.   But the crafty fifteenth-century king was, "in the duty of a good prince and as a lover of his country, much wanting ".[40]   It is plain, therefore, that "it is not yet a hundred years complete since the liberties of Franco-Gallia and the authority of its Annual General Council still flourished in full vigor and exerted themselves against a king of ripe years and great understanding ". [41]

[36] Hotman, pp. 89, 51-2.

[37] *Ibid.*, p. 104. I cannot, on the evidence of the *Franco-Gallia*, concur in the opinion of Baudrillart, *Tableau du XVIᵉ Siècle*, pp. 61-3, that Hotman spoke for the aristocracy.

[38] Hotman, *op. cit.*, p. 108. *Cf.* La Boétie.

[39] *Ibid.*, p. 113.

[40] *Ibid.*, p. 118.

[41] *Ibid.*, p. 122.

In conclusion, Hotman, like a number of the historians examined previously, protests against the application of Roman Law to French institutions,[42] notably in the matter of the Salic Law. He realizes that the original Salic Law confined itself to private law.[43] But maintaining as he does the legislative power of the Nation through Custom, he recognizes the great value of its able misconstruction in the national crisis of 1328.[44] The real harm done to the nation by the legal-minded comes not only from excessive litigation,[45] nor from the fact that nearly a third of the population takes its profits from the numerous *Parlements* which have sprung up all over France,[46] but that these " pleaders and pettyfoggers " have subjected by their craft the nobles and the princes as well as the General Council.[47] They try to exercise a veto over royal edicts, to enforce an oath of office for all positions in France, and to prohibit appeal from their judgments.[48] These regrettable institutions, born of the study of Roman Law, Hotman believes are to be permanent, but he protests against the resulting misuse of the term *Parlement,* properly applicable only to the former legislative councils of the province or nation.[49]

This work of Hotman, though disavowed in part by its own author some years later, nevertheless had a great influence on his own generation.[50] The notions of a national

[42] Hotman, *op. cit.*, p. 125.

[43] *Ibid.*, pp. 57-8.

[44] *Ibid.*, pp. 54, 127-34.

[45] *Ibid.*, p. 136.

[46] *Ibid.* There were in Hotman's day seven fixed parlements and one circuit council.

[47] *Ibid.*, p. 135.

[48] *Ibid.*, p. 137.

[49] *Ibid.*, pp. 136, 144.

[50] Thierry, *Récits*, p. 35.

elective monarchy and a sovereign national council became for a time the doctrines of the party of the League that was to be so powerful at the Estates of 1588.[51] The historical good faith of the author, the visible mass of quotations in his book, convinced not only himself but many of his readers that his thesis was sound. More than a century later, the hypercritical Pierre Bayle asserted " That book of Hotman is at bottom a fine piece, well-written and full of learning, and so much the more vexatious to the opposite party because the author contents himself with citing matters of fact. . . ."[52]

The chief merits of Hotman were his plan—that of the historical method applied as a guide to contemporary policy[53] —and his originality in the collection of primary sources. He composed the *Franco-Gallia* before the full publication of the *Researches* of Pasquier or of the *Republic* of Bodin, at a time when the erudite compilations that appeared in the succeeding century had not even been projected.

If Hotman was reproached as if his work were " the production of a drunken furious mad-man ",[54] it may have been because of the intellectual progeny it engendered. With the *Vindiciae Contra Tyrannos* of Hubert Languet,[55] the firmness of Hotman becomes violence, and is indeed directed equally against the king and the people, which is represented as a wild beast. Disobedience, deposition of kings and tyrannicide are the three steps in the revolt preached by this inflammatory pamphlet,[56] which is men-

---

[51] Picot, *op. cit.*, vol. iii, p. 374, n. 3.

[52] Bayle, *Dict. Hist. & Crit.*, London ed., Art. Hotman, vol. iii, p. 522n.

[53] Suggested in Bodin's *Method of History*, pub. 1566. See above, p. 72.

[54] Bayle, *op. cit., ibid.*

[55] Some say Duplessy-Mornay hid behind the pseudonym of Junius Brutus.

[56] This account based on Flint, *op. cit.*, p. 187; Baudrillart, *op. cit.*, pp. 68-9; and Bonnefon, *Oeuvres de La Boétie*, p. xxxi *et seq.*

tioned here only as an indication of the passions to which Hotman's erudition willingly or not furnished weapons.

As in Bodin's earlier *Method,* the remainder of the historical ammunition used by the sixteenth-century pamphleteers derives chiefly from the Bible and aims at enthroning regicide. Hotman's use of French history was not to bear fruit until the first half of the eighteenth century when French historians representing the views of distinct social classes, and the notion of a common origin for Gauls and Franks, reopened the combat that was to involve Boulainvilliers and Dubos, Montesquieu and Sieyès.

Meanwhile an essentially different expression of the sixteenth-century spirit of revolt must be cited if the transition to the historical preoccupations of the seventeenth century are to be understood. This other contemporary sentiment, which may be called the " natural rights " theory, is voiced in the *Contr'Un* of Etienne de la Boétie,[57] famous in his day for the eloquence of his book, and since, also for the affection showed him by Montaigne.[58]

Written in La Boétie's eighteenth year, this *Discourse on Voluntary Servitude* is a passionate and brilliantly-conceived appeal to non-resistance and non-cooperation with the king. The youthful author combats the idolatry which has always hedged about the kingship, ridicules the " pretty stories " told of Clovis and other French kings as sources of present political conduct.[59] This is the negation of Bodin's and Hotman's efforts. It will be also the rationalist attitude of Rousseau,[60] opposed to the historical point of view of Montesquieu.

[57] La Boétie, *Oeuvres,* ed. Bonnefon, Bordeaux, 1892.

[58] *Essais,* bk. i, ch. xxvii.

[59] *Contr'Un,* p. 43.

[60] *Discours de l'Inégalité,* p. 4; *cf.* also Dezeimeris, R., *Renaissance des Lettres à Bordeaux,* p. 42.

In effect, La Boétie is only pointing out with convincing warmth the lesson taught in the twelfth century by Wace [61] that the king differs in no whit from other men; that he is one and they are many.[62]   His solution is non-resistance to, and non-cooperation with the king.[63]   Whatever historical examples are adduced by the young enthusiast are drawn from classical sources or from contemporary Italy.[64]   Not unmindful of the connection between liberty and patriotism,[65] La Boétie by his pamphlet, widely read in the sixteenth century, not only gave text to all the succeeding proponents of liberty, but was construed in his own day as agitating for revolt.   An anonymous reader of his pamphlet penciled on its margin " Seditious against the monarchy ";[66] and a practical application of his ideas regarding tyranny was made in the *Réveille-Matin des Français,* a publication of the year 1574 under the name of Eusebius Philadelphus, reproducing a large fragment of La Boétie's treatise.

Under the reigns of Henry IV and his successors, the work fell into quasi-oblivion, only to be resuscitated at the time of the French Revolution, when it was reprinted twice [67] and again in a mélange composed of extracts from two other libertarians—Benjamin Constant and Alfieri.[68]

La Boétie was thus a noticeable factor at the outset of the politico-racial struggle we are examining, though he differs from the pamphleteers who invoked Frankish liberty and

[61] *Cf. Roman de Rou,* ed. Pluquet, t. ii, p. 303 *et seq.;* also, Beaumanoir, *passim.*

[62] *Contr'Un,* p. 8.

[63] *Ibid.,* p. 14.

[64] *Ibid.,* pp. 24-5.

[65] *Ibid.,* pp. 8, 33.

[66] Bonnefon, p. xxxvii.

[67] In 1789 and 1790.

[68] In 1852 as a protest against the coup d'état of December: *Tyrannie, Usurpation, et Servitude Volontaire* . . . Bruxelles, 1852.

the constitution of France on behalf of their party and the
" people ". From its reputation as well as from its contrast in method, it was necessary that the *Contr'Un* be opposed to the *Franco-Gallia*; the chief glory of the sixteenth-
century rationalist school confronted with the numerous
examples of the historical school.

In the realm of non-partisan historical research, the sixteenth century contributed almost as much usable materials
as did the pamphleteers, and inasmuch as the historiographers will, in the course of the seventeenth and eighteenth
centuries be referred to almost as sources, a brief glance at
their works and tendencies is here in order.

Following the *Grandes Chroniques de France* of the fifteenth century, known later as the *Chroniques de Saint-Denis*
and incidentally the first printed [69] history of France (1476),
Nicole Gilles (died 1503) made a fanciful abstract [70] which
won great popularity by its more palatable French dress.[71]
Gilles repeats, of course, the story of the Trojan origin
given such prominence in the *Chroniques*. But an interesting passage [72] of the work is that dealing with Charlemagne,
made a giant, a hero, nearly a god, in accordance with the
popular traditions remarked above.[73]

Throughout Gilles' work, in spite of the interspersed
Latin phrases, the words *Francus* and *Francicus* are translated as *François*, regardless of chronology. The distinction
that Pasquier, for example, made towards the end of the
sixteenth century between the Gallic and the Frankish origins

---

[69] Thierry, *Lettres sur l'Hist. de France*, p. 51. The *Chroniques* are
reprinted in Bouquet, *op. cit.*, vol. iii, p. 155 *et seq.*

[70] *Les Chroniques et Annales de France depuis la destruction de Troye
jusques au Roy Louis unziesme*, Paris, 1566.

[71] Thierry, *Dix Ans*, p. 335.

[72] *Chroniques et Annales*, folio 45.

[73] See above, p. 52 *et seq.*

of the French is utterly unknown or ignored a hundred years earlier.

Of Pasquier's admiration for previous historians a fair share was allotted to the one he calls Paul-Emile.   Paulus Emilius (died 1529) was a Veronese scholar imported by Louis XII for the purpose of writing the history of France in the " new " Italian manner, imitative of Thucydides and the classic historians.   Emilius' *De rebus gestis Francorum* [74] is a sort of transposition of French history into Graeco-Roman terms.   The result, even though based on all the extant sources, finds again the Renaissance civilization of France in the time of Clovis, with the consequent removal of all barbarism, invasion, and violence from French history.

Not only Mézeray in the next century, but Dubos in the eighteenth, relied upon Emilius for certain details, although the work was not very popular in its own day owing partly to its precious latinity.   One incident—Anastasius' conferring the consular dignities upon Clovis [75] — was given by Paulus-Emilius all the solemnity and significance which it will assume in the hands of the abbés who believed in the imperial " right " of Clovis to rule Gaul and who cite the Veronese manufacturer of speeches almost as if he were a contemporary witness.[76]

Another historian, cited by Hotman, but no more popular than Paulus-Emilius, is Gaguinus (died 1520) whose *Chroniques de France* [77] is notable only for its rejection of popular legends, such as those perpetuated by Gilles, and for the historic directness the author feels free to use regarding the reigning house of kings.   Speaking of Hugh Capet, the sixteenth-century author says: "And he had himself crowned

[74] *Libri quatuor et seq.*, Basel, 1601.

[75] *De rebus gestis Franc.*, p. 12.

[76] See below, ch. ix.

[77] Appeared 1515.

king of France and put Charles in prison, to whom that
kingdom belonged—Hugh the Great it was begot this Hugh
Capet, usurper of the kingdom of France. . . ." [78]

Thus far, the sixteenth century had had little more than
collections and rearrangements of medieval chronicles offered it. The " new " historian appeared in the person of
Bernard de Girard, seigneur du Haillan (1537-1610), whose
Histoire générale des rois de France, already quoted from,
is contemporaneous with the Estates of Blois and Bodin's
Republic (1576).

Du Haillan's thesis is that history must deal only with
affairs of state; his secondary point is that the history of
France should be written in French.[79] Contrary to the
anachronism of Emilius, du Haillan finds that polite learning and letters in France do not go much farther back than
fifty years.[80] He recognizes the barbarism of the times of
Gregory of Tours, and indirectly the violent characters
of the nations that invaded Gaul.[81]

Du Haillan's realization does not correspond to his plan.
The classical speeches, the chroniclers' inventions are largely
re-worked into his " history ". *Frank* is still *French* for
the historian, who follows the medieval notion that the fiefs
date from Charlemagne, under whom occurred a perfectly
legitimate division of the lands wrested from " so many
barbarian nations ". [82]

The gentleman du Haillian has the distinction of being
the first " historiographer of the king ", a title that super-
seded that of chronicler. And in his protest against the local
color of the medieval narrators, he can indeed be ranked as

[78] *Chroniques,* folio 58.
[79] *Histoire,* Preface to the reader, p. vi.
[80] *Ibid.*
[81] *Ibid.*
[82] *Histoire,* vol. i, p. 204.

the first of a long line of political, not to say royal, historians who in their turn had to yield before Voltaire's revolution, when the " new " history once more reverted to
manners and customs.[83]

Three years after the publication of the *Histoire générale*
a work directly opposed to it in tendency was given in the
first volume of the *Antiquitez gauloises et françoises* of
Claude Fauchet, president of the *Chambre des Monnaies*.
Fauchet has a clear notion of the race difference between
the Gauls and the *French* [84] undoubtedly gained from Gregory of Tours, whose importance as a source he fully appre-
ciates.[85] Interested in presenting " the manners of our old
French " [86] (fathers) Fauchet prefers to " base himself on
good memoirs " [87] rather than to invent eloquent speeches.
The result is an extremely conscientious piece of work,
" purged almost entirely of fables ",[88] and " free of favorit-
ism or hatred, to which I have no leaning ".[89]

Another officer of the Parlement, Jean du Tillet, was
working about the same time as Fauchet, on a *Recueil des
Roys de France* published posthumously in 1517. The history of early Frankish times assumes in his hands—this is
his chief contribution—a philological aspect dear to many of
his seventeenth and eighteenth-century continuators. But it

[83] Du Haillan says of the chroniclers: " They amuse themselves with
recounting the conversations between one gentleman and another; or a
captain and a soldier; this and that; banquets, precedence, ceremony, their
sauces and jellies, the dress of the Princes, how they sat and how embraced one another . . . which do not belong in history at all." Pref.,
p. ii.

[84] *Antiquitez,* ed. 1610, folio 147.

[85] *Ibid.*

[86] *Ibid.,* folio 103.

[87] *Ibid.*

[88] Thierry, *Dix Ans,* p. 363.

[89] *Antiquitez,* folio 1.

has the merit of establishing once more in the last quarter of the sixteenth century the Germanic origin of the Franks: [90]

Those who have written that the French were originally true Germans have done them more honor than those who have thought them come from the Trojans, since honor is due only to virtue. For there has been no nation which has suffered less from corruption of morals, and which has so long and valiantly preserved its liberty with arms, than the German, which even today would be the best maintained, were it united.[91]

The year 1579 again saw the appearance of a general history, that of François de Belleforest,[92] who established in no uncertain terms not alone the Gallo-German origin of the Franks [93] (occasionally called by him *Francs*),[94] but the fact of their conquest of Gaul [95] and the conception of Hugh Capet's accession as the end of German royalty.[96] He refutes Hotman on the elective character of the French monarchy.[97] He coins the word *Francs-Gaulois* in an effort at greater exactitude, not followed by Mézeray and Daniel in the succeeding age.

The last few years of the sixteenth century saw other histories on the market, each characterized by some critical or political bent; from the *Grandeur, droits, prééminence des rois et royaumes de France* [98] by Francois Pithou, who sought to defend Henri IV from the bulls of Gregory XIV;

[90] *Recueil*, ed. 1618, p. 8; he still calls them French, to be sure.

[91] *Ibid.*

[92] *Les Grandes Annales et Histoire générale de France*, 1579.

[93] Foreword, folio 1.

[94] Subtitle—"*dès la venue des Francs*", but ". . . *contenans la conqueste d'iceux François.*"

[95] *Ibid.*, vol. i, folio 362.

[96] *Ibid.*, vol. i, folio 364.

[97] *Ibid.*, vol. i, folio 1.

[98] Published 1594.

to the *Inventaire général de l'histoire de France* [99] by Jean de Serres, the second royal historiographer, whose sole object in his mediocre compilation is to arouse the interest of his countrymen in past French history, that a reciprocal understanding may result from its collation with contemporary history.[100]

Incidental to another work on contemporary history, the *Histoire de France* [101] of Lancelot de la Popelinière, is to be found a more scholarly and definitive refutation of the Trojan origin of the French,[102] which, added to those already enumerated, warrants the conclusion that, outside popular histories,[103] the myth is definitely dead by the end of the sixteenth century. It is only to be regretted that it was not also buried at the same epoch.

At least one author, unfortunately anonymous, attempted that undertaking in a pleasant little pamphlet, *Discours non plus mélancolique que divers, de choses mesmement qui appartiennent à notre France,* etc.,[104] in which learned discussions of the Trojan story and the accompanying " etymologies " are laughed out of court by the invention of equally plausible and no less absurd substitutes.

A second conclusion warranted by the works of the sixteenth-century historians is the growing distinction between

[99] Published 1597.

[100] *Inventaire*, p. 4.

[101] Published 1581.

[102] Pref. to vol. i, p. iii. Bossuet cites him as trustworthy, though he was a Calvinist. *Hist. des Var.*, p. 1.

[103] Such as that of Jean le Maire des Belges, *Illustrations des Gaules et singularitez de Troie,* published 1509-13 but popular till the time of Ronsard who borrowed the " facts " to write the first four books of his *Franciade*, would-be national epic, published 1572. *Cf.* also the works of Jean Bouchet, *Généalogies des rois de France,* 1527; Ferrand de Bez' history of the kings of France, 1577; Du Bellay de Langeay, *Epitome de l'antiquité des Gaules de France,* 1556.

[104] Poictiers, 1557, pp. 1-16.

Frank and Gaul. Third, it is clearly the prevailing notion that the Franks (or French) who left Germany, were only descendants of a colony of Gauls. Lastly, something like national patriotism [105] pierces through nearly every writer's " thesis " or " appeal ", allied very frequently to passionate pleas for liberty,[106] which is invoked as an immemorial right of the French and not infrequently based on the well-battered etymology of *Frank* as *free*. That these last two sentiments pervaded to some extent the active part of the population seems confirmed in two different ways. Writing shortly before the middle of the century, the Venetian ambassador, speaking of the French nation's resented loss of liberties, says:

The thing has gone so far that some of the French themselves, who see more clearly than others, say: ' Our kings used to be called *Reges Francorum,* now they should be called *Reges Servorum!* ' [107]

The consciousness of national unity on the part of the French, on the other hand, may be shown in the demands of the Third Estate at Blois, regarding the abuse of naturalization as a privilege conferrable by the king. Aimed primarily at the foreign bishops and favorites of Catherine de' Medici, the request was finally concurred in patriotically [108] by all three orders as the re-enforcement of an

---

[105] *Cf.* for example, Pasquier's 1st chapter, and Hotman, and La Popelinière, *passim;* or in an incidental remark in Jean de Serres: " O Frenchmen, it is to you this history is addressed, as to men who have the chiefest interest in the State of your Mother, which foreigners can only admire." *Inventaire,* " Touchant l'usage de ce sien."

[106] What d'Aubigné calls the " malady of the kingdom ", referring especially to La Boétie, Hotman and Junius Brutus. *Hist. Univ.,* t. ii, bk. ii, ch. ii, p. 1072.

[107] *Relations des Ambass.,* vol. i, p. 273.

[108] Picot, *op. cit.,* vol. iii, p. 108.

ancient law of the kingdom.[109] A residence requirement of ten years or more was demanded by the Estates, together with a minimum of 200 livres income, and wife and child, before letters of naturalization might be granted. These were revocable after an absence of one year on the part of the beneficiary.[110]

Finally, a section on indications of French national unity in the sixteenth century cannot come to a close without mention of the *Satyre Ménippée,* the joint work of half a dozen jurists and historians who, in this parody of the Estates of the League of 1593, attacked the private and public corruptions perpetuated by the civil wars and the unholy antinational alliance of the League party with the Spaniards.[111] To the second part of the satire, Pierre Pithou, learned jurist, and brother of the historian already cited, contributed a " Harangue . . . on behalf of the Third Estate " in the course of which is vented a noble indignation at the invasion of Paris and the free cities by foreigners—Spaniards, Walloons, Neapolitans.[112] The representative of the nobility, though he ironically affects lack of comprehension at the attacks on the League, shows the temper and conviction of the authors when he says:

. . . I have also heard my grandmother say as she brought her butter to market that once upon a time there were such as Gaston de Foix, Dunois, La Hire, Poton, and Captain Bayart, who strove but for honor and to acquire glory for the French . . .[113]

---

[109] Picot, *ibid.*

[110] *Ibid.,* pp. 249-50.

[111] Speech of de Rieux, *Satyre,* ed. Ch. Read, p. 161.

[112] Speech of d'Aubray, *ibid.,* p. 175 *et seq.*

[113] *Satyre,* pp. 161-2.

CHAPTER V

CAYET—LOYSEAU—THE ESTATES OF 1614

WITH the accession of Henry IV to the throne in 1589, the parties which had agitated for contradictory reforms or innovations in government, or created disorder for their special ends, were gradually subjected to the royal authority and lost their reason for existence. The thoughts of the seventeenth century upon history, politics, and the government of France naturally reflect the permanent establishment [1] of the absolute monarchy. Three main points of view on the royal authority are discernible amid the mass of writings, less diverse but no less voluminous than those of the preceding century.

The first, which concerns this essay most closely, is the historical approach to the conditions of monarchical supremacy existing in France. By looking into the past, after the manner of Bodin and Hotman, but with the advantage of the vast works of historical erudition produced, as will be seen, in the interim, certain writers at first supported and later criticized the absolute government of France in all its parts. Loyseau, Mézeray, Fénelon, Bayle, Audigier, Daniel and Boulainvilliers were such writers.

The second stream of opinion may be called the rationalistic, and derives its tenets almost wholly from reflections on the nature of government, although it is not averse from historical illustration as a secondary prop. Seventeenth-century rationalizers include Claude Joly, Montchrétien, Jean Savaron, Le Bret, and Louis XIV himself.

[1] In spite of the Fronde; see below, p. 124 *et seq.*

Lastly, the question is attacked *pro* or *contra* in a theological manner by Bellarmin, Richelieu, Dupuy, Bossuet, and Jurieu.

On the specific issue of racial, national, and institutional origins, the seventeenth century completely changes the grounds of argument. The shift results not from historical research alone—though the progress in that direction is indeed considerable — but also from the more fundamental change in the bases of the political conflict. Under a Henry IV, a Richelieu, even a Mazarin, and especially a Louis XIV, history must take the presence of the absolute king as a given fact, an inescapable premise. History must either laud the kingship or remain duly compilative. Historical parallels or contentions injurious to the monarchy are visited with effective disciplining: Mézeray loses his pension,[2] Claude Joly's *Maximes* are publicly burnt.[3] Even as late as the reign of Louis XV, Montesquieu's ordinarily tolerant pen feels justified in administering a rebuke to the Abbé Dubos on the mere ground of casting a shadow upon the title of the reigning families in France.[4]

By the end of the sixteenth century, Pasquier and Bodin, Hotman and du Haillan had discredited as French history the notion of a Trojan origin, and forgotten or disregarded the division between Frank and Gaul, victor and vanquished, last heard of at the end of the twelfth century— and had substituted for these the more palatable fiction of a common origin for Gauls and Franks, made reasonable by the semi-historical emigration across the Rhine of certain Gallic tribes under Sigovese. Now, the notable contribution of the seventeenth-century historiographers is that, driven back, partly by absolutism, partly by the growing scientific

[2] Larroque, D. de, *Vie de Mézeray*, Amsterdam, 1726, p. 37.

[3] Sée, Henri, *Les Idées Politiques au 17ᵉ Siècle*, Paris, 1923, p. 109.

[4] *Esprit des Lois*, bk. xxx, ch. 25, p. 287.

spirit, to documents, sources, and early chronicles, they rediscovered the duality of races which had once existed on French soil. Simultaneously, the nobility, likewise restless under the tutelage of the king, driven from one government retrenchment to another by the ambitious bourgeoisie, handmaiden of absolutism, also rediscovered the ancient racial conflict and used it to challenge the king's rights, contemn the Third Estate, and rally its own emasculated forces.

Apart from these political events and apart from the current literature they evoked, often non-historical in content, the birth and growth of the new historical controversy is unintelligible. Since it was, moreover, the outstanding feature of the eighteenth century, gathering extraneous elements as it went, the scope of this and succeeding chapters shall include representatives of the three currents of thought mentioned above, and discuss them in their chronological interrelations.

The transition from the sixteenth to the seventeenth century is most visible in a polemical way in the *Institution au droict des Français*[5] of Guy Coquille, who though a monarchist of the previous age, a *politique,* admits that the Parlements and Estates have advisory powers for the king's convenience, but in no way constitute either a democratic or an aristocratic feature in the government of France.[6] Clearly, the work of Hotman has in the interim lost credit and authority. The " chronologist " of Henry IV, Pierre Victor Cayet, refers to Hotman slightingly in his preface to the *Chronologie Novénaire,* a history of the wars of Henry IV, published in 1608.

The Malcontents [says Cayet] joined themselves to the

[5] Paris, 1608.

[6] *Discours des Etats de France, Oeuvres,* 1703, vol. i, p. 276.

Huguenots, none of whom began to write any differently from their speech in the past, and Hotman, jurist, in his French Gaul undertook to show, ' that the French people had had sovereign authority not only to elect their kings, but also to repudiate the sons of kings, to elect foreigners.' And he says on the subject many things praising peoples who limit the licence of their kings and lead them to reason. . . . In short he scrimmaged with old histories, rightly and wrongly, according to his passion . . . I leave it to the reader who has read . . . whether these wars were for the public good and religion, or for the private interests of so many nobles who took up arms at that time.[7]

Elsewhere in his voluminous contemporary chronicle, Cayet reveals himself a monarchical, patriotic, yet singularly free-spoken historian. He asserts that the Crown of France is not hereditary, but simply patrimonial or feudal, in accordance with the Salic Law. This system prevents the kings of France from ever becoming tyrants, since they know that their own blood will succeed to them, for which the kings conserve the kingdom as a personal patrimony.[8] The kings of France, furthermore, are free, possessing the oldest kingdom in existence.[9] It had its origin more than four hundred years before the birth of Christ; was the first to shake off the yoke of the Roman Empire, the first to accept Christianity, whence " these kings . . . have always held the first rank and dignity among Christian kings "— *nemine contradicente*.[10]

With André Duchesne, also a scholarly [11] but nonetheless

[7] *Chronologie*, Avant-Propos, p. 10-11 (not paginated).

[8] *Chronologie*, vol. i, folio 18b.

[9] An allegation common in the seventeenth century and even the eighteenth century.

[10] *Chronologie*, vol. i, folio 4b.

[11] *Cf.* his *Bibliothèque des auteurs qui ont écrit l'histoire et la topographie de la France*, Paris, 1627.

tendencious compiler, the monarchical doctrine gains further substantiation. The *Antiquitez et recherches de la grandeur et majesté des Roys de France* published in 1609, without adding any new system or theory to history, not only ascribes sovereign power to the king within his realm,[12] but the divine-right theory of kingship finds a clear statement, which antedates Bossuet's classical exposition of the doctrine as applied to Louis XIV, though it follows by ten years the *Basilikon Doron* of James I of England.[13]

Even more adulatory is the work of Jérome Bignon, who in his treatise, *De l'excellence des rois et du royaume de France,*[14] links again the supremacy of the king in France with his superiority to all other kings.[15] Similarly, the kingdom is superior to all others because it is " successive and hereditary, not elective ". [16]

Thus in the desire for peace and unity, pamphleteers and partisan historians stress the unlimited power of the French king, ascribe to his line the antiquity with which the more individualistic spirits of the preceding era had imbued the " constitution "; but, abating not a jot from the latter's feeling of nationality, the writers of the early seventeenth century set up the superiority of the French kingdom for the very reasons of hereditary absolutism disavowed by their immediate ancestors. With such " points " to make, it might be assumed that questions of racial and institutional origins would seem neither relevant nor useful. Yet one disinterested jurist was found to revive these issues.

Charles Loyseau, evidently influenced by Bodin, produced

[12] *Antiquitez,* bk. i, disc. 4, p. 163 *et seq.*

[13] *Antiquitez,* Avant-Propos, pp. 2-3.

[14] Paris, 1610.

[15] *De l'excellence,* etc., p. 255.

[16] *Ibid.,* p. 265.

in 1608-10 a series of treatises [17] in which his primary purpose was to find the fundamental nature of the state. Loyseau shows that in the Middle Ages the public suzerainty
(*seigneurie*) and the private were often confused,[18] which
they no longer are. The problem of establishing the distinction in law undoubtedly led the scientific-minded inquirer
to find the origins of the confusion in fact. And in his
treatise on the nobility, he advances a thesis—unchallenged
in his day—but which the best minds of the eighteenth century were to wrangle about.

The nobility of France [says Loyseau] had its origin in the
long-past mixture of the two peoples who came to live together
in this kingdom, namely the Gauls, and the Franks who conquered and subjected them without at the same time desiring
to harry or exterminate them; but they (the Franks) retained
this superiority over them that they wished alone to hold
public offices, to bear arms and to partake of the fiefs without
being held to pay any taxes, either to the local lords, or to the
sovereign for the needs of the state; instead of which, they were
only required to give aid in wars. As for the conquered people,
they were for the most part reduced to semi-servitude.[19]

Naturally the seventeenth-century jurist does not escape
the anachronism of calling the Franks, *Français,* though
when he uses the word *Franc,* it is only to fall into the other
tradition of deriving it from " free ". To Loyseau, upholder of both king and privileged orders, it is the Franks
who seized and maintained supremacy in the French nation
from the time of their invasion to this. " In regard to our
French (ancestors) it is certain that when they conquered
Gaul, they made themselves lords of the people and goods

[17] *Des seigneuries,* 1608; *Du Droit des offices,* 1609; *Des Ordres de la
Noblesse,* 1610.

[18] *Des seigneuries,* bk. i, ch. i, p. 4.

[19] *Des ordres de la noblesse,* ed. 1701, p. 24.

thereof—I mean complete lords, as much of the public suzerainty as of the private, or property." [20]

In consequence, Loyseau exalts *honor* as the mainspring of the monarchy—a view which his spiritual descendant Montesquieu will not be loath to adopt.[21] But the privileged order is not to encroach upon the rights of the monarch, by making their offices hereditary,[22] any more than the Estates need be consulted to grant subsidies. Yet Loyseau, as a careful student, does not fail to recognize that the king's right to levy taxes is a recent accretion to the suzerainty, since from the organization of the nation sketched above it has been seen that the " subjects " of the king are in reality " free " [23] except as warriors. In fact, as in law, it is only as warriors that the king has the right of life and death over them.[24] These are customs of the kingdom, though Loyseau cites as " fundamental laws " the Salic Law,[25] the inalienability and indivisibility of the kingdom, and the registration of royal edicts by the Parlement. The last two were of course not traditional for any long period before Loyseau's time, and they point to a liberal, semi-constitutional doctrine running counter to the trend of absolutist opinion current during the first decade of the century, and especially noteworthy in the year of Henry IV's assassination.[26]

Loyseau's book was nevertheless not revolutionary, apart from the notion of the racial division in France. Yet the

[20] *Des seigneuries*, p. 5.

[21] *Esprit des Lois*, bk. iii, chs. vi-vii, pp. 24-5; Loyseau, *Des offices*, bk. i, ch. vii *passim*.

[22] *Des offices*, bk. iv, ch. iv.

[23] *Des seigneuries*, p. 16.

[24] *Des offices*, bk. iv, ch. iv.

[25] I.e. the pseudo-Salic Law of 1317, see above, ch. iii.

[26] *Cf.* H. Sée, *op. cit.*, p. 30.

influence of his theory of races pierces through the indignation he feels at the mistreatment of the agricultural classes. Although in the *Traité des seigneuries* he says with great historical acumen: " As to their persons, the natives of the country were made serfs, not in complete slavery, but nearly such as the Romans called *Censitos, seu adscriptos,* or *seu glebae addictos,* who were two kinds of semi-serfs . . . ; [27] yet in the Treatise on the Nobility, he exclaims:

In the government of France, we have so lowered them, nay oppressed them, both by tallages and by the tyranny of the nobles, that there is good cause to wonder how they can subsist. . . .[28]

In the same place, he calls the inferiority of their rank below that of townsmen unjust and protests their being held " vile ". In point of fact, Loyseau's grievances against the nobility were not peculiar to him. The chief energies of the Third Estate as a class were bent against the same oppressions, not against the royal assumption of extraordinary powers. That this was the case even after the prosperous short reign of Henry IV is shown by the records of the Estates-General of Paris, convoked in 1614 by the Queen Regent.

Strangely enough, the most powerful nobles had likewise demanded the meeting of the Estates on the grounds that they were being sidetracked from public employments.[29] Indeed, the first speech of the nobility was a lively attack against the Third Estate as upstarts, and against their " self-sufficiency based on the occupancy of a few positions ". [30] However contradictory the two statements, it would seem

[27] P. 5.
[28] P. 43.
[29] Picot, *Histoire des Etats-Généraux,* vol. iv, p. 175.
[30] *Ibid.,* p. 182.

that the forms of servility were still enforced upon the lowest estate, whose orator had to harangue the king in a kneeling position.[31] Notwithstanding, it was clear throughout the sessions of the Estates that the Third had a growing consciousness of its dignity, an increased sense of self-respect, which led to a good deal of plain speech before the other two orders, including references to the race question.

Jean Savaron, Lieutenant of the Sénéchaussée of Auvergne, was chosen by the Third as one of its first representatives, and proved himself not only learned but courageous. In concluding his polished challenge to the nobility, he uses the accepted historical fiction of the Franks delivering the Gauls:

Gentlemen of the nobility, regain the merit of your predecessors and the doors to honors and offices will be opened to you. History teaches us that the Romans placed such duties upon the French [Franks] that they finally shook the yoke of obedience and thereby laid the first foundations of the French monarchy. The people are so heavily laden with taxes that it is to be feared the same might happen again. May God prove me a false prophet![32]

Before the king, Savaron, definitely uniting the grievances of the " common people " with those of the bourgeoisie, painted a touching picture of the misery of the lowest classes, pleading on paternalistic grounds: " Sire, they are not insects and worms who demand your justice and pity; it is your wretched people — reasonable creatures, children of whom you are the father and protector. . . ."[33]

The nobility strongly objected, being defended before the

[31] Picot, *ibid.*

[32] *Procès-verbal et cahier de la noblesse ès Etats de l'an 1615. Cf.* the slightly different text in the *Procès-verbal du tiers,* 20 novembre, 1614. (Quoted in Picot, *op. cit.*, vol. iv, p. 190).

[33] Florimon de Rapine, *Des Etats généraux,* vol. xvi, pp. 198-9.

Third by the young bishop of Luçon, Armand Duplessis, the future Richelieu.   Savaron answered that, having served the king as a judicial official and soldier as well, he could reply to everyone in either capacity.[34]   To put an end to the dispute between the two orders, a new orator was selected by the Third Estate, President de Mesmes, of Paris.   His speech, however, brought no conciliation.   To disclaim any intention of offense, he told the nobility on November 24, 1614 that France was " the common mother of the three orders, that the Church was the Eldest brother, the nobility the second born, and the Third Estate, the youngest." [35] He added after recognizing a degree of superiority in the nobility, that there had existed families in which the youngest had redeemed the fortunes ruined by the elder.[36]   At once the president of the nobility objected, and the order as a whole decided to complain to the king before whom the baron of Senecey charged the lowest order with forgetting its condition and with insulting the nobility by comparing the kingdom to a family of three brothers.   " Into what wretched state have we fallen if these words are true !" [37]

Whatever subjacent idea may have been entertained of a common origin for Frank and Gaul, or even common ignorance of the racial question, it is plain that the nobility of 1614 did not consider themselves related " to the vulgar in the closest of society, which is fraternity ".[38]   Maintaining that the nobles owed their preeminence to the right of arms by which they gave peace and order to the realm, the noble speaker defined the Third Estate as " an order composed

[34] F. de Rapine, *op. cit.*, p. 207.   A member of the nobility threatened on report of this to have Savaron beaten by his servants.

[35] *Ibid.*, p. 226.

[36] *Ibid.*

[37] Quoted in Picot, *op. cit.*, vol. iv, p. 194.

[38] *Ibid.*

of the people of town and fields, the latter nearly all justici-
able of the first two orders; the former being burghers,
merchants, artisans, and some public officers ". [39]   And the
bulk of the delegation withdrew from the Louvre shouting
" that they would not have sons of cobblers and shoemakers
call them brothers, and that there was as much difference
between the nobles and the Third as between master and
menial ". [40]

Though there succeeded temporary union on questions of
immediate interest, a second split occurred between the two
upper orders and the commoners over the question of the
Gallican liberties.   The support of the king's independence
by the Third Estate was never more visible than on that
occasion which gave rise in reality to an expression of
national autonomy.[41]   At all times, moreover, the strife
against the privileged orders was more popular than any
protests against the abuses of royal power.   The mob of
Paris itself followed the debates and gave vent to feelings
of rancor accumulated through centuries.[42]   The populace
solaced itself by repeating a topical quatrain on the Gallican
question embodying as well President de Mesmes' emphatic
words :

O nobles, O clergy, the elders of France,
If your king's own honor ye weakly uphold
And the Third in your duty is far in advance
Then you'll see younger sons take the place of the old.[43]

[39] Picot, *ibid.*

[40] Rapine, *op. cit.,* p. 228.

[41] Picot, *op. cit.,* vol. iv, p. 201 ; Thierry, *Histoire du Tiers Etat,* p. 176.
" The Gallican Liberties of 1682 is but a reproduction of the statement of
the Third Estate in 1615." *Ibid.,* p. 178.

[42] Picot, *op. cit.,* vol. iv, p. 218.

[43] Ms. Bibl. Nationale, Fontanieu, *Pièces, Lettres,* etc.

At the same time, the Third demanded in its cahier periodic meetings of the Estates every ten years, the enfranchisement by lords and clergy of all their serfs, freedom of professions and the abolition of internal customs barriers.[44] In all these reforms which seem " advanced " indeed for the early seventeenth century, the clergy was more often concurrent than the nobility.[45]

The latter order not only labored for the maintenance of its former real privileges, but took every opportunity to decry the ambition and ability of the Third Estate, to insist upon enforced differentiations of dress,[46] prohibitions against the commoners' bearing arms or keeping hunting dogs; and at the same time to request the privilege of engaging in wholesale trade without derogation to rank, as a means of tapping the wealth which was in truth transferring the power from the upper class to the middle.[47]

These class principles enunciated in 1614 will serve to explain the attitude of a Boulainvilliers at the end of the century, and possibly account for the last regrettable incident before the cloture of the Estates in February 1615. On the fourth of that month, at a joint meeting of the Third and the nobility, le Sieur de Chavailles, commoner, neglected to salute Messire de Bonneval, noble deputy, and was insulted and beaten over the head with the gentleman's stick.[48] This attempt to " teach manners and duty " to the Third Estate immediately assumed large proportions. The lowest order considered the act *lèse-majesté,* as the deputies were met by royal order.[49] The king promised that suit would

[44] Thierry, *Hist. du Tiers,* p. 181 *et seq.*

[45] *Ibid.,* p. 183 *et seq.*

[46] Thierry, *op. cit.,* pp. 184n. and 185n.

[47] *Ibid.,* p. 185.

[48] Rapine, *op. cit.,* vol. xvii, p. 3.

[49] Picot, *op. cit.,* vol. iv, p. 232.

be brought, but the noble gentleman escaped with having his head cut off—in effigy.[50]

Finally, on February 23, the presentation of the cahiers to the king occurred, in which only Richelieu's speech for the clergy and that of Milon for the Third Estate expressed any serious opinions. The latter speaker assailed the nobility with specific charges which can be summarized as the non-performance of the duties for which the privileged order was in the past granted its prerogatives.[51] This was a startling historical assumption, to which the speaker gave substance by recalling the Field of May of the early French (Frankish) monarchy as the ancestor of the present Estates-General.[52]

The regent, profiting by these divisions,[53] made only vague replies to the two vigorous speeches, and finally intending to do nothing,[54] resorted to the simple expedient of closing the session by locking the Third Estate out of its meeting-hall. The device, repeated in 1789, did not meet with the success it achieved in 1615. The first time the bewildered commoners exclaimed, " Are we any different today from what we were yesterday before the king, or has one night changed our status and authority?"[55]

But in 1789 the answer was not in the form of a question at all. " We are today," affirmed Sieyès, [56] " everything that we were yesterday; let us deliberate."

---

[50] Rapine, *op. cit.*, vol. xvii, p. 149.

[51] Picot, *op. cit.*, vol. iv, p. 243.

[52] *Ibid.*

[53] The motto of the earlier Medici regent had been " *Divide et impera* ".

[54] Three concessions were made by the king on March 24.

[55] Rapine *op. cit.*, vol. xvii, pp. 111, 119.

[56] The contrast was first pointed out by Thierry, *op. cit.*, p. 188, and has been reproduced since then without acknowledgment by every historian of the Estates.

In the same year that the Estates convened, there appeared a small volume entitled *Traité de la Loi Salique, armes, blasons, et devises des Français,*[57] which lends a curious confirmation of the theory uttered by Loyseau regarding the racial origin of the nobility.   The author, Claude Malingre, accepts without question the antiquated story of the Trojan origin, repeating the common notion of the brotherhood of Turcus and Francio, whence the Turks and the French. But he credits as an opinion of the Turks, " Thus may no man be called a gentleman unless he be Turk or French, from the greatness of courage of Hector and Troilus, whence their first dukes are issued." [58]   Also, indirectly, the Trojans under Aeneas caused the flight and settlement of Brutus at Nantes in Bretagne, the founding of Tours in honor of Turnus, his nephew, and finally the conquest of Albion and birth of New Troy or London.[59]   Thus is the antiquity of the ancestors of the French upheld.   But it is a question which strikes Malingre elsewhere in his work, why and when the French obtained their name, since " there is nothing more certain in our history than that the French are descended from the Sycambrians, Caucians, Antuarians, Canifates [*sic*] and other peoples formerly called Gauls though born and residing in the Germanies ".[60]

Malingre having explained previously how the Trojans made a stay in Pannonia on their way westward, and founded the city of Sycambria which he thinks is modern Buda, he goes on to repeat the story of the Trojans' refusal to pay tribute to the Romans after helping them to repel

[57] By Claude Malingre, Paris, 1614; reprinted in Leber, *Collection de Pièces,* vol. i, p. 39 *et seq.*

[58] Leber, *op. cit,* vol. i, p. 41.

[59] *Ibid.,* p. 40.

[60] *Ibid.,* p. 295.

the Allans.[61]   The seventeenth-century author characteristi-
cally feels and admits the confusion of traditions without
attempting to conciliate them by trimming.

Rather than submit to the Romans, according to him, the
Gauls abandoned their city, crossed the Rhine and in this
manner spread the fame of their magnanimity, nobility, and
frankness in courage, whence their given name of Franks
or French.[62]   The last distinction is of interest, but one
which is not sustained by the writer.   He postulates a better
reason for the name French, which the Gauls took of their
own accord; it is owing to their freedom from the Romans
and customary franchise.   An alternative name they assumed
to indicate their constituting a league or a united nation—
the name of the Allemans, i. e. all men![63]

Obviously, Malingre did not think in terms of system or
theory.   Only accidentally do his prejudices and anachron-
isms pierce through the text.   In a word, they comprise the
idea of single reality beneath the names of *Frank, French,
Gaul, Allemand,* and conquered Trojan; the faint adumbra-
tion of a contradictory relation between race and nobility,[64]
and lastly the feeling of national unity common to his
century.

What difference results from different beliefs regarding
the ever-latent race question in all its implications, is seen in
the fact that even the courageous tribune of the Third
Estate, Jean Savaron, five years after his impressive treatise

[61] Malingre, *op. cit.,* p. 296; his authority, Jean Guyart, in his book on
the Salic Law, calls these Trojans Gauls, ch. iv, *passim.*

[62] Leber, *Collection de Pièces,* vol. i, p. 297.

[63] *Ibid.,* 298.

[64] The mere form of words favored, in French, this conception destined
to grow: ". . . and let the offices of your sovereign courts be given to
gentlemen by *race* as they were formerly . . ." *Cahier de la Noblesse,*
1615; folio 278.

showing the vices of the *paulette*[65] and sale of offices, reasserts in an essay on the sovereignty of the king his divine
right and absolute power, but limits it in respect of the inalienability of the king's domain, which belongs to the
nation.   The king is only " administrator and life-benefi-
ciary of his kingdom ".   He is also governed by the Salic
Law and the fundamental laws of the kingdom, which, however, do not include the control of legislation by the Estates-
General or Parlement.[66]

Disregarding noble privileges, the increasingly uncondi-
tional power of the king is accompanied, for thoughtful
men, by the growing sense of the king's responsibility.   The
poet Montchrétien, for example, outlines in his epoch-making
Traité d'oeconomie politique the rigorous discipline and self-
devotion incumbent upon the monarch.[67]   On the other hand,
Montchrétien's most particular conception—that of social
solidarity and community of interests — runs counter not
only to the class animosities manifested the very year of his
writing, but also to the essential prepossessions of his age.

Only the ultramontanist movement, led by Cardinal Bellarmin, in any way challenged the authority of the king, and
that chiefly for asserting the supremacy of the Pope rather
than destroying the monarchical doctrine.   The resulting
paradox was that Bellarmin and his followers partly revived
the theory of popular sovereignty,[68] while the Gallicans,
usually members of the Third Estate, in order to uphold
national independence by means of the king, had to refute

[65] Fee by which judicial offices were made proprietary and thereby
taken out of the king's control.

[66] H. Sée, *op. cit.*, p. 31.

[67] Published 1615, ed. Brentano, p. 125; *cf.* again Frederick the Great,
Oeuvres, vol. ix, p. *227 et seq.*

[68] " It is the consent of the people which makes kings, consuls or any
other government ".   Quoted in Sée, *op. cit.*, p. 36.

the popular theory in question. Duchesne, the historian previously cited, affirms in his *Antiquitez:*

Religion and the state are the first and oldest pillars of human society, two brothers of the same blood . . . who have established in France foundations of indefinite lasting power for eternity, being as they were at all times under protection of the authority of our great kings, who have never been wholly secular, but imbued with the priesthood and kingship all at once.[69]

Another historical source of support for the monarchy was found by Jacques Charron in the works of the distinguished forger Jean Nanni, better known as Annius of Viterbo. From the latter's supposed Antiquities of Gaul, Charron included in his own *Histoire universelle de toutes les nations, et spécialement des Gaulois ou François* a complete genealogy of kings from Gomer, grandson of Noah, to Henry IV and Louis XIII.

It will have been noticed in his title that Charron accepts the identity of Frank and Gaul. In his scheme, Gomer was the father of the Gauls; a second dynasty was begun by Sicamber, son of Francus and the daughter of Rhemus; lastly, the dynasty of another Francus, first king of the French properly so called, ruler in Gaul as well as in Germany. The first line of kings, in Charron's *potpourri,* have names drawn in general from Gallic customs or places. The second comprises Trojan, Greek, Latin and Germanic names (not omitting Theuto). The last boasts altogether German names, ending with Pharamond, ancestor of the fourth dynasty, first king of France, twenty-eighth of the French, seventy-eighth of the Gauls.[70] The would-be historian devotes nearly half his space to the predecessors of Pharamond

[69] *Antiquitez,* bk. i, disc. 4, pp. 164-5.

[70] This account drawn from Thierry, *Dix Ans,* p. 385 *et seq.*

in justification of his claim to original research, alleging
that the remainder of French history is so well known that
he will touch only the high spots.[71]

This confusion of Gauls and French is not to be taken
as absence of national pride. On the contrary, in dealing
with Charlemagne's customary dress, Charron quarrels with
many of his colleagues, and chiefly with his sources, to deny
that the kings of France were Germans. " Charlemagne
used to dress . . . just as the French of his time did; from
which it is clear that the Germans (*Alemans* [*sic*]) are entirely mistaken in saying that dressing in the French mode
means in the fashion of their Nation; since at that time no
Germans were called French. . . . Germany cannot be taken
to have been his country, but only Gaul, over which his
father had reigned. . . ." [72]

More worthy of respect is a work of the same year
(1621) by Scipion Dupleix, historiographer of the king,
who on the strength of his *Histoire et Mémoires* [73] became
the most popular and best known historian of France for a
quarter of a century. Dupleix has a keener sense of the
racial mixture of France than his predecessors, probably
because as a Gascon and ardent regionalist he wishes to
single out the glory of his " nation ", come from the Span-
ish Pyrenees, in mitigation of the over-emphasis laid by
French historians on the exploits of the French (Franks)
in Gaul.[74]

Dupleix took advantage of André Duchesne's learned as-
sistance regarding the lives and deeds of the Frankish kings;

[71] Charron, *Hist. univ.*, Preface, quoted in Thierry, *ibid.*, p. 387.

[72] *Ibid.;* in Charron, *op. cit.*, p. 777.

[73] *Histoire générale de France avec l'Etat de l'Eglise et de l'Empire, et
Mémoires des Gaulois depuis de déluge jusques à l'establissement de la
monarchie françoise*, Paris, 1621.

[74] *Mémoires des Gaules*, Preface, pp. 3-4.

yet in spite of it, he introduces a good share of Annius'
fables and a number of supposititious speeches of his own.
The result was that when Mézeray undertook to rewrite
French history towards the end of the reign, he discarded all
of Dupleix's borrowed erudition together with his fables.[75]

[75] For this remark, see Thierry, *Dix Ans*, p. 392.

CHAPTER VI

Mézeray—Audigier—Père Daniel

BEFORE the advent of Mézeray's book, France witnessed the rise to power of the bishop of Luçon, formerly deputy of the clergy, and with him, as Cardinal de Richelieu, the complete independence of the king—or to speak with less conscious irony—of the Crown. The king's power was to be limited neither by the Church, nor by the Estates, nor by any forms or customs of legality.[1]

Nevertheless, Richelieu's point of view is anything but favorable to leveling tendencies on the part of the Third Estate. "A low birth rarely produces the capacities necessary to a magistrate, and it is certain that the virtue of a well-born person has something nobler in it than that found in a man of lesser extraction. . . ."[2] Far from designing theoretically the extinction of the nobility, Richelieu saw it as "one of the principal sinews of the state, capable of contributing a great deal to its conservation and stability".[3]

The political complexion of France is therefore noticeably different when François Eudes, who called himself de Mézeray, decided at the age of twenty-six or twenty-seven to write a new French history. Richelieu, recognizing the power of the printing press, had gathered about him or his purse a number of writers;[4] and young Mézeray either before or immediately after conceiving his project was sub-

[1] Richelieu, *Testament Politique*, in Petitot, *Collection . . . des Mémoires*, ch. iv, *passim*.

[2] *Ibid.*, vol. ii, ch. ix, sect. i, p. 205.

[3] *Ibid.*, ch. iii, sect. i, p. 184 *et seq.*

[4] Such as le P. Joseph, Fancan, Cassan, Le Bret, etc.

114

stantially gratified by the minister.[5]   Mézeray was thirty-
two years old when the first folio appeared in 1643 and
won immediate success.   " It seemed," says Larroque, " as
if he were the only Historian of France." [6]

Attacking all his predecessors, the newcomer completely
eclipsed Dupleix, though without in any measure improving
on his historical method.   The imaginary speeches, the false
portraits with which the history is " enriched ", together
with the lame quatrains beneath the historical engravings,
constitute in fact a retrogression upon the early part of
Duchesne-Dupleix.   What Mézeray popularized definitely
was the idea that a great many of the stories concerning
the origins of the French were mere inventions and that in
any case they did not matter.   He regrets the scanty sources
left by the ancients, dismisses the descent of Noah, and appears dubious of Annius of Viterbo.[7]

The substance of Mézeray's belief is that the Celts were
the original race out of which Gauls, Germans, Britons—
and some say Illyrians and Spaniards—are descended.   The
Gauls spread over Europe and as far as Asia, at a time
when their " impetuous valor " made them feared, especially
by the Romans, then a struggling unknown nation.   It was
the luxury and idleness engendered by contact with the
Greeks through the colonists of Marseille that laid the Gauls
open to invasions first by Rome, then by the Germans.   The
latter were related to the Gauls, who had followed Sigovese
into Germany two hundred years before.   And in truth, it
was thought by Strabo that the Germans were so called
from *germanus*, brother, attesting the resemblance between
them and the Gauls: tall, blond, and white-skinned.[8]

[5] Larroque, *Vie de Mézeray, Amsterdam,* 1726, p. 9.

[6] *Ibid.,* p. 14.

[7] Mézeray, *Hist. de France, Avant Clovis,* ed. 1685, p. 3.

[8] *Ibid.,* bk. i, p. 4 *et seq.*

The last volume of Mézeray's work appeared in 1646—
a date to be remembered for another publication about to be
mentioned—and such was the success of the whole history
that an abridgment was suggested, upon which the historiographer spent some ten years. It appeared in 1668, and
proved, though lacking exactitude, even more popular than
the two editions of the larger work. As it is the *Abrégé* [9]
which really built for Mézeray his fame of more than a
hundred years' duration, the main thoughts of the author
are here extracted from it.

The antiquity of the kingdom of France forms the starting point of his nationalistic appeal, which looks at the English as " ancient enemies " and regards the French as, by
common opinion, " native Germans ". [10] Mézeray's reluc-
tance to use the name *Frank* leads into such absurdities as
" . . . the authors of the third and fourth centuries always
mean *French* when they use the word *Germans* ". [11]

Resolutely tackling the question of the invasion, Mézeray
lays the foundation of the later anti-Frank system of Dubos
when he says that Clovis not only gained the " esteem " of
the Gauls by his conquest, but also their affection by adopting their religion. " Hitherto their obedience had been
forced; so happy a change rendered it voluntary." [12]

The French loved their liberties, which they defended
successfully in the Armorican League [13] from the tyranny
of the Romans, who left them in free possession of the
second province of Germany. [14] Under "Faramond," first

---

[9] *Abrégé Chronologique, ou Extraicts de l'Hist. de France, par le Sieur
de Mézeray*, Paris, 1668. References are to the ed. of 1676. Sixteen
editions appeared before the last in 1755.

[10] *Abrégé*, vol. i, p. 25.

[11] *Ibid*. He likewise says *Allemands* more frequently than *Germains*.

[12] *Abrégé*, vol. i, p. 3.

[13] See above, ch. i.

[14] *Abrégé*, vol. i, pp. 33, 45.

king of the French, the Salic Law was compiled during three *malla,* or assizes, and named after the noblest of the French.[15] That the kingship was elective is shown in the case of Mérovée,[16] who took advantage of the "Fall of Rome" to extend his kingdom.[17] But his son Childeric revolted the French by his licentiousness, "to which infamies they were not accustomed". [18]

The story of Clovis' glory reaching the Orient and resulting in Anastasius' conferring consular dignity upon him, likewise finds favor in Mézeray's eyes. The ceremony increased the obedience of the Gauls, who still revered the old forms.[19] In the matter of Frankish overlordship, Mézeray, though conscious of the racial division of France, makes no point of its perpetuation. He merely says that the French "took a third or a fourth part (of the land) which they divided among themselves—that is, among their freemen, who were the weapon-bearers".[20] The slaves of the French tilled the soil, together with the native Gauls, and thus the land which had been nearly devastated came under cultivation and was gradually repeopled. The Gauls paid tribute to the French but the latter paid only with their person.[21]

Mézeray, without qualifying further the condition of the conquered race, nonetheless indicates that much of the Roman culture, many of the habits and institutions remained in Gaul, and even influenced the kings who, believing themselves as absolute as the emperors, created counts, dukes,

---

[15] *Abrégé*, p. 49.

[16] *Ibid.,* p. 59. *Cf.* also the election of Aegidius, *ibid.,* p. 66 *et seq.*

[17] *Ibid.,* p. 63.

[18] *Ibid.,* p. 65.

[19] *Ibid.,* p. 90.

[20] *Ibid.,* p 93; *cf.* also vol. i, p. 257 on "free-born and serfs".

[21] *Ibid.*

and generals.[22]   But that absolutism was limited by the
Field of March, in which the French " signified approbation
to royal undertakings by the noise of weapons; disapproved
by confused murmurings ". [23]   In this statement, the reading of Tacitus is visible, and with it the historical indifference which permitted the application of recorded German
customs to the Franks, nowhere mentioned by the Roman
author.

At the Field of March, the bishops, the lords, and the
people attended; but it is clear from the very vagueness of
Mézeray's reference to " the people ", that in his own words
elsewhere, " the kings presided and with the *lords* [*sic*] deliberated on the year's business ". [24]   The assembly levied
taxes upon the Gauls alone, " for it was considered odious
by the French to suffer levies ".   The king's revenue therefore consisted of the income of his private domains and the
free gifts of the French in *mallum* assembled.[25]

The assembly likewise elected the kings, chosen from the
reigning house and succeeding upon three conditions: birth,
the choice of the late king, and the consent of the great.[26]
Again, of the free citizens those who were nobles were such
by birth and ancientness of family—not by exemptions; of
the nobles those were great (*optimates*) either by right of
distinguished services or large possessions.[27]   These were
granted for life by the king from his own share of the best
lands.[28]   In the early monarchy, as seen by the king's historiographer, there was no nobility of the robe.   Justice was

22 *Abrégé, ibid.*
23 *Ibid.,* p. 247.
24 *Ibid.,* p. 247.
25 *Ibid.,* p. 245.
26 *Ibid.*
27 *Ibid.,* p. 252.
28 *Ibid.,* p. 249.

rendered " by the armed men who hung their axes upon a post in the midst of the mallum ". [29]

Under what is called the. " first race ", i. e. the Merovingian dynasty — to summarize Mézeray's doctrines — the Franks enjoyed an aristocratic government and elective kingship, supremacy of a territorial and financial nature over the conquered Gauls, and the services of serfs or slaves in agricultural pursuits, while men of law and war were drawn from their own ranks. The Gallican Church already enjoyed in full freedom the former gifts of the Gauls to which the liberality of the French was constantly adding.[30]

Consistent with the nomenclature which only modern nationalism has made a self-contradiction, the popular historian declares, " The native tongue of the French was Teutonic or Germanic. The Austrasians,[31] at least those nearest the Rhine, always kept it and still do, though much altered. Those farther this side of the Rhine dropped it to take up the language of the Gallic people, which was Romanic or Romance. . . .",[32] which has grown " out of the rust and the corruption of the Roman or Latin language, and has been twisted and pulled according to the genius of the nation. . . ." [33]

Charlemagne, in numerous other ways a hero to Mézeray, enriched his native tongue, " which was the Teutonic ", by reducing it to rules, composing its grammar, and naming all the months and winds in that language.[34] In view of the fact that Charlemagne is called king of France and is re-

---

[29] *Abrégé*, p. 252.   *Cf.* the Anglo-Saxon " Sacred Tree ", J. R. Green, *Short Hist. of the English People*, ed. 1916, ch. i, p. 15.

[30] Mézéray, *Abrégé*, p. 263.

[31] The eastern Franks of the Carolingian empire.

[32] *Abrégé*, p. 258.

[33] *Ibid.*, p. 259.

[34] *Ibid.*, p. 535.

ported as fond of collecting " all the old verses as memoirs for their history ",[35] it is difficult to conceive how Mézeray escaped observing the two streams of racial influence in France and how he could continue applying the name French as indiscriminately as he does.[36]

It is relevant to note in this connection that Mézeray was no more interested than his readers in historical accuracy. Like many before and after him, he thought it would be " too much labor for too little glory " to verify his sources.[37] Note also, that Mézeray wrote his history with a partisan purpose—" to recall to men their former rights, natural and inalienable ".[38] He was fond of telling truths unpleasant to the authorities, and incurred in so doing the hatred of the court and the loss of his pension at the hands of Colbert.[39]

When the contents of the histories are critically examined it is hard to find what seditious and impolitic assertion may have annoyed the great minister. It appears that Mézeray's account of the origin of taxation in France was the offending statement, softened in subsequent editions but without the return of the pension.

Despite his purpose there is in Mézeray no class system, no heretical governmental theory. He recognizes the conquest of Gaul but believes in a survival of Roman culture. Besides, the Franks and the Gauls were ultimately brother-Celts. From a practical standpoint, Mézeray is proud of France, of its liberties, and even of its stubborn regionalism;[40] he maintains the unity of the kingdom existed at all

[35] *Abrégé*, ibid.

[36] But *cf.* " Even the German king went to the general assembly of the French ", meaning the sons of Charlemagne. *Abrégé*, vol. ii, p. 153.

[37] Larroque, *op. cit.*, p. 33 and *cf.* Lelong, *Bibl. Hist. de la France*, vol. iii, Appended Memoirs, p. lxxxiv.

[38] *Hist. de France, Avant Clovis*, Preface.

[39] Larroque, *op. cit.*, p. 37.

[40] *Abrégé*, vol. ii, p. 23.

times,[41] he looks back with longing to the days of the aristocratic assemblies,[42] and he idolizes Charlemagne with a sort of naive wilfulness not wholly popular in origin. His praise of the great emperor is all the greater that he was not a usurper,[43] that he spent his substance " civilizing barbarous nations and carrying the name of the French nation with *éclat* into the most remote kingdoms." [44] In short, Charlemagne was " the Great Frenchman who built Franciac, that is to say the castle of the French . . . the king whose name one cannot hear without immediately conceiving some grand image." [45]

Even fifty years after the appearance of his shorter work Mézeray was still " illustrious ", and for the best reason he could have wished: that he had successfully worked to " immortalize a Nation as persistently glorious as ever was ".[46] But in the meantime much unobtrusive scholarly work had been accomplished that was to sweep not only the old histories from the shelf but the old forms of the racial issue from the books themselves.

The very year that Mézeray's third volume appeared (1646), the learned but little known historian Adrien de Valois published in Latin under the title of *Gesta veterum Francorum* [47] the first of three folio volumes, intended as the introduction to an imposing history of France present-

[41] *Abrégé*, vol. ii, p. 13.

[42] " Louis Debonair was reinstated and given back the crown and insignia, *but on the advice and consent of the French people*" (Italics his), *op. cit.*, vol. ii, p. 42.

[43] *Ibid.*, vol. i, p. 462.

[44] *Ibid.*, vol. i, p. 465.

[45] *Abrégé*, vol. i, pp. 461, 465.

[46] Larroque, *op. cit.*, p. 94.

[47] Adriani Valesii, *Gesta veterum Francorum sive rerum Francicarum usque ad Chlotarii senioris mortem, libri VIII.*

ing within a critical narrative in Latin all existing trustworthy accounts of the early monarchy of the Franks.   The
work stopped from its own magnitude at the end of the
Merovingian line of kings, but nevertheless within that
period of five centuries Adrien de Valois was able to extract
from a careful collation of the reported facts a clearer concept of the duality of races than had hitherto appeared in
French history proper,[48] a concept to be given all the greater
weight by the perfect impartiality of the author and his
judicious apportionment of credit among sources.[49]

Discarding all the fabrications of Annius and others,
Valois goes back to Gregory of Tours as the " foundation
of our history ".[50]   It is inevitable that in studying this
author, de Valois should feel the same consciousness of
national difference which animated the sixth-century bishop,
though de Valois insensibly softens the brutality of the
Frankish invader in his second-hand report.[51]   It was in
collecting later documents for his *Notitia galliarum* that
de Valois came across a striking but isolated twelfth-century
chronology which, after reciting the usual traditions, asserts
that the Franks " thus freed from taxes [by Valentinian]
never would pay any after that, and nobody could force
them, whence it is that they are today known as Frank, in
the tongue of that nation, those who enjoy full liberty.
. . ."[52]   So far there is nothing noteworthy in this chronology, but its anonymous author goes on to deduce from its
statement a sociological distinction of the greatest originality: ". . . as for those who among that nation [the Franks]
live in this condition of bondage, it is clear that they are not

[48] See above, ch. v, the obiter dicta of Maitre Charles Loyseau.
[49] Thierry, *Récits*, p. 39, supports this statement.
[50] Valesii, *Gesta*, vol. ii, Pref.
[51] Thierry, *op. cit.*, pp. 38-9.
[52] *Notitia*, p. 209.

Franks in origin, but that they are the sons of the Gauls, subjected to the Franks by right of conquest." [53]

The seventeenth-century critic was particularly struck by this inference, to which he adds in his text, " These words, worthy of recollection, I do not remember to have seen anywhere else; but they indicate that at the time they were written, about the year 1200, the Franks who dominated Gaul were free from tribute, and only the Gauls were subject to it. [54]

In an epoch preoccupied with another regency and its turmoils, a work so voluminous, so learned, and stylistically so lifeless as Adrien de Valois' could not compete with the " journalistic " [55] Mézeray. For if the latter had no system, he nonetheless had a point of view tending in general towards limiting the king's power as in the past by a general assembly. This, as has been seen, was not a suggested return to Frankish democracy, but it suited the spirit of the Fronde which was not an attempt at democratic revolution. [56] It was largely a reaction, strongest among the judicial class, against royal absolutism. Talon, attorney-general at Paris, characterizes the muzzling of the Parlement in regard to legislation as " a despotic and sovereign government . . . fit for the Scythians, the most remote and northern barbarians, whose faces are not even human ". [57] " Despotic government," according to an anonymous author of 1652, " is not compatible with our customs, neither Christian nor French." [58]

[53] *Notitia, ibid.*

[54] *Ibid.*

[55] *Cf.* Mézeray's project of a " Journal Littéraire Général " for which privilege was accorded him, in B. T. Morgan, *Hist. du Journal des Sçavans,* p. 41.

[56] H. Sée, *op. cit.,* pp. 86, 122.

[57] Quoted in Sée, *op. cit.,* p. 87.

[58] *Mazarinades,* vol. ii, p. 459.

This ministerial despotism is seen by the protesting writers as a recent thing, not older than the rule of Richelieu,[59]
and they invoke history to prove both the importance of
other organs in the State than the Crown and the elective
nature of the monarchy. Says one " Reasonable Plaintiff ",
Hugh Capet was " elected by the Estates of France to reign
equitably according to the laws of the country; he swore it
at his coronation, and therefore transmitted the kingdom to
his posterity on the same conditions." [60]

The nobility are covertly attacked as " the ones [who]
instead of contributing to the expenses of war have taken
advantage of these baneful occasions to enrich and gorge
themselves with the goods and blood of their brothers." [61]

But while confusion reigns over the triangular duel of
Court, Princes, and Parlement, the majority of opinions
still holds a monarchical course.[62] Only one contribution
of any importance is made that may be construed as liberal
in tone, and even that is based on monarchical premises.
Claude Joly, in his *Recueil de Maximes . . . pour l'institution du Roy . . ,*[63] which was at first intended to be merely
a collection of extracts from Commines illustrating his
views, seeks the origin of royalty and finds it a creation of
the people. He cites and uses many sixteenth-century authorities, such as de Seyssel, du Haillan, and especially Bodin.
He concludes with Hotman that " it seems to some ill-
informed of the nature of sovereigns that the people are
made only for the king, whereas on the contrary it is truth
that kings have only been made for the people. For at all

[59] Sée, *op. cit.,* pp. 90-93; Lavisse, *Hist. de France,* vol. vii, pt. i, p. 17.

[60] *Mazarinades,* vol. ii, p. 458.

[61] *Mazarinades,* vol. ii, pp. 428-9.

[62] Sée, *op. cit.,* p. 101 *et seq.*

[63] Published in 1652, attacked, condemned and burned by the Châtelet
(police jurisdiction of Paris).

times there have been peoples without kings, but there have never been kings without peoples." [64]

Joly's whole effort is directed at a return to the old traditions of the monarchy [65] and historical examples are his chief weapons, seconded by a perspicuous logic derived from his ecclesiastical milieu and legalistic family tradition.[66]

Simultaneously with these topical and polemical works, that combine the traditions of the early monarchy with contemporary issues, certain mid-seventeenth-century Frenchmen were developing historical criticism into something of a science and collecting all available original documents into large compilations, often unsurpassed to this day for scholarliness.

Beginning with Pierre Dupuy, known otherwise for his *Commentaire sur le traité des libertez de l'Eglise gallicane de Pierre Pithou,* the *Trésor des Chartes* was catalogued, at the instigation of Mathieu Molé, First President of the Paris Parlement. By purchasing with his brother the office of librarian, he was able to systematize the king's collection, accomplishing the preliminary groundwork for tasks others were to undertake.

It was left to André Duchesne, also mentioned above as a polemist, to acquire the title of "Father of French History" by his *Historia Francorum scriptores* published in five volumes from 1636 to 1649—the first *national* collection of writers, antedating de Valois' more interpretative work as well as the "Monuments" of nineteenth-century Germany or Guizot's corresponding work in France.

No less useful was the *Glossary* of Charles du Fresne

---

[64] *Maximes,* ch. v, pp. 130-1.

[65] On Claude Joly, see Jean Brissaud, *Un Libéral au 17ème siècle.*

[66] He was son of a *lieutenant-général de la maréchaussée,* grandson of Loisel, codifier of customs, and he himself in holy orders.

Ducange, published in 1678,[67] and offering a mine of information on medieval sources and facts, even before its continuation by the Benedictines of St. Maur in 1733.

Between the *Glossary* and the work of these monks briefly noted below, comes the Collection of Capitularies completed by Etienne Baluze in 1674, which gave for the first time some historical bases to modern dissertations upon the status of persons and property under the " second race " of French kings.

Lastly, the greatest of the Benedictines, Mabillon, by working on lives of the saints under the guidance of d'Archery, applied his rising talents to authenticating accounts of his subjects and using them to depict the civil and ecclesiastical history of the Middle Ages. His great work, however, is the *De re diplomatica,* which establishes the principles of source criticism for his period. His work bore additional fruit in the labors of his disciple and friend Th. Ruinart, whose edition of Gregory of Tours in 1699 shows the judicious emphasis already placed by de Valois on the significance of the text to French history.

Of the further work of the Benedictines more will be said in a later chapter. Here the works of the Jesuit Sirmond, of Labbé, of Sainte-Marthe, of Claude de Rubis on the early monarchy; of Jean-Jacques Chifflet [68] on the Tomb of Childeric [69] need merely be cited as notable items in the body of seventeenth-century historical research dealing with the periods of interest to this study.

The first results in narrative history of the mass of documents appeared in the work of the Jesuit Father Gabriel Daniel (1649-1728), whose completed *History of France*

[67] *Glossarium ad scriptores mediae et infimae latinitatis,* 3 vols.

[68] For the foregoing, see Michaud, *Biographie Universelle.*

[69] Discovered at Tournai in 1653.

appeared in 1713, but whose earlier dissertations upon the subject were published in Paris in 1696 as a tentative essay to test public opinion before launching his large work. That public opinion had been brought up, so to speak, upon the work of Mézeray—and worse yet misled by such treatises as Audigier's *De l'origine des Français et de leur Empire,*[70] and a learned Jesuit's *Historia coloniarum.*[71] The latter carried to its absurdest limits the story of Gallic emigrés into Germany later returning as Franks into their native land. The system of Audigier, similar in purpose, is based on Book V of Livy, and expands casual hints found in Pliny and other classical historians to establish the popular fable.[72]

It is significant that Audigier tries to give his theories an appearance of sound historicity by being extremely circumstantial. He puts the migration at 590 B. C., makes Bellovese and Sigovese—leaders of the expedition—the nephews of "Ambigate, king of the Celts", who fears the overpopulation of Gaul.[73]

But to return to the more important work of Père

---

[70] Paris, 1676, 2 vols.

[71] *Aegidio Lacarry auctore, Historia coloniarum tum a Gallis in exteras nationes missarum,* etc. Paris, 1677.

[72] Leber, *Collection de Pièces,* vol. i, p. 16.

[73] *Ibid. et seq.* To the work's detailed fancy, the author adds a more useful survey of twelve different opinions he encountered in his readings upon the place of origin of the French (Leber, *op. cit.,* vol. i, p. 19 *et seq.*). Not all of them show distinct divergence of belief, and all twelve may be reduced to the three encountered so far in the course of this study : 1. From Troy (Pannonia, Scythia, Palus Meotis) ; 2. From Germany (middle, high, low, etc.) ; 3. From Gaul (Provence, Rousillon, etc.). A fourth adduced by Audigier is almost wholly foreign to French history (Turnebius (1512-1565) was primarily a philologist) and altogether incidental to the main purpose of the writers cited : Vopiscus, Eumenius, Freculphus, Adrian Turnebius and Ptolemy derive the French from Scandia, a geographical term in itself so variously applied as to add little precision to theorizing.

Daniel.[74] The Jesuit father in dealing with his predecessor is harsh but just: " Mézeray ignored or was ignorant of the sources." Constructively Daniel makes a point, for the first time in French history, of observing details of phraseology, avoiding anachronism and, " scrupulously reproducing the aspect and language of the period ". [75]

In the prefatory essay, Daniel deals with three important points: first, the foundation of the French monarchy in Gaul, " for as I contend, against the belief of all our historians, that it was Clovis who founded the French empire this side of the Rhine, and who established and fixed the nation . . . I cannot dispense with an account of the reasons which have led me to stray from the ordinary path . . . and begin the history of France with Clovis." [76]

After this revolutionary start, which literally enthrones the Frankish invaders, Daniel asserts that the deposition of Childeric and the election of Count Gilles (Egidius) is " pure fable ". Lastly, he proposes to discuss whether the " French empire is an hereditary or an elective one ". [77] These conclusions making for unlimited absolutism had naturally not lost relevance to the politics of this the fifty-third year of Louis XIV's reign. Daniel proves that the kingship was hereditary under the first race (Merovingian), that there was a change to election under the second (Carolingian), and a return to hereditary rule under the third (Capetian).[78] The political inference is obvious and emphatic, ". . . This right of succession which the descendants of Hugh Capet

---

[74] *Deux dissertations préliminaires pour une nouvelle histoire de France,* etc. Paris, 1696. Reprinted as Parts I and II of Preface to the *Histoire de France* of which first vol. was published the same year.

[75] Thierry, *Lettres,* p. 45.

[76] Leber, *op. cit.,* vol. i, p. 365.

[77] *Ibid.,* p. 366.

[78] Leber, *op. cit.,* vol. i, p. 366.

enjoy since nearly eight centuries is as old as the establishment of the monarchy in Gaul." [79]

By the "strictest rules of criticism", Daniel hopes to
"make it seem very likely" that Clovis was the first Christian king of the French and the first king of the French in
Gaul as well. To establish this point, so necessary to his
thesis in favor of the Capetians, he boldly denies the reign in
Gaul of the first four kings [80] by indicating the silence of
contemporary writers concerning them. He ironizes very
wittily about Sidonius Appolinaris' failure to write a single
verse on Mérovée who supposedly "took Paris, made other
conquests and was the darling of his people." [81]

Showing in the same adroit manner the growth of false-
hoods based on a perverted scintilla of truth, Daniel is able
to rule out of French history many incidents and conclusions
accepted in his day. He brilliantly ridicules the extravagant
story of Childeric's promiscuous love-making [82] and, by
making Gregory of Tours contradict himself in different
passages, establishes the appearance of Childeric in Gaul as
a mere incursion, after which that chieftain recrossed the
Rhine.[83]

On the matter of the origin of the French, Daniel cites
Procopius and adopts his view that they came from the
marshes of Germany, situated between the Rhine and the
Ocean. The Frankish League with the much-disputed Ar-
boricans, also mentioned by Procopius, is a further argument in favor of Daniel. The League resulted in the

[79] *Ibid.*

[80] Pharamond, Chlodio, Mérovée, Childeric, cited by Gregory of Tours
and popular in French literature from then to the time of Mézeray and
of Chateaubriand.

[81] Leber, *op. cit.*, vol. i, p. 371.

[82] *Ibid.*, p. 381 *et seq.*

[83] *Ibid.*, pp. 383-4.

intermarriage of the two peoples because both were Christian, says Procopius. But, argues Daniel, the French were not Christians before Clovis' reign.[84]

Whatever the ultimate worth of his thesis, the clarity and logic of Daniel are refreshing amidst the confusion of previous chroniclers, including de Valois, who too often hesitates on the brink of conclusions. In the same manner as sampled above, Daniel proves to his satisfaction and on the basis of texts that Clovis cannot have inherited the kingdom of France, but was in the aggressive position of a raiding barbarian prince.[85]

Such an assertion, in the eyes of a later student[86] will furnish good grounds for the theory that the Franks seized Gaul by conquest and have remained its masters.[87] The matter of " Thuringia " or " Tungria " mentioned by Gregory of Tours[88] as the place to which the French went after leaving Pannonia (Hungary) and crossing the Rhine, does not bother Daniel at all; though it did many of his predecessors and subsequent scholars. The difficulty with the text is that the French need not have crossed the Rhine to go from Pannonia to Thuringia since both places are *east* of the river. Was Gregory ignorant of geography? One manuscript of Gregory was found with the word *Tungriam* in place of *Thuringiam*. Whence Vignier,[89] and others evolved a theory by which Tungria meant the region of Tongres, around Liège.

[84] *Ibid.*, p. 388.

[85] Leber, *op. cit.*, vol. i, p. 391.

[86] Boulainvilliers, who shows familiarity with Daniel's history though not wholly uncritical of it. See below, ch. vii.

[87] In the mind of Abbé Sieyès that mastery changed hands in the French Revolution. See below, ch. xiv.

[88] Bk. ii, ch. ix.

[89] In his *Traité de l'origine, estat et demeure des anciens Français,* Preface to his *Sommaire de l'Histoire de France,* 1579.

Daniel combats the specious interpretation which would destroy his point, by showing that Gregory reports the facts as hearsay and that no other contemporary confirms it.[90] The point, apart from its scholarly interest, may appear trivial, but many inductions yet to come from it are possible. In his second dissertation, Daniel refutes in the same painstaking manner the entire story of Childeric. This done, he can vindicate his right to begin with Clovis his *History of France since the establishment of the monarchy in Gaul.*[91]

The facts advanced and the inferences from them referred to above were warmly contested, especially by Dom Liron [92] (1665-1748) who maintains that not only Childeric, but his predecessor Mérovée, were established in Gaul " not by force but because the emperor gave them lands ".[93] The same blasting criticism of sources that Daniel employed is now turned against him, the rebutting author being caught in the dilemma of keeping the Franks glorious and mighty without making them mere barbarian invaders. It is undeniable, though it may seem difficult to prove, that the connection between the monarchical absolutism of Louis XIV and the nature of the original " French monarchy " was close enough to affect historical systems and even scholarly research.

Yet, never before the reign of the Grand Monarch had the press law been so severe, never had the number of printers been so ruthlessly reduced, nor the days of imprudent authors so frequently spent in prison. The office of police lieutenant created for repressing libel and sedition became a separate branch of the arbitrary power, no longer regarding

---

[90] Leber, *op. cit.*, vol. i, pp. 399-400.

[91] *Ibid.*, p. 407.

[92] *Singularitez historiques et littéraires,* Paris, 1734-40, 4 vols.

[93] Leber, *op. cit.*, vol. i, p. 416.

even the forms of justice.[94]   It is nevertheless during this climax of absolutism that Fénelon, bishop and man of letters, learned in the history of France,[95] and imbued with a high sense of justice and statesmanship, strove by recourse to history and logic to moderate the despotism and personal pride of his monarch.

[94] On practices of Louis' government, see Lavisse, vol. vii, pt. i, p. 267 et seq.

[95] Confirmed by Ch. Urbain, *Ecrits et Lettres Politiques de Fénelon*, p. 18 and Thierry, *Récits*, pp. 52-3.

CHAPTER VII

FÉNELON—BOULAINVILLIERS

FRANÇOIS DE SALIGNAC DE LA MOTHE-FÉNELON, famous
in French literature for his masterpiece, *Télémaque,* ought
to be no less distinguished in the history of liberalism for his
Letter of Remonstrances to Louis XIV.[1]   Appointed in
1689 tutor to the Duc de Bourgogne (1682-1712), grandson of Louis XIV, Fénelon exercised upon the mind and
spirit of that prince a liberalizing influence that can be fairly
judged from the works the tutor wrote for his pupil.   The
Télémaque[2] and the *Dialogue des Morts* abound in critical
allusions to the reign of Louis XIV, but it is in the more
direct *Examen de conscience pour un roi*[3] that the full import of Fénelon's views may be gathered.

Belonging to the old nobility, Fénelon was

imbued with the privileges of his race [that is to say, class]
and could join with extraordinary artistry the proud dignity of
the gentleman to the Christian humility inspired by a deep and
sincere piety.   His birth and his character enabled him to regard
the majesty of the throne without being dazzled, and gave him
enough daring to notice and censure, sometimes too severely,
the errors and faults of Louis XIV.[4]

[1] *A Louis XIV, Remontrances à ce prince sur divers points de son
administration,* 1694.   Ed. Ch. Urbain, p. 143 *et seq.*

[2] Published 1699, but caused the author's disgrace while still in Ms.,
1695.

[3] Translated into English by Lord Granville in 1746 under the title of
Proper heads of self-examination for a king.

[4] Urbain, *op. cit.,* p. 17.

Fénelon reveals the nobiliary prejudice throughout his precepts to the son of the heir-apparent by insisting on the importance of the laws and customs of the kingdom, which should be part of a king's study [5] since they limit his authority and he must " observe them religiously ".[6]   These laws cannot be comprehended without a thorough knowledge of the nation's history.   The king must place the national interest before his own,[7] refrain from engaging in wars for his own glory,[8] and observe the nation's fundamental and natural rights.[9]   These used to be safeguarded by the Parlements or national assemblies,[10] according to Fénelon who, like his contemporaries, is thinking of " origins " and " tradition " when he sketches the importance of historical knowledge:

Do you know [he addresses the young duke], by which forms the kingdom was governed under the different races [of kings] ? What were the *anciens Parlements*, and the Estates-General which succeeded them; what was the subordination of the fiefs; how things have come to be in their present state, upon what [events] the change was based; what anarchy is, and what a kingship, regulated by laws, midway between the two extremes ? [11]

Fénelon is obviously a believer in the limited monarchy under which the Carolingian kings are supposed to have

[5] Fénelon, *Examen*, p. 33; *Lettres*, p. 165.

[6] *Examen*, pp. 35, 51; *Lettres*, p. 165.   See examples drawn from French history, p. 167 *et seq.*

[7] *Examen*, p. 58.

[8] *Ibid.*, pp. 44-7.

[9] *Ibid.*, pp. 34, 36.

[10] *Ibid.*, p. 35.   Fénelon uses the very words " *anciens parlements* ", which were later to appear in the important work of Boulainvilliers. See below, ch. vii.

[11] *Examen*, p. 35.

ruled. The control by the "nation", which to Fénelon meant the nobility,[12] is to extend to taxation. "You know that formerly the king never took anything from the people on his sole authority: it was the Parlement, that is to say the assembly of the nation, which granted him the moneys necessary for the extraordinary needs of the State."[13] On the important question of the relation of the modern Parlements to the old, Fénelon keenly discerns their difference and the inferiority of the first-named.[14]

Again and again the pupil is warned against his own pride and the temptations of luxury. Not Charlemagne in these instances, but Saint Louis is held up as a model of simplicity.[15] Not even the empire of Charlemagne is to be desired at the cost of injustice and violence, nor is it likely to survive the energies of the founder.[16] Threatening as he is, Fénelon lets it be seen that it is love of country[17] that makes him predict internal disorders. In the later years of his disgrace and retirement, he still sees despotism as the source of all France's ills.[18] He therefore plans with the Duc de Chevreuse "reforms" in the government amounting to a revolution, but which in reality embody a return to an idealized government by the nobility that Fénelon imagined in the past.

He proposes three orders of assemblies—local, provincial, and the Estates-General of the nation. These are to meet every three years, grant all extraordinary taxes, deliberate

---

[12] *Plans de Gouvernement,* art. 2, sect. 3, p. 102 *et seq.;* and below.

[13] *Examen,* p. 48.

[14] *Ibid.*

[15] *Ibid.,* p. 41.

[16] *Ibid.,* p. 86.

[17] *Ibid.,* p. 83; *patrie* occurs rather frequently, and specifically, "... with what fondness I love my country..." *Lettre au duc de Chevreuse,* p. 182.

[18] *Ibid.,* p. 181.

on war and commerce, and as long as they see fit. The membership of the provincial assembly shall come from the old nobility and the highest ranks of the Third Estate, both freely elected.[19] Though by no means popular assemblies, the Estates should abolish undue privileges, make an end of *lettres d'état* and illegal encroachments by the nobility, forcing the latter to bring all their lands under cultivation.[20]

The nobility is to be regenerated, however, by the strict registration of its titles; is to be educated at the king's expense; is to provide exclusively all the officers of the Court and army; is to participate in wholesale commerce without losing caste;[21] and to furnish judges on an equal footing with the Third Estate. Further letters of nobility and all misalliances and illegitimacy should likewise be forbidden, to keep the order intact in rank and composition.[22]

Fénelon likewise sees Church and State as cooperating equals, neither subordinated to the other. To make this point acceptable to the royal dignity he points to the historical fact that the Christian and Catholic religion is less anciently established than the State, at the same time as it is of older establishment than the royal line, which it "accepted and authorized: Examples: Pippin and Hugh Capet ".[23]

Lastly, to insure the stability of the government thus outlined and guarantee justice, " chosen jurists " are to be assembled " to correct and gather all the customs, abridge procedure, etc."[24] This old idea worked upon by Colbert and the Revolutionary Convention though not ful-

[19] *Plans de Gouvernement*, Nov., 1711, pp. 101-4.

[20] *Ibid.*, pp. 102-5.

[21] " The nobility, whose entire wealth lies in (royal) decrees, lives only by (means of) letters of state." *Lettre à Louis XIV*, p. 150.

[22] *Plans de Gouvernement*, pp. 116-7.

[23] *Ibid.*, p. 109.

[24] *Ibid.*, p. 121.

filled until the Consulate of Bonaparte, is in keeping with Fénelon's keen consciousness of national unity. In the cruelly just remonstrance to Louis XIV, he speaks frequently of the monarch's relation to " France and the French nation " in contexts that leave no doubt of the words' modern acceptation.[25] His sentiment is not even free of self-consciousness : " I love my country " comes before his " attachment to the person of the king ", and he concludes, " If I loved France less, the king, the royal house . . . ," [26] showing the order of his loyalties.

It was this deep devotion, spurred by a generous feeling of class and a sense that age-old traditions were being dangerously abandoned, that made Fénelon call for an assembly of Notables as a first step before the calling of the Estates General.[27] The same feelings had led him in 1695 to propose for the duc de Bourgogne's education a comprehensive survey on the condition of France. The reports of the intendants (1695-8) in the *généralités* constitute two score of folios packed with information which received scant attention at the hands of learned or even thoughtful men. It was left for the disappointed scion of another noble family, the Comte Henri de Boulainvilliers,[28] to attempt to give historical background and narrative continuity to the principles of reform.

[25] *Lettre à Louis XIV*, pp. 144, 145, 146, 147, 150, 154; " *France* ", " *nation française* ", and " *peuple* " occur nine times taken altogether to seven mentions of " *état* " and two of " *royaume* "; *loc. cit.*, pp. 163-4; *Lettres*, pp. 172, 174. In this letter, " *France* ", " *nation* ", " *patrie* ", " *tout le corps de la nation* ", " *la nation entière unie* " occur 25 times together, against " *Etat* " once and " *royaume* " 3 times.

[26] *Ibid.*, pp. 182-3.

[27] *Ibid.*, p. 174.

[28] Born 1658, died 1722.

Prolific but quasi-unpublished historian, Boulainvilliers found his true vocation only after making a start in the profession of arms and being brought back to civil life by the premature death of his father. As in the strikingly similar case of Montesquieu later, it was in an effort to straighten out tangled family affairs that the young Boulain-villiers became interested in the titles and history of his ancestors and developed that passion for the past to which we owe most of his works. These, composed for the in-struction of his children or the perusal of friends, were circulated freely in manuscript and often copied. Some im-perfect printings of his ever-changing originals did see the light of day, but it was chiefly after his death in 1722 that his ideas reached the historical world. Two personal ac-quaintances of which we know may have been respectively sources of, and channels for, his ideas. That he knew Fénelon is revealed by his collaboration with him in a politico-theological refutation of Spinoza.[29] And his friendship in the opening years of the eighteenth century with young Nicolas Fréret, of which more will be said later, probably resulted in the epoch-making essay of that young man on the name and significance of the Franks.

Like Fénelon, Boulainvilliers deplores and attacks the "despotism" of royal officers which makes it impossible that the truth should ever reach the king,[30] whence it is that he seeks to instruct the Duc de Bourgogne at his own re-quest, just as he does his children. In addition, he confesses "an almost supernatural love for his country",[31] and takes permission from the Duke's high regard for the nobility to attack the "odious magistracy of the intendants and sub-

[29] Bruxelles (Amsterdam), 1731.
[30] *Etat de la France*, ed. Londres, 1737, 6 vols., vol. i, p. 33.
[31] *Ibid.*, p. 37.

intendants ",[32] the " worst enemies of the nobility ".[33] In attempting to cure the evils of the century, Boulainvilliers asserts the uselessness of uncritical memoirs, and urges attention to the experimental truths to be drawn from history.[34]

The plight of the people no less than the abasement of the nobility touch him, and he is ready to fulfill the most exacting demands that Fénelon ever made of the ideal historian—that he should show the form of the government together with the detail of the manners and customs of nations. With respect to France, the good historian must know the origin of the fiefs, the growth of the communes, the rise of the Third Estate, etc.[35]

This program, Boulainvilliers, animated by class pride, though modest about his learning, carries out to the best of his abilities, seconded by voluminous reading.[36] Thus accidentally the pendulum swung back toward the end of the seventeenth century to the " new " history so loudly decried by du Haillan a hundred years before. But in addition to being a political, social and economic historian, it is easy to discern amid the repetitious mass of his works that he is also a maker of systems. The particular theory which he reiterates again and again has been mentioned in this study every time one of its multifarious elements appeared in a previous historian. It is simply that the Franks by their conquest of Gaul acquired certain rights over the territory and certain privileges over the conquered Gauls, which are the origin and legitimate source of the nobles' prerogatives throughout French history. In other words, the nobility are

[32] *Ibid.*, p. 39.

[33] *Ibid.*, pp. 57, 59.

[34] *Etat de la France*, vol. i, pp. 43, 41.

[35] *Lettres sur les occupations de l'Académie française*, 1714, ch. viii.

[36] *Mémoires historiques sur l'ancien gouvernement*, 6 vols., Londres, 1737, vol. i, p. 60.

the descendants of the Franks, the Third Estate those of the Gallo-Romans.

In perhaps his most characteristic *Essais sur la Noblesse de France contenans une dissertation sur son origine et abaissement,*[37] the influence of his predisposition may be seen on the details of French history. Though the epigraph of the work is *Heu! fuimus Troes,*[38] Boulainvilliers is too careful a scholar to adopt in more than an allegorical way the story of the Trojan origin. In fact, contrary to his habit of beginning by citations showing prevalent opinions he later disproves, the author establishes the usefulness of the nobility by reason. " At common law," he says, " all men are equal. Violence introduces distinctions, but the usage is so ancient that it has acquired the force of natural law." [39] The nobility existed among all ancient peoples, and its decadence heralded the fall of Rome. " Virtue needs rank to signalize it and birth is the means." [40]

All of French history proves the value and independence of the nobility. " The kingdom was established in the course of thirteen centuries by means of the blood, toil and liberality (*dépenses*) of the old nobility." [41]

Turning to historical justifications, Boulainvilliers repeats his ideas on the origins of the Franks more fully expressed in his *Dissertation sur les premiers François et sur leur origine.*[42] The French [43] formerly lived beyond the Rhine,

---

[37] Amsterdam, 1732.

[38] Title-page.

[39] *Dissertation*, p. 1.

[40] *Ibid.*, p. 5.

[41] *Ibid.*, p. 11.

[42] *Essais*, p. 301 *et seq.*

[43] Boulainvilliers uses *French* more often than *Frank* but with a clear conception of its limited meaning, since his very system rests upon the distinction of race formerly slighted.

and whether it is true, as Mézeray reports,[44] that the Gauls, Germans, and Britons were originally of one race, the fact remains that the distinction of Gauls and Germans is subsequent; that the Gauls were conquered by the Romans and that it is the glory of the Franks to have in turn subjugated the conquerors of the world.

From the outset, obviously, the right of conquest is for Boulainvilliers the ultimate title to fame and property.[45] " It is perhaps this memorable feat," the Count goes on, " whence derives this unconquerable repugnance of the French to any slavery. . . ." [46] In Rome's conquest of Gaul, Britain, and Germany, began the hatreds which finally undermined the Empire by elevating the Franks, who reached the highest point of their glory under Charlemagne.[47]

The last statement contains two of Boulainvilliers' major propositions: the principle of racial hatred and the conviction that the golden age of mankind existed in the government of Charlemagne. On the first issue, the writer is not unaware of the early mixture between Germans and Gauls, but he indicates that the ultimately victorious group was that in the region of Tongres, and to them Boulainvilliers applies the classical description of Tacitus: tall, blond, chaste, hardy, bellicose, without towns or trade.[48] He distinguishes among them four categories: nobles or *Adalinges*; freemen or *Fridlinges*; serfs or *Lazzes*; freedmen or *Frilazzes*. These categories persisted among the Carolingian

---

[44] Of the authors dealt with in the preceding chapters, Boulainvilliers cites Mézeray, Daniel, Loyseau, du Haillan, Pasquier, Bouteiller, Tacitus, Gregory of Tours, du Tillet, Fauchet, Bignon, Chantereau, Pithou, Dupuy, Duchesne, G. de Nangis.

[45] *Etat de la France,* vol. i, p. 134.

[46] *Essais,* p. 304.

[47] *Ibid.,* p. 310.

[48] *Ibid.,* p. 318. Boulainvilliers' Teutons are more communistic than individualistic, however.

Franks. At the same time there were also four orders among the Gauls: Druids, Knights, People, and Serfs; but "there is evidence to show that among the French, even when Christianized, no prelacy was conferred upon servile persons, or persons of a low class." [49] The third important point in Boulainvilliers' system follows, that the first *two* orders are therefore noble in origin.

The hardihood of the German conquerors noted previously is, to Boulainvilliers, a sign that their blood was unmixed with that of aliens. Among these Germans, known also as Sicambrians, and including the Chamavi, Bructeri, etc., was the "cradle of our monarchy, established when Clovis in 481 combined in his person the dignities of king and Mayor or duke." [50] The numbers of the Franks were swelled by colonies of Goths, Huns, Ostrogoths, Burgundians, Saxons, Britons and Normans, and they possessed themselves of two-thirds of Gaul; [51] one-third being left to the natives on condition of service and tribute. The distinction between the two kinds of land is "shown by the term *Salic land* or *Franc-aleu,* from *alles leuthe: all compatriots*". [52] The Franks being too few to till all the land at their disposal, and their temperament being averse to it, the Gauls became the farmers of the nation,[53] were excluded from military service, the government, and the administration of justice, which latter was in the hands of the Frankish elders.[54] The Gallo-Romans were thus "thrown into the order of the clergy".[55]

[49] *Essais,* p. 329.

[50] *Ibid.,* pp. 11, 340.

[51] *Ibid.,* pp. 11-12.

[52] *Mémoires Hist.,* pp. 5, 130.

[53] *Ibid.,* p. 145.

[54] *Essais,* pp. 13-17.

[55] *Ibid.* and *Mémoires,* p. 134 *et seq.*

Benefices and honors came as rewards for services and from newly-conquered lands on certain conditions, such as life interest, tribute, etc.[56]   In that government noble was equivalent to master and lord and to " Salian ", meaning Frankish conqueror of Gaul.[57]   By their possession of land, therefore, the nobility alone constituted the State.[58]   To summarize, in his own words, and show the double direction of Boulainvilliers' system :

I. The conquest of Gaul is the foundation of the French state under which we live . . . it is from it that we have received our primary rights.[59]

II. . . . I have always been annoyed by the mistake of our historians . . . who regard France as the patrimony of Clovis and his successors.   It has been forgotten that he was but the General of a free army that had elected him to lead it in its enterprises, of which the profit and glory were to be shared in common. . . .[60]

III. . . . the advantages [of the French nobility] I reduce to four : exemption from all charges, save military service ; participation in all profits from conquest—lands or booty ; the right to judge their peers . . . and to deliberate in all matters brought before the general assembly of the Field of March ; lastly, the right to defend themselves and their property.[61]

The history of his class since that time Boulainvilliers shows as the gradual loss of prerogatives, the formation of three estates in the place of one, the precedence of the clergy, and finally, the adjunction of lawyers as a nobility of the robe.[62]   Preeminent in the Estates of 1302, the nobility was

[56] *Essais*, p. 22.
[57] *Mémoires Hist.*, vol. i, p. 133.
[58] *Ibid.*, vol. i, pp. 133-4.
[59] *Ibid.*, vol. i, pp. 126-7.
[60] *Ibid.*, pp. 127, 129.
[61] *Mémoires*, vol. i, p. 135.
[62] *Ibid.*, pp. 133-4.

attacked by Philip V and Charles-le-Bel, and, though it sustained by means of its Salic Law the claim of Philip of Valois to the throne, it was, as a result of French flightiness, outdistanced by the magistracy.[63] Taking precedence over the clergy at the *lit de justice* of December 26, 1407, the nobility finds itself displaced from the Estate of Tours in 1470, deprived of its right of life and death over its peers—shorn of its power.[64] By the abuse of tax-exemptions granted by the king,[65] the old and the new nobility have become hopelessly entangled; [66] since Charles VII it is impossible to distinguish the true from the false, so that any noble family that does not antedate 1443 must be suspect to experts; and since that time, confusion and usurpation of rights have brought the upper order to its present desuetude.

Now, in Boulainvilliers' mind the importance of the Estates-General, or " former parlements ", as he calls them, is that if in the beginning only the nobles had the privilege of attending, the presence of the modern three Estates is a usurpation on the part of the First and Third. But it has been shown that these two orders were ultimately drawn from the conquered Gauls.[67] The modern state of France is therefore in no respect conformable with the original monarchy. By the time of Hugh Capet, owing to the Gauls' having in many cases obtained freedom from servitude by military service, the lower orders of the two races intermingled and were " confounded in the same laws and in a single national group." [68] Boulainvilliers thus admits that he is clamoring for a lost cause.

[63] *Lettres sur les anciens Parlemens*, vol. iii, p. 65 *et seq.*, p. 93 *et seq.*

[64] *Ibid.*, vol. iii, Letters xi-xiv.

[65] From the time of Philip IV onwards. *Ibid.*, vol. i, p. 130; vol. ii, pp. 38, 75, 89.

[66] *Ibid.*, vol. iii, pp. 71-2 ; 98-114 ; *Essais*, p. 274.

[67] *Essais*, vol. i, p. 41.

[68] *Essais*, vol. i, p. 67.

Some features of Nordic government still remained, however. Charlemagne's aggrandizement at the expense of the Armorican, Saxon, Norman, and Breton provinces led to the establishment of fiefs, a Nordic custom possibly derived from the conquered tribes themselves.[69] It was then that the possessors of benefices usurped title to their property in the form of fiefs. The result was nonetheless admirable, for the hierarchy of rights and duties was such as to prevent a mixture of upper and lower classes even in time of common danger.[70] Justice remained in the hands of the holders of benefices, and Gauls were subjected to the Salic Law in case of litigation with a noble.[71] Charlemagne by re-establishing the general assemblies once more gave deliberative power to the well-born.

But after Charlemagne this beautifully equilibrated system began to decline. Two important factors have helped the disintegration: the liberation of the serfs who were " either native Gauls subjected to the French, or unfortunates whom necessity and accident had reduced to servitude; and the progress by which these serfs have risen, without any right, to the condition of their former masters." [72]

To Boulainvilliers this topsy-turvyness seems servitude. "Woeful wretchedness of our age," exclaims the Count, indignant at being dispossessed, "which, not being satisfied even with the submission in which we live, tries to discover slavery back in a time when it was not thought of!" [73]

Having thus righted himself with the past, Boulainvilliers entered into contemporary politics with a vigorous

---

[69] *Essais*, vol. i, p. 102.

[70] *Ibid.*, p. 112.

[71] *Ibid.*, p. 120.

[72] *Lettres sur les anciens Parlemens*, vol. i, pp. 130-1.

[73] *Notes et préface critique sur le journal du règne de St. Louis.* (Ms. Bibliothèque de l'Arsenal, B.L.F., No. 131.)

protest against the " dukes and peers " [74] who in certain
memoirs of 1663, 1664, and 1716 pretended to form a body
separate from the nobility and to place themselves at its
head. The political occasion was of course the question of
the regency for Louis XV's minority, and Boulainvilliers
valiantly entered the breach on behalf of his whole order,
thereby incurring the wrath of Cardinal Fleury, among
others, who stated that the Count of Boulainvilliers " knew
neither the past, the present, nor the future ". [75]

Whatever truth there is in the accusation that the voluminous and rambling historian did not know the past, it remains a fact that he gave new life to a very provocative
thesis of far-reaching consequence. Against the absolute
monarchy,[76] against the dukes and princes of the blood,[77]
against the magistrates, against the Third Estate, he appealed on a peculiarly *national* [78] platform to the " original
liberties " [79] of France, to the tradition of the Estates-General,[80] to the right of self-taxation by the assembly of the
nation,[81] to the whole apparatus of constitutionalism so
much admired in England by eighteenth-century Frenchmen
and which the disgruntled noble found in the history of his
own country.

From a scholarly aspect, the work of Boulainvilliers is also
important despite his prejudices and lacunas. By recalling

[74] *Mémoire pour la Noblesse de France contre les ducs et pairs,* published in 1717 but immediately withdrawn.

[75] Michaud, *Biog. Univ.,* Art. Boulainvilliers.

[76] *Lettres,* vol. i, p. 174; vol. iii, p. 10.

[77] See above.

[78] The words *nation* and *patrie* abound in his works, and by no means
in the restricted sense of *nobility.* The entire people shared his interest
if only they were distributed in their proper places.

[79] *Mémoires.,* vol. i, p. 128 *et seq.*

[80] *Ibid.,* p. 198 *et seq.*

[81] *Lettres,* vol. i, p. 45; vol. iii, p. 180 *et seq.*

the former racial division of France, he focussed the interest of men of learning on a problem which royal absolutism had tried to bury within the terms of the emigrant Gauls fiction. These two points were in fact to be resolved on a critical basis early in the eighteenth century, long before historians would agree on the nature of the Frankish settlement itself. Lastly, Boulainvilliers' explicit critiques of Mézeray and Daniel were based on a very judicious understanding of the historical writer's function.   Of the first he says:

" He had no just notion of the history of the first race of Our Kings, although in his time it was hardly possible to do better. . . ." [82]   He had nonetheless the merit of being " a good citizen and a good Frenchman ".[83]   Daniel, in Boulainvilliers' estimation, is scarcely superior to Mézeray for reducing, in spite of his pretensions, all the old laws and usages to the terms and practices of his own day.[84]

Remarking on the scarcity of historians under a monarchy, Boulainvilliers sketches the desiderata of an historian who would write the history of France.   In addition to a good style, he must have " a sufficient knowledge of the old authors, as well as of the moderns; he must have consulted two or three thousand charters, to obtain a true notion of the character of each century's manners and customs, as well as to learn an infinity of details of which historians have never spoken. . . . " [85]   It cannot be said that Boulainvilliers was such a complete historian, but it might be argued that he inspired one, whose talents auspiciously came to light at the beginning of the eighteenth century.   This historian was the young prodigy Nicolas Fréret.

[82] *Anciens Parlemens*, vol. i, p. 23.
[83] *Ibid.*, pp. 24-5.
[84] *Ibid.*, vol. i, pp. 26-8.
[85] *Ibid.*, p. 16 *et seq.*

CHAPTER VIII

Fréret—Saint-Simon—Leibnitz

Born in 1688, the son of a Procurator of the Paris Parlement, Fréret was educated in a legal atmosphere that suscitated in him a deep interest in history; while his friendship with the older Boulainvilliers helped to foster that interest and defend it against family objections to the career of letters.

Having already made something of a local reputation as a member of a literary society, Fréret was admitted as " pupil " to the newly-reorganized *Académie des Inscriptions et Belles-Lettres* in 1714. It was as his maiden address that he presented the now famous memoir on the origin of the French, in which he establishes three points. The first is that the Franks were a league formed in the third century A. D. among several tribes of Low Germany; the same tribes that Caesar referred to as the Sicambrian League; and which subsequently served in the Roman army. The second is corollary to the first. Since the Franks do not constitute a new nation or a race separate from the German, the attempt to trace their migrations and ultimate origin is futile.[1] Finally, the name *Frank* does not mean *free*. In various German dialects, *frek, frak, frenk, frank, vrang,* all are equivalent to the Latin *ferox,* meaning alike proud or fearless and wild or cruel. [2] Fréret in this etymology was following that of Isidore of Spain, but based his conclusions on the study of old franco-teutonic verses showing that in

[1] *Oeuvres de Fréret*, Paris, 1798, vol. v, p. 164 *et seq.*

[2] *Ibid.,* p. 203 *et seq.*

148

the time of Louis le Débonnaire, the Franks were also called *Frenk,* to which *fright* and *verachten* (to despise) seem related. From the Frankish point of view, the word must have been a title of honor by which they noted their courage and valor.[3]

For a reason which has remained obscure but not inexplicable, the Monarchy appeared to the Academy in some way offended by the Memoir, and on the denunciation of the influential Abbé de Vertot, Fréret was clapped into the Bastille where he remained six months. It is difficult to determine what part of his Memoir hurt the royal dignity; whether the reducing of the Franks to a group of marauding tribes, or the denial of either a Gallic or a Trojan or yet a distinct racial origin. It remains a fact, however, that with the exception of a short paper on the name Merovingian read in 1746, Fréret's experience turned him definitely away from French history and directed his many talents into the less dangerous field of Roman and Greek antiquity.

With Fréret unable to follow up his advantage, contradictory opinions still prevailed on a question which had in reality been definitely settled. It is true that Fréret's own delator, Abbé de Vertot, had concluded in a memoir of 1705 before the same Academy that the French were originally Germans. Descended, like Boulainvilliers, from an old but impoverished noble family, the Abbé took pride in establishing the ultimate superiority of the French over the Romans they conquered.[4] His method is to establish an exact parallel between the general account of the Germans' customs and manners by Tacitus and the specific accounts of the Franks' customs and manners by contemporary chroniclers.[5]

---

[3] Fréret, *op. cit.,* p. 206 *et seq.*

[4] *Dissertation sur . . . la véritable origine des Français,* in Leber, *op. cit.,* vol. i, p. 59.

[5] Leber, *op. cit.,* vol. i, p. 43 *et seq.*

Out of his memoir, however, it arises that " France is the name of a nation, rather than of a country "; [6] and it is possible that Fréret's destruction of this point may have animated his resentment.

The military monarchy of the Franks, their general assemblies, and above all their simplicity of life appeal to the historian's pride of ancestry. " The Franks in early times were not eager for gold or silver. Health, strength, courage and freedom they held as the only solid goods . . . and this warlike people, on quitting Germany to burst upon Gaul, brought only iron to conquer it." [7]

The loyal and monarchical Abbé [8] is not afraid to assert that the great assemblies of the Franks were " *the general parliament of the nation* ",[9] and that the ordinances and decrees — called capitularies under the second race — had no force of law until approved and received by the consent and concurrence of the whole nation.[10] Yet he makes it clear that only the clergy and the nobility composed these assemblies, all other orders being servile.[11]

De Vertot's system seems an academic modification of Boulainvilliers', at least regarding the early phases of the French monarchy, for he says: " It may at first sight seem strange that the Romans or Gauls (i. e. the clergy), living under the recent domination of a foreign and victorious nation, should have been granted such an important role in the government." [12] He goes on to explain that they per-

[6] Leber, *op. cit.*, p. 67.

[7] *Ibid.*, p. 62.

[8] *Cf.* his *Traité de la mouvance de Bretagne*, denying the former autonomy of Brittany ; and also: *Hist. de l'établissement des Bretons dans les Gaules.*

[9] Leber, *op. cit.*, p. 63 (italics are his).

[10] *Ibid.*, p. 69.

[11] *Ibid.*, p. 70.

[12] Leber, *op. cit.*, vol. i, p. 92.

haps contributed as much as the Franks themselves to the establishment of the monarchy, for by converting them to Catholicism they made legitimate a possession based only on force and violence.[13] This view was apparently not at all displeasing to the absolutism of the French king, and de Vertot sincerely believed, divergently from Boulainvilliers, that even originally " the Franks were subordinated to sovereign princes, though they in turn were subject to military laws they dared not violate." [14]

Simultaneously, but in England, a French soldier of fortune, Paul de Rapin-Thoyras, deceived in his hopes of recognition at home, was using the same magazine of facts to exalt the transplanted Germanic form of free government in England, at the expense of his native land's institutions. Disregarding entirely the Celtic and Roman and Norman-French heritage of Britain, Rapin, in his popular *History of England*,[15] establishes an exact parallel between parliamentary government as he saw it and the customs of the Anglo-Saxons. There were " two things the Saxons did not think suitable to entrust to their kings . . . the power of changing the laws enacted by the consent of king and people, and the power of raising taxes." [16] By further asserting popular rights to liberty and property,[17] Thoyras not only appealed to the opinions favoring the Revolution of 1688, but also completed the first ideal picture by a Frenchman of eighteenth-century parliamentary government in England.

[13] Leber, *op. cit.*, pp. 72-3.

[14] *Ibid.*, p. 60.

[15] *Histoire d'Angleterre*, La Haye, 1724, 8 vols., Trans. Tindal, London, 1726.

[16] *Hist. of England*, " Essay on Origins of the English Government," pp. ii-iii.

[17] *Ibid.*, pp. iii-iv.

To be sure, Montesquieu's *Persian Letters*,[18] published in 1721, contain a glimmer of admiration for England and her system of liberty,[19] but Montesquieu had not yet visited the country by that date, nor had he discovered the close kinship existing between the Germanic tribal assembly and the Parliament of Walpole's ministry.   Besides, there is every reason to believe that Rapin-Thoyras' historical investigations antedate Montesquieu's by some fifteen years.   On the other hand, it must be said in defense of Montesquieu's originality and to qualify the importance of the Frenchman's *Histoire d'Angleterre,* that, despite Voltaire's belief that it was the best history of England, it had very little circulation in France.[20]

While the abbés and the academies were discussing matters of origin, men closer to the vortex of "despotism" were raising their voices in increasingly loud protest.   The Duc de Saint-Simon, whose memoirs form such a vivid, albeit partisan account of the period 1692-1723, reveals himself not less aware of the state of France than Fénelon, and not less critical of the crown's historical encroachments on the nobility than Boulainvilliers.   It may in fact be from the latter that Saint-Simon adopted the view that the Frankish sovereign who conquered Gaul, in giving out the confiscated lands to his warriors, thereby created the " nobility, the sole body of the nation, who were first called men of war, the nobles, to differentiate them from the conquered who, from their complete servitude were called serfs." [21]

And yet, the same anti-despotic passion as Boulainvilliers' animates his present sympathy towards the lower classes.

[18] *Lettres Persanes*, Rouen, 1721, ed. Tourneux, Paris, 19—.

[19] Letter CV, vol. ii, p. 27.

[20] See Michaud, art. Rapin.

[21] *Mémoires*, ed. Chéruel, Paris, 1872, 20 vols., vol. ii, p. 367.

In a letter to Cardinal Fleury, the duke, protesting his public spirit, paints of the French people a picture of wretchedness comparable to that of Fénelon in his letter to the Duc de Chevreuse. Saint-Simon concludes, " the people will soon be thrown into despair ". [22]   Saint-Simon and Chevreuse were in fact associated in a plan to save the government by transferring the power from the king's ministers to special councils of the nobles, who were to supplant both king and parlement in the manner Boulainvilliers might have wished.[23]

The aristocrat in Saint-Simon inveighs against the deplorable practice of the king's choosing commoners to be his ministers of state, so that " he may throw them back into the abyss from which he has drawn them ".[24]   He refutes the idea that the Parlement is the foremost body in the State.[25]   Since it is drawn from the Third Estate it cannot be a separate order.   There are three orders in the state, of which the nobility alone is of any account.   " The nobility, now second, was formerly the only estate which by right of superiority represented and formed the state." [26]

The clergy has obtained its wealth and station only by reason of the charity and piety of the nobles, and it is only its religious character which entitles it to first place.   As for the Third Estate, it became an order from the day that Philippe de Valois began to tax it; since then, it has raised itself from servitude, and become property-owning in various ways.[27]

As might be inferred, Saint-Simon divides the nobility as well as the state, and deplores the confusion in both its ranks

[22] *Ecrits inédits*, vol. iv, p. 175 *et seq.*

[23] *Mémoires*, ed. Chéruel, vol. vi, p. 288.

[24] *Parallèle des trois premiers rois bourbons, Ecrits*, vol. iv, p. 231.

[25] *ibid.*, p. 402 *et seq.*

[26] *Ecrits*, p. 402 *et seq.*

[27] *Ibid.*, p. 407.

as a sign of political decadence. It is his chief grievance against Louis XIV. By subtle and apparently trivial means, the dukes and peers have been driven from their rightful high place. It was at Louvois' instigation that the Ministers began to call dukes *Monsieur,* whereas these must title the ministers *Monseigneur.*[28] " Such was the art of everywhere lowering the great, the lordships, the nobility, the special bodies [in the nobility] by persons of no account in themselves. . . ." [29]

Saint-Simon thus differs from Boulainvilliers on the matter of a hierarchy within the nobility, and he assails the lesser gentry for their hostility to the dukes and peers in the Assembly of 1717.[30] He vituperates against the idleness and incompetence of ". . . this nobility accustomed to being good for nothing except getting killed, to carrying on war because of mere seniority, and to stagnating in the most deadly uselessness, bred by indolence and distaste for any instruction save war, and by incapacity to use instruction if it had it." [31]

The noble duke's proposed reforms are easily imagined: the restoration of his order, by the creation of a regulating body, and by forbidding further ennoblings; [32] a return to the " fundamental laws " of the nation, which seem to consist almost exclusively of the Salic Law; [33] and the substitution of noble councils for the ministers, under the authority of a Council of State.[34] The absolute monarchy, though he

[28] *Mémoires*, vol. ii, p. 179.

[29] *Ecrits*, vol. iv, p. 285.

[30] See above, p. 146.

[31] *Mémoires*, vol. xi, pp. 427-8.

[32] *Projets de gouvernement*, Paris, 1860, p. 55 *et seq.*

[33] *Ecrits*, vol. ii, p. 121.

[34] *Projets*, p. 18 *et seq.*

does not say so[35] outright, is thus limited, though not, of course, by any popular institutions.[36] The Estates-General, being now composed of three orders, conflict with the " fundamental laws ". To give them the legislative power would be an extraordinary abuse. The Estates, therefore, reduced to 36 deputies, should simply ratify without discussing the laws presented to them.[37]

Fénelon, Saint-Simon, Boulainvilliers, singled out in this study as reacting against absolutism and exalting the conqueror nobility, invoked early French history on behalf of their pleas, but are not for that reason to be regarded as the only opponents of the despotism which the eighteenth century after bitter discussions finally shattered.

As early as 1689, the anonymous author of the *Soupirs de la France Esclave* cried aloud against the " fearful tyranny under which [France] groans beholding the happy liberties enjoyed by all the neighboring nations . . . in the possession of their ancient laws." [38] Originally the monarchy was not absolute; indeed it was elective; furthermore in the Estates resided the sovereignty as deputies of the people; and later the Parlement succeeded to their power " as a brake to the enterprises of the Crown ". [39]

With these views the author does not combine egalitarian principles. He deplores on the contrary the dizzy height to which Louis XIV has raised himself, so that " all human beings are but dust under his feet ".[40] He wishes, as do all

[35] H. Sée, *op. cit.* points out in this connection Saint-Simon's occasional word of praise for the English and Dutch governments.

[36] *Projets*, pp. 20, 22, 55, 59, 61.

[37] *Ibid.*, p. 4; *Ecrits*, vol. ii, p. 401.

[38] *Soupirs, First memoir*, quoted in Sée, *op. cit.*, p. 194.

[39] *Eighth Memoir*, p. 167, *ibid.*, p. 199.

[40] *Second Memoir*, p. 21, *ibid.*, p. 197.

opponents of Louis XIV, that " the monarchy be brought back to its old forms ". [41]

To these reiterated demands were added indictments of absolutism from the pens of protestant writers, refugees in Holland after the revocation of the Edict of Nantes: Levassor (to whom the *Soupirs de la France* have often been attributed), Claude, Basnage de Beauval, Jurieu, and especially the author of the *Dictionnaire Historique et Critique,* Pierre Bayle.

What the protestants undermine in the theory of the French monarchy is the divine right of kings.[42] In his *Lettres Pastorales,* Jurieu, to escape this doctrine, arrives at the notion of the social contract [43] and substantiates his point with historical examples.[44] Bayle likewise in his *Commentaire philosophique* (1686). Eleven years later, in his *Dictionnaire* he applied to the ends of tolerance the same method of rational doubt and comparative history.

He insists on the precise citation of sources. Writers must " never advance anything which they do not find in witnesses worthy of faith "; [45] must " carefully hide their prejudices and avoid appearing passionate ".[46] His use of the comparative method in the history of religions, by throwing into relief similarities of beliefs as well as of errors, is nothing more nor less than the weapon which Voltaire is to use.[47] From our point of view, the significant

---

[41] *Twelfth Memoir,* p. 217, *ibid.,* p. 197.

[42] Boulainvilliers himself attacked Bossuet for his misuse of Scripture to bolster up the king's power. *Anciens Parlemens,* vol. i, p. 68.

[43] *Lettres Pastorales,* xvi, p. 363 *et seq.*

[44] *Lettres,* xvi and xvii.

[45] *Dict.* art. *Démocrite,* vol. ii, p. 636. Ref. are to the London edition of 1734, as above.

[46] *Ibid.* art. *Bellarmin,* vol. i, p. 542.

[47] Voltaire calls him " the immortal Bayle . . . an honor to human nature, the author of the first dictionary that teaches thinking." *Oeuvres,* vol. l, p. 312.

thing is that Bayle turns this weapon on every question—political, social and historical, as well as religious.

Speaking of Bodin's contention at the Estates of 1576, that the power of monarchs is limited and that they govern according to laws, Bayle clearly shows his sympathy with those views: " He maintained the former when he saw the king's flatterers . . . propose what might create great abuses and the oppression of the people; and he maintained the latter when he saw France full of factions . . . which gave birth to a great number of manifestoes and other books, in which the most essential and fundamental laws of the government were undermined. . . . He had the misfortune of contradicting himself after the death of Henry III . . . but the fall of a sinner does not spoil the good actions that he has done." [48]

Speaking of Hotman, Bayle again says: " He wrote a book entitled *Franco-Gallia* to show that the French monarchy is not what it is thought to be, and that of right the people are the true sovereigns in it. . . . That book of Hotman is at bottom a fine piece, well-written and full of learning, and so much the more vexatious to the contrary party because the author contents himself with citing matters of fact. . . ." [49]

If it be objected that some of the previously cited attacks on despotism launched against the French Crown in the thirty years from the Revocation of the Edict of Nantes to the death of Louis XIV, were topical and without influence, the same doubt cannot be raised about Bayle's *Dictionary*. Eleven editions appeared before 1741, and its plan and method undoubtedly shaped those of the Encyclopedia. Critic and methodologist, Bayle paid little continued attention to the special historical questions upon which, as has

[48] *Dict.* art. *Bodin*, vol. ii, p. 53, n.
[49] *Dict.* art. *Hotman*, vol. iii, pp. 521-522 n.

been seen, various conceptions of the French monarchy hinged. But his opinions and his gigantic footnotes, packed with arguments and citations, found their mark. Turning now once again from destructive criticism to the establishment of historical systems, we must take up academic controversy where it was left by the memoirs of de Vertot and Fréret.

In his actionable memoir of 1714 Fréret had refuted the belief that the Franks were a separate nation directly descended from the emigrant Gauls led by Sigovese. Fréret did *not* deny the possible common origin, at a very remote period, of the peoples of Germany and the greater part of Gaul.[50]   In allowing this possibility, Fréret adroitly combats an essay on the subject by the celebrated philosopher and mathematician, Leibnitz,[51] who had taken a distinctly nationalistic tone to refute the Gallic origin of the Franks.

Leibnitz attacks especially the erudite but biased work of Lacarry mentioned above [52] and points out maliciously that that author, " together with several other learned men of his nation, has imagined with misguided zeal for the glory of his country (*patrie*) that it would be a greater honor to derive the modern inhabitants of Gaul from the Gauls themselves . . . that is maintaining what one would wish, and not what one has found." [53]

The philosopher's own zeal is unusual. He takes seeming pride in the assertion that the French (he does not use Frank) are a Teutonic people come from the shores of the

[50] Leber, *op. cit.*, vol. i, p. 129.

[51] *Essai sur l'origine des Français*, vol. ii, p. 287, of *Recueil de Diverses Pièces*, Amsterdam, 1720.   First published in Latin, 1715; Leber, *op. cit.*, p. 97 *et seq.*

[52] See above, ch. vi, p. 127.

[53] Leber, *op. cit.*, vol. i, pp. 102-3.

Baltic Sea.[54] His chief authority is the anonymous geographer of Ravenna published by Dom Porcheron, a monk of St. Germain. Other testimony, he thinks, indicates that the French were a seafaring people descended from the Danes, as late as the reign of Louis le Débonnaire.[55] The French, whose dominion extended as far as the Elbe river, are therefore related to the Angles, Saxons, Rugians, Cimbrians, etc.[56]

The German historian states that he makes these remarks partly because they are unknown, and partly because they are honorable to the French and Saxons, " peoples formerly neighbors " and who were described by an old source as " swift, agile, well-built, well-dressed[!], handsome of face, and very tall." [57]

The third proof of Leibnitz' thesis is drawn from his opponents themselves—at least from those who, disregarding the work of Cluwer and de Valois, still hold for the Trojan origin. Leibnitz suggests that as that theory rests on the fact that the French were said to come from the Palus Meotis, it is very probable that the Baltic Sea is meant since the two bodies of water were often confused by the old geographers.[58] As far as can be discovered, then, the first settlement of the French was between the Baltic and the Elbe; the second between the Weser and the Rhine, whence they passed into Gaul and " founded a very flourishing Empire ". [59]

Leibnitz is also anxious to give the French a sort of copyright on the Salic Law, which he thinks was published long

[54] Leber, *op. cit.*, vol. i, p. 103.

[55] *Ibid.*, pp. 104, 106.

[56] *Ibid.*, pp. 105, 108.

[57] *Ibid.*, p. 106.

[58] *Ibid.*, p. 110.

[59] *Ibid.*, p. 111.

before their conversion to Christianity, and which was named, not after the river Issel, as the Dutch would have us believe, but after the Sale in Franconia.[60] He draws a flattering picture of Charlemagne in his palace on the Sale, making a treaty with the Saxons to give them equality with the French, " as if they were one people ". [61]

After having generally been known as Germans, the people between the Main, Sale, Elbe rivers and Harz Mountains were called Franks or French.[62] They became pirates and were swept off the sea by their cousins the Saxons, but regained new vigor when they submitted to a king of their own,[63] named Priam (short for Pharamond). His son was Clodio, " which is the same as Clogion, Clovis, Illudevic or Louis ". [64]

The same inverted patriotism, so to speak, operates to make the philosopher " prefer " one interpretation of documents relating to Charlemagne's ancestry so that the emperor should descend from Clodio, instead of from a Roman family, as he should according to M. du Bouchet, " which would make Charlemagne not of the *French* race ". [65]

Leibnitz concludes his essay by venturing the opinion that the *Arboriches* of Procopius were Gauls, whose territory extended from Brittany to the Scheldt, and who soon after the invasions " began to leave the Romans to submit themselves to the French ". [66]

[60] Leber, *loc. cit.*, p. 116.

[61] *Ibid.*, p. 117.

[62] *Ibid.*, p. 119.

[63] *Ibid.*, p. 122.

[64] *Ibid.*, p. 124. Leibnitz probably did not mean to tickle the vanity of his political bugbear Louis XIV.

[65] *Ibid.*, pp. 123-124 (italics mine to clarify, if possible, the nomenclature).

[66] *Ibid.*, pp. 125-6.

The weak point in this pro-German theory was discerned by Fréret, who objects that the various migrations of the Franks are not only not supported by testimony but that if they took place from the shores of the Baltic westward, the inhabitants of Lower Germany and northeastern Gaul must have been driven out; a conflict of races of which the Romans who were on the spot have left no testimony.[67]

Another refutation of Leibnitz from the French side appeared in 1716 in the *Journal de Trévoux*[68] over the well-known name of its editor, the Reverend Père Tournemine. The versatile critic, who was open-minded enough to be a protector of young Voltaire and gracefully to disperse his own talents among varied subjects of passing interest, is the last upholder in France of what Thierry calls " the patriotic hypothesis of the unity of race ".[69]

Tournemine begins by doubting the authenticity of Leibnitz' chief source, the geographer of Ravenna. Then he shows that, even if it is to be credited, Leibnitz has misconstrued the passage.[70] " If it were a matter for wishing," he goes on, consciously laying bare possible grounds of agreement, " perhaps we should hesitate between the honor of being a compatriot of Leibnitz and the glory of descending from a people which, after having taken Rome, ravaged Greece, and vanquished the troops of Alexander . . . ,"[71] i. e. the Gauls. But ". . . let us follow the tradition of the best accredited and most famous historians: it leads us straight to the Gauls who under Sigovese conquered the most beautiful regions of Germany."[72]

[67] Fréret, *op. cit.*, Leber, vol. i, p. 131.

[68] *Mémoires pour l'Hist. des Sciences et des Beaux-Arts* (Journal de Trévoux), vol. 61, January, 1716, p. 10 *et seq.*

[69] *Récits*, p. 42.

[70] *Réflections*, in *Mémoires* cited, pp. 10-13.

[71] *Ibid.*, p. 14.

[72] *Ibid.*, p. 15.

Tournemine shows that Lacarry, whom he is defending, did not originate the theory, but developed the ideas and suggestions of Bodin and Trivorius.[73]   They do not rest upon invention but result from this convincing reasoning that the French left the country which the Gauls had occupied without having been driven from it from the time of their invasion.   The French were therefore originally Gauls. Historically, proofs are to be found in Caesar, Tacitus, and Livy.   There is also philological confirmation in the fact that the Gauls first bore the name German, or Herman (Hermian), meaning warlike men.   *Allemands* and *Français* are simply the names of two sub-groups.[74]   The language of the French was Teutonic, as Leibnitz asserts; but Teutonic, according to Pontanus, is related to Gallic.   To clinch the matter, the Jesuit Father restates his point syllogistically:

The French are Germans; the Germans are the Gauls who crossed the Rhine; *ergo,* the French are Gauls. [75]

After Tournemine it was a Benedictine monk, Dom Joseph Vaissette, who in 1722 concluded the matter by leaving no alternative but the German origin of the French,[76] and thus shifting the whole ground of controversy for the eighteenth-century historians, just as the work of Pasquier, Bodin, and Hotman had swung the issue away from a Trojan origin for those of the seventeenth.[77]

[73] Author of *Observatio Apologetica,* 1631.

[74] *Mémoires,* pp. 16-18.

[75] *Ibid.,* pp. 19-20.   Leibnitz replied in his *Responsio ad R. P. Turnominium,* Eccard, *Leges Francorum Salicae,* p. 261 *et seq.*

[76] In his anonymous *Dissertation sur l'origine des Français, etc.,* Paris, 1722, 1 vol.

[77] That the Trojan myth still survived among some portion of the reading population may be indicated by the nth blasting of it in the *Philosophie du Bon Sens,* by the Marquis d'Argens (vol. i, p. 120) La Haye, 1740.   The tone of Voltaire in his *Dictionnaire Philosophique,* Art.

Dom Vaissette recognizes explicitly the attraction which " a system so glorious to the nation " exerts, but he puts truth above patriotism and seeks to find out whether the French are lineal heirs of the *Tectosages,* the tribe of Gauls who settled in Germany.[78] As the last writer on the subject, Tournemine, had put forth " with his usual clarity " the elements of the adverse position, Vaissette proposed to refute him, and through him, all his longer-winded predecessors.

The Benedictine monk picks up the phrase " convincing reasoning " to turn it against his opponent by showing that there is nothing to prove that the country out of which the French came into Gaul is the same region in which the Tectosages, that is, the emigrant Gauls, originally settled.[79] Having first caught the Jesuit in a *petitio principii,* the monk proceeds to examine the very historical authorities adduced by Tournemine, and does so with the searching care for which his order was already famous. He gradually turns the " convincing argument " into the sheerest of possibilities.

Tacitus, for Dom Vaissette, is the most exact and careful historian of the Germans; if, therefore, Tacitus fails to mention the Tectosages among the Germans, and he accounts otherwise for their origin, Vaissette feels he has proved the Tectosages cannot have been the progenitors of the French.[80] Indeed, the only people mentioned by Tacitus as speaking the Gallic language settled ultimately along the Danube in Pannonia and on the frontiers of Dacia and Sarmatia.[81]

Français is merely narrative in reviewing the Trojan story. See below ch. xii.

[78] Leber, *op. cit.,* vol. i, p. 134.

[79] *Ibid.,* pp. 136-7.

[80] *Ibid.,* pp. 144-5.

[81] *Ibid.,* p. 146.

Without going more deeply into the geographical details which Dom Vaissette handles with such virtuosity, it is worthy of note that he incidentally deals a heavy blow at " etymology " as a means of historical research. He shows that if theories are to be based on similarities of names it will be easy to " confuse, if one wishes, the *Anglais* and the *Angevins,* the *Warnes* and the *Auvergnats,* the *Thuringians* and the *Tourangeaux* ". [82]

In corresponding fashion, Vaissette undermines the syllogism of Tournemine by showing that its premises rest on confusions of names, wilful or accidental.[83] For example, the name of Celt, given by the ancients to many peoples of northern Europe indiscriminately cannot be construed to establish a common origin for Gauls and Germans, simply because later writers applied it more specifically to either Gauls or Germans, but never to both.[84] Further he shows that the name German was given and taken by all barbarian peoples outside the Roman empire, and that it is impossible to infer any particular identity from a general name so improperly applied.[85] The Turnominian logic did not in any case take into account the migrations and revolutions that must have occurred in regions so wide and bitterly contested by the Germans; by which the unimpaired unity of the Tectosages is put sadly in doubt.[86]

Obviously to ward off in closing any imputation of lack of patriotism, Dom Vaissette makes it clear that Caesar's praise of the Tectosages does not imply any lack of courage on the part of all the other German tribes; that on the con-

[82] Leber, *loc. cit.,* p. 151. The last association had in fact been made by Audigier, see above and Leber, vol. i, p. 18.

[83] *Ibid.,* p. 153 *et seq.*

[84] *Ibid.,* pp. 156-7.

[85] *Ibid.,* p. 165.

[86] *Ibid.,* p. 166.

trary they may have lost their valor in the three centuries before the *Catti* and other " French tribes " invaded Gaul; that, in short, the Tectosages or Gauls " were not the only ones capable of founding the French empire ".[87]

After this masterly destruction of a well-entrenched position, Vaissette again makes a curtsy to the national sentiment: ". . . we are compelled to admit that we wish an opinion [Tournemine's] so glorious for the nation could be found to be true . . . we dare hope for [substantiation of it] either from Père Tournemine, or from some other person equally versed in our antiquities."[88]

That person never came. With the growing self-consciousness of the bourgeoisie, patriotic pride took the more menacing form of disputing the community of origin between the Gauls and the lower classes, as a challenge to Boulainvilliers and Saint-Simon. An anonymous author, purporting to be a councillor of the Parlement at Rouen, published in 1730 a " Letter " in answer to the count.[89] Speaking almost with the vehemence of Savaron and de Mesmes at the Estates of 1614, he asserts his will to " put back the nobles on a level with the burghers . . . and give them brothers instead of slaves ".[90]

The claims of the councillor are based upon the continuity of self-government in the communities of both southern and northern France, the immemorial liberty of the French towns of which mention has already been made.[91] The point of view exhibited is that of the upper middle class,

---

[87] Leber, *op. cit.*, vol. i, p. 174.

[88] *Ibid.*, p. 177.

[89] *Lettre d'un conseiller du parlement de Rouen au sujet d'un écrit du Comte de Boulainvilliers*, Desmolets, *Mém. de litt.*, vol. ix, p. 115 *et seq.* Quoted in Thierry, *Récits*, p. 61.

[90] Desmolets, *loc. cit.*, p. 115.

[91] *Ibid.*, p. 203.

which refuses to recognize privileges of birth but willingly admits those of wealth.[92]

The townsmen's rights to liberty were founded on the fact that they were not personally serfs, but merely owed certain feudal dues and were subject to the lord's justice.[93] It is unfair, the anonymous author complains, to lower the status of the majority of the nation in order to enhance the glory of three or four thousand persons.[94]   These are ridiculed for believing themselves descended from the Germans, more accurately the camp of Mérovée, depicted as

. . . French barbarians who flooded unhappy Gaul, who overthrew the Roman laws that governed the inhabitants according to the principles of humanity and justice, and put in their place barbaric ignorance, greed and cruelty.   What desolation for town and country to behold justice administered by a barbarian corporal in the place of a Roman decurion![95]

This attachement to and vindication of the Roman heritage in France was ill-supported and worse expressed by the anonymous Gallic bourgeois.   The thesis was not indefensible, but it required a trained mind, vast reading, not to mention patience and a reputation with which to launch the result before the public opinion.   The man who united in himself these qualities, and had in addition every inducement from a personal and social point of view to present the " Gallic " viewpoint, was the distinguished Perpetual Secretary of the French Academy, Jean-Baptiste Dubos, whose monumental *Histoire Critique de l'Etablissement de la Monarchie Française dans les Gaules,* manuscript in 1732,[96] was first printed two years later.[97]

---

[92] Desmolets, *loc. cit.,* p. 125.   [93] *Ibid.,* pp. 220-1.

[94] *Ibid,* p. 188   [95] Leber, *op. cit.,* p. 253.

[96] *Cf.* the approbation of Secousse, 22 Oct., 1732, *Hist. Crit.,* vol. i, p. 72.

[97] Paris, 3 vols.   Dubos was already known for his works on esthetics.

CHAPTER IX

Abbé Dubos

On the course of the antagonism between Gaul and Frank, the centuries from the sixteenth to the eighteenth had shed little light beyond that cast by polemics or particular researches often centered on a side issue. The moral animadversions of Tacitus, the religious bias of Gregory of Tours, the democratic protests of the Middle Ages were not more remote from the genesis of the conflict than were the fiery pamphlets of Hotman or the counsels of Fénelon. Indeed, throughout the entire period surveyed to this point, only one " system " of facts has been erected that really pretends to explain the conflict genetically. That is the system of Boulainvilliers. With him as percursor bridging the dividing years, the eighteenth century could distinguish itself from the previous ones, not by an attempt at impartiality, but rather by a certain seriousness, maturity, completeness of viewpoint, fitting complement of encyclopedic rationalism. This conclusion is supported almost as much by the scope and number of the works produced on our subject during the seventeen hundreds as by their intrinsic merit. Moreover, their diversity defies all but the most general classification of Pro-Gallo-Roman, Pro-Frank, and compromise-theories; though it marks a high point in the Nordic-Latin strife. The work of the Abbé mentioned at the end of the last chapter ably opens the case for the supposedly conquered race.

It is an interesting coincidence that the three solid volumes by Dubos that were to center controversy for twenty-five years saw the light of day the very year that Montesquieu, whose fame has eclipsed the less spectacular Abbé's, turned to historical work with the production of his *Considerations on the Romans,*[1] of which more will be said later. But at this point, particular detailed attention must be given to the lesser man's work.

The wide erudition of the latter is concentrated to establish one principle, namely that the "conquest" of Gaul by the Franks is an historical fiction. To this, all other ascertainable historical generalizations subserve; and from it, deductions of great contemporary significance regarding the nation and the monarchy are made to follow.

Recent historians, according to Dubos, have given a false idea of the establishment of the monarchy. The Franks are considered wild men just out of their native woods and marshes, who seized Gaul by armed force.[2] This error is traceable to the blind following of chroniclers who themselves suffered from the general decline of learning in sixth-century Gaul.[3] So that the misconception is very old indeed; nor did rising scientific interest destroy it in the sixteenth century, because the religious wars drew attention away from sound historical investigations.[4]

Dubos respects and shares the patriotic interest that animated such men as du Haillan, Vignier, and de Valois, who began to study the history of their country (*patrie*).[5] What arouses the indignation of our author is that Fredegarius'

---

[1] *Considérations sur les Causes de la Grandeur des Romains et de leur Décadence*, Amsterdam, 1734, 1 vol., no author's name.

[2] *Hist. Crit.*, Disc. Prélim., vol. i, p. 1.

[3] *Ibid.*, bk. i, pp. 17, 19-20. See above ch. ii for Gregory's testimony.

[4] *Ibid.*, p. 53. See above Hotman, etc.

[5] *Ibid.*, p. 53.

falsification of Gregory of Tours [6] has contaminated all histories, as well as the "abridgements destined for the hands of children to whom it is desired to give a first notion of the history of their country." [7]

From the outset, therefore, Dubos' interest is avowedly conditioned towards a vindication of disregarded rights. Yet his intentions are scholarly. He proposes to use contemporary sources wherever possible and to report his citations exactly.[8] His history is critical because he has "an accepted system to destroy and a new system to establish ".[9]

The "History " is divided into six Books, of which *the first* treats of the state of the Western Empire and Gaul at the beginning of the fifth century; *the second,* of what happened in Gaul from 407 to 456 A. D.; *the third,* of the reigns of Childeric and Clovis to the time of the latter's conversion; *the fourth and fifth,* of affairs in Gaul to Clovis' death; and *the sixth,* of the state of Gaul under Clovis and his successors.

Within this comprehensive plan, certain sub-topics guide the otherwise fairly chronological account.

I — The establishment of the Franks in Gaul was to a large extent peaceful and desired by the native inhabitants.

II—Treaties, titles, and honors legitimized the Frankish power in Gaul as a continuation of Roman rule.

III—The mingling of the two races—Franks and Gallo-Romans—began almost at once; and no social or political differentiation between them was made by the settlement of " our kings ".

IV — Christianity and the influence of the powerful Ar-

[6] *Hist. Crit.*, vol. i, p. 19. (In Fredegarius' *Epitome* of the *Hist. Franc.*)
[7] *Ibid.*, p. 58.
[8] *Ibid.*, pp. 61-2.
[9] *Ibid.*, p. 64.

morican Republic (in northwestern Gaul) [10] contributed chiefly to the founding of the monarchy.

V—Freedom and the *absence* of slaves among the Franks are historical facts hitherto perverted, so that the present distinction in France among the three orders is a vestige of the Gallo-Roman government rather than a Frankish innovation.

VI—Absolute monarchy existed in a military way among the Franks, and the present sovereignty of the Crown in France is therefore not a usurpation of power by one noble family over its former equals.

By the end of the fifth century, Dubos relates, when Gaul passed under the rule of " our kings ", the Franks had occupied the right bank of the Rhine for more than two hundred years.[11] Their nation was divided into closely allied tribes, whom the Romans tried to keep friendly and from whom they even drew brave soldiers. In a word, the Empire treated the Franks as if they had been its natural subjects, giving them land in return for peaceful submission to Roman laws.[12] New invasions did occur, but the law-abiding Franks often helped the Romans against new aggressors and all attempts of marauding bands in the fifth century were thus made unsuccessful.[13]

By that time, the Franks, polished by contact with Romans for two centuries, " no longer showed physical differences greater than that now existing between the people on the two banks of the Rhine . . . which is nil." [14] The hostility of the Franks and the incursions mentioned by historians

[10] See above ch. ii, p. 34 and n.

[11] Dubos, *op. cit.*, vol. i, p. 2.

[12] *Ibid.*, p. 3.

[13] *Ibid.*, p. 4.

[14] *Ibid.*, pp. 207, 225, 241.

were merely the work of a tribe or two, or of a discontented group disavowed by the rest of the Nation.[15] It was in reality the destruction of the Roman army in 439 that enabled the French monarchy to be established in Gaul. About 443 Clodio, king of the Salian Franks, began the work of penetration, but news of Attila's projected incursion brought about a general cessation of hostilities and union against the invaders. Whence many regions were given to the Franks peacefully under their own Kings.[16] The two Frankish tribes with which this capitulation was made were the Salians and Riparians.

Dubos further "supposes"—and that is his besetting sin— that there was anarchy in Gaul until the accession of Clovis. No remaining civil officer had sufficiently wide or recognized authority.[17] Gaul was "probably" ruled by numerous Imperial officers who no longer obeyed Rome, but who, like the civilized Frank, Arbogastus, enjoyed local authority as Count. Of this anarchy, Childeric, succeeding Clodio, did not take advantage as did many Roman officers who made themselves dukes and counts, for he left his son Clovis but a very small patrimony.

What made Clovis powerful was that he was invested with the dignity of the Empire. . . . He also took advantage of trouble and disorder in Gaul and in 30 years gained two-thirds of that territory without at the same time becoming an enemy of the Empire. By negotiations he added part after part of Roman Gaul to his domain.[18] In 496, he was baptized, his conversion led the Armorican League to submit their possessions to him, and the last of the Roman troops pledged allegiance to

---

[15] *Hist. Crit.*, vol. i, p. 243.

[16] *Ibid.*, pp. 6-7.

[17] *Ibid.*, p. 11.

[18] *Ibid.*, vol. i, p. 11.

him soon after.   Then it was that Anastasius, the Eastern
Emperor, gave him civil power with the title of consul.[19]

The constant implication Dubos would have us draw from
these incidents is that the entire process of " founding " the
monarchy was one of treaty-making and the legislation of
emergency acts by the remaining Roman authority.   Thus
we are told that Clovis' " four sons continued his system,
fighting the Burgundians—not the Empire ", and making a
treaty with the Ostrogoths which Justinian ratified: " He
transferred by that act to the French Monarchy all the rights
that the Roman Monarchy could still exercise over Gaul." [20]

In the course of his narrative the pro-Gallo-Roman historian cites no less than eight treaties and ratifications made
by various emperors and powers with the Franks to authorize their government.[21]   And these treaties were not victors'
treaties forced upon a helpless people at the sword's point.
Throughout, Dubos insists on the voluntary character of the
transactions: Far from the Romans and Gauls being under
Clovis and his successors oppressed nationalities, every piece
of testimony shows them to us as a Nation voluntarily submitted to the princes ruling over them." [22]   The Romans encouraged their settling down to agricultural life; promoted
them to high office.[23]   It was as Master of the Militia that the
Romans accepted the king of the Salian Franks, an accep-

[19] *Hist. Crit., ibid.*

[20] *Ibid.*, p. 14.

[21] The first Franko-Roman treaty, lost to history, vol. i, p. 221; its
renewal recorded, *ibid.*; *Treaty with Zeno*, vol. ii, p. 274; *Treaty with
Vitiges*, vol. iii, p. 211; ratified by Justinian, *ibid.*, p. 218; second treaty
with latter, *ibid.*, p. 228; *Confirmation of Treaty with Ostrogoths*, vol.
iii, p. 231; recognized at Marseille and elsewhere, *ibid.*

[22] *Hist. Crit.*, vol. i, p. 14.

[23] *Ibid.*, p. 224.

tance ratified by Justinian's recognition of the cession of Gaul to the Franks in 542.[24]

Clovis' marriage with Clotilde, the Burgundian princess who eventually converted him to Christianity, had the result of inducing the Armorican League of northwestern Gaul to conclude an alliance with Clovis, giving him civil jurisdiction over it, in addition to the military obedience due to the Master of the Militia. This diplomatic marriage "did more to establish the French Monarchy than any feat of arms".[25] Thereafter the wealth of Clovis and his soldiers led other Gallo-Romans to " capitulate " with him.[26]

A third event of major importance in the establishment of the French Monarchy is the honorary consulship conferred upon Clovis by the Eastern Emperor. " He governed thereafter with as much authority [over the Romans] as he did over the Franks in his quality of king." [27] It meant " being Emperor of Gaul " though he was already master of all its soldiers.[28]

Dubos further insists on the " legality " of Clovis' acts at all times, and is forced frequently to " suppose " likely conditions to explain away possible objections. For instance, Clovis' name not appearing in the *Fastaeas,* Dubos indicates that perhaps the jealousy of Theodoric, king of the Visigoths, is responsible, since the *Fastaeas* were drawn up in his cities.[29] Again, "a letter of Justinian written about

[24] *Hist. Crit.,* vol. ii, pp. 333, 339.

[25] *Ibid.,* pp. 442, 460.

[26] *Ibid.,* vol. ii, p. 569.

[27] *Op. cit.,* vol. iii, p. 2.

[28] It is curious to compare modern opinions upon that point. Says Mommsen: " Clovis can have worn the diadem only as king, and as for the title of Augustus, he can only have assumed it of his own accord." Quoted in Lavisse, vol. ii, pt. 1, pp. 103 n., and Brehaut, " We know it was a mere honorary post," *op. cit.,* p. 263 *et seq.*

[29] *Hist. Crit.,* vol. iii, p. 6.

534 " to Theodebert, grandson of Clovis, is lost, but we
have Theodebert's reply in which we learn that Justinian
accused Clovis of not having kept certain promises. . . ."
He infers from such a vague document that these promises
had been made by Clovis to obtain the consulship.[30]

Nevertheless, it should not be gathered, as a number of
his critics have, that Dubos invents his sources or uses them
superficially.   On the contrary he is most scrupulous in his
choice; he relies chiefly on the authors accepted by his fellow
scholars—Gregory of Tours, Zosimus, Procopius, Orosius,
the Capitularies of Charlemagne, the compilations of Duchesne, Ducange, Baluze, Eccard, and the best monographs,
such as that of Le Blanc on the Numismatics of the Merovingians.[31]   Dubos' fault is precisely that he scrutinizes his
texts too deeply and begins to read in them what was never
meant.

In the latter part of his work, Dubos stops his narration,
and plunges into our old labyrinth—the social and political
relations of Gauls and Franks after their settlement.   Dubos'
reason for minute detail is not obscured: he directly attacks
the system of Boulainvilliers.

At the beginning of the fifth century, says Dubos, the
completely Romanized Gauls were divided into freemen and
slaves, slavery being of the " German type ", according to
Tacitus, that is, based upon cultivation on shares.[32]   Yet
there is nothing in the law of the Franks to show that some
were nobles and others *roturiers*.   On the contrary, the laws
indicate the presence of only one order.[33]   Dubos argues

[30] *Hist. Crit.*, vol. iii, pp. 14-18.

[31] *Traité historique des monnaies de France*, 1690.

[32] *Hist. Crit.*, vol. i, bk. i, pp. 17-18.

[33] *Ibid.*, vol. iii, p. 331.

ingeniously from the price of " composition " for murder—
as ingeniously as most of those who have made the simple
provisions yield support to their theories. But Dubos belongs to the eighteenth century and the passion for reasonableness overcomes historical commonsense:

According to natural law, all men are born equal . . . and
one must not suppose without proofs that a Nation has acted
counter to this law by awarding to citizens who have the good
fortune of being born in certain families, distinctions and
prerogatives prejudicial to citizens born in other families.[34]

From which basis, Dubos with persistent egalitarianism
tries to show that " no special privileges were granted to
oldest families " as such; public service and high office were
the only distinctions rewarded. " The constitution of society in the Frankish nation was in this respect the same as it
is today in the kingdom of England." [35] This statement,
erroneous as it is, is highly important in showing in Dubos
the tendency to admire England, which was characteristic of
the century as early as 1725.[36]
The Franks had two assemblies, the Field of March and
the Mallum, which was a kind of district circuit court, in
which subsequently other barbarians and even Romans participated. The Field of March, a representative assembly,
was at first annual, but was later abolished when the country
extended its boundaries.[37] The Franks' principal officers
were the elders or *seniores*, whence the subsequent *seigneur*.
The common idea that at this time the Franks were the only
warriors is false. And since " on it is built the notion that

[34] *Hist. Crit.*, vol. iii, p. 330.

[35] *Ibid.*, p. 348.

[36] *Cf.* Bernois de Muralt, *Lettres sur les Anglais et les Français*, 1725;
and Thoyras cited above.

[37] *Hist. Crit.*, vol. iii, pp. 361-3.

the order of the Nobility comes from their kingdom ", Boulainvilliers must be wrong.

At the same time, Dubos is bolstering up the king's sovereignty. Elsewhere he specifically avows these aims: " It is an erroneous belief . . . that the Franks were an aristocracy, the king being powerless without the consent of the nobles, rather than a Monarchy." [38] ". . . It is our erroneous belief that the Franks paid no tribute to the princes . . . a belief which is prejudicial to the old inhabitants of Gaul, to the kings, and is favorable to the Franks." [39] The remarks are pointedly directed at Boulainvilliers:

The laws which supposedly indicate this state of things exist only in the imagination of those who have had the self-assurance to affirm them. The facts that they allege, they misinterpret according to their original preconception; they quibble and confuse the general rule with the exception.[40]

No better condemnation of *either* party from an impartial historical viewpoint could be desired, though Dubos himself is unmistakably sincere. And this in spite of purely systematic difficulties. He is driven, for example, in his support of the monarchy and of the Franks' " legitimacy ", into pointing out that Clovis was subordinated " *in a sense* " to the Roman Empire, " though only in name " owing to its distance from Gaul. " Regard and veneration for the Empire on the part of the Nations of the west were such that there was no derogation to Royal dignity in accepting the service of Rome." [41] On the same principle of pride in Roman dignities, Dubos explains the frequently-cited example of Charlemagne, who ordinarily dressed like a Frank,

[38] *Hist. Crit.*, vol. i, pp. 58, 60.
[39] *Ibid.*
[40] *Ibid.*, p. 59.
[41] *Ibid.*, vol. iii, p. 20.

donning the consular tunic and robe when, to please Popes Adrian and Leo, he consented to wear Roman habit.[42]

Regarding the treatment of Gallo-Roman rights and property by the Franks, Dubos has no difficulty in finding data suitable to his thesis, since in fact these same data are even now accepted as the most likely historical approximation to the truth.[43] It is mainly the National Council assembled at Orléans in 511 that serves the Abbé " to show that Clovis let the Romans of Gaul live according to Roman law ", and that " this prince allowed the bishops, who were still almost all of that nation [i. e. Romans] to enjoy in peace all rights, distinctions, and prerogatives that they possessed in the reigns of the last Emperors." [44]

Although he often tries to prove too much by parallels with later times, the national aspect of the situation does not escape the eighteenth-century historian. " Today," he says, " all the inhabitants of France who were born within the kingdom are reputed to be of the same nation. . . . They are all Frenchmen. . . ." [45] But before the Capetians, the inhabitants of Gaul, were "compatriots without being fellow-citizens. . . . [46] Now birth rules nationality; in those times it was filiation through the male line. . . . ' People ' and ' nation ' then meant very different things " [47] whereas now " these two words . . . in common speech have the same signification ".[48] But although Dubos is conscious of the

---

[42] *Hist. Crit.*, vol. iii, p. 10.

[43] See above the modern conclusions of Ernest Lavisse and Ferdinand Lot.

[44] *Hist. Crit.*, vol. iii, pp. 43, 46.

[45] *Ibid.*, p. 260.

[46] *Ibid.*

[47] " A nation consisted of persons living according to the same laws or customs. A people was a collection of Nations," *ibid.*, p. 262.

[48] *Ibid.*, pp. 261-2.

national minorities denied "self-determination" in the
Europe of his day, he is quite certain that "there was a
greater difference between the conquerors of Mexico and
Peru and the Indians they conquered, than between the
Franks and Germans and the Gauls."

Clovis, as successor to the Emperor, had the right to dis-
tribute military benefices, or Salic lands, which had formerly
been conferred by Rome upon its soldiers.[49] These lands,
however, were not taken from the Gallo-Roman proprietors,
first because the Franks, between 24,000 and 25,000 fighting
men in all, were not numerous enough to need spoliation in
order to satisfy their wants; and second, because the wars
of the fifth and sixth centuries in Gaul must have created
many vacancies.[50] Completing thereby his circle — logical
and historical as well—the Secretary of the Academy decides
that " the Frankish Kings' absention from rapine was one
of the motives that made the Romans wish to come under
the domination of our kings." [51]

Returning to the Salic lands, the critic explains that being
military benefices, these lands could not be inherited by
women,[52] but under the Carolingians these lands became
fiefs and passed into the hands of women who gave military
service by proxy.[53] Now, the Crown is the chief fief of the
kingdom, and as such subject to the Salic Law, which Dubos
believes of great antiquity though possibly not written down
until the time of Clovis' sons.[54] The Salic Law is therefore

[49] *Hist. Crit.*, vol. iii, pp. 292-3, 535.

[50] *Ibid.*, pp. 536-7. These wars must be taken to mean the internecine
quarrels among barbarians and among Romans. See the *Hist. Crit.*, vol.
i, pp. 229-30, 43. Dubos here argues, as he often does, negatively from
the silence of witnesses—Gregory and Procopius.

[51] *Hist. Crit.*, vol. iii, p. 552.

[52] *Ibid.*, p. 292.

[53] *Ibid.*, p. 293.

[54] *Ibid.*, vol. i, p. 44.

coeval with the monarchy, and its control of the succession is of cardinal importance in preventing civil wars.[55]

The indivisibility of the kingdom—the second major principle of the French monarchy—dates only from the Capetian line, whence it follows that the " constitution of the Monarchy was practically the same under the second race as under the first ". Therefore those who misunderstand the first race do likewise the second, and believe that the strengthening of the royal authority in the course of time was against the constitution of the first race.[56] " Louis le Gros, Philippe Auguste, etc. are looked upon as tyrants "—this was Boulainvilliers' view [57]—" although all they did was to vindicate the rights of the crown and of the people. . . . They only re-established, so far as they could, the ancient order." [58] This vindication of the " rights of the crown and of the people " refers of course to the exemptions from taxation and indicates Dubos' consciousness of the long alliance between the king and the bourgeoisie.

Naturally, the survival of Roman traditions of self-government in the towns could not fail to catch the eye of the historian, who sees the royal granting of charters as a " reassertion of old rights ". [59] Senates subsisted in the cities under the Merovingians and to them is due the continued Right of Commune which they preserved against infeodation,[60] as they had enjoyed it " from time immemorial ". [61]

---

[55] *Hist. Crit.*, vol. i, p. 44.

[56] *Ibid.*, p. 60.

[57] *Lettres sur les Parlemens*, vol. i, p. 130; vol. ii, p. 219 *et seq.*

[58] *Hist. Crit.*, vol. i, p. 60.

[59] *Ibid.*, vol. iii, pp. 505-10.

[60] *Ibid.*, p. 501.

[61] *Ibid.*, pp. 502, 513-4.

Regarding the nobility, Dubos asserts that only under the weak kings of the second race did the Dukes and Counts usurp an hereditary right to their commissions, a usurpation not only against the Prince, "but in many places, they usurped further the liberties and privileges of the People ".[62] Furthermore, at the origin, everybody in the Frankish state paid tribute, or taxes, except for the occasional exemption of churches.[63]   Even the Salic lands were taxable, as they had been under Roman law,[64] and it is certain that the Carolingian kings, who were anything but unfavorable to the Franks, did not exempt the Franks from tribute.[65]   It was therefore after the substitution for the ancient laws of new ones " dictated by caprice . . . some provisions of which, as odious as they are bizarre, clearly show that they must have been accepted under duress " that " Gaul became in truth a conquered nation ".[66]   " Our usurpers," as Dubos calls the ninth and tenth-century nobles, " reserved the right of judicial appointment and imposed taxes at their pleasure." [67]

Nor is the common opinion that the Franks by their superiority as the weapon-bearers gained by force an imprescriptible right, at all founded.   The soldiers came from all the nations, and the Franks in turn were admitted to all the professions; there were Franks even among the clergy, as is evidenced by their names.[68]   Those Franks who were not warriors or ecclesiastics lived on their land or by their

[62] *Hist. Crit.*, vol. iii, p. 502.

[63] *Ibid.*, p. 582.

[64] *Codex Justinianus, Lib.* xi, *Titul,* 74.

[65] *Hist. Crit.*, vol. iii, pp. 589-90.

[66] *Ibid.*, p. 503.

[67] *Ibid.*

[68] *Ibid.*, pp. 364-9.

industry. Salic lands were subject to partible inheritance; consequently the military did not often get rich; and other Franks as well were to be found cultivating the soil like Gallo-Romans.[69]

The large majority of the tillers of the ground, however, were slaves, who, under the Franks, owed their condition to capture, purchase, punishment, or the accident of birth. But as there were already more slaves than freemen at the time of the Frankish settlement in Gaul, " one must not attribute the great number of serfs [under the third race] to the harshness of the Franks, nor suppose that they reduced the former inhabitants of Gaul to a species of slavery." [70] Dubos is naturally eager to prove that serfdom did not debar from bearing arms, in order to deny the special valor assigned by Boulainvilliers to race.[71] He shows also from a law of Louis le Gros that serfs had to be fought against like any other defendant [72] in the trial by combat imported from the Burgundians into Frankish manners.[73]

In concluding this proportionately voluminous account of Dubos' system, set forth here at such length to make intelligible its subsequent demolition, it is fitting to notice the Gallic Abbé's admiration for Clovis — in contrast to the grandeur Charlemagne assumes in the eyes of Boulainvilliers, Montesquieu, and Mably.

Dubos admits that as mere king of the Salian Franks, Clovis had other Frankish kings put to death in order to " persuade the tribes to elect him as their king ",[74] but he alleges the corruption of the victims as well as reasons of

[69] *Hist. Crit.*, vol. iii, pp. 382-3.

[70] *Ibid.*, p. 321.

[71] *Ibid.*, p. 325.

[72] *Ibid.*, p. 327.

[73] *Ibid.*, p. 393.

[74] *Ibid.*, p. 24.

state which make all kings behave alike in similar circumstances. No, Clovis' peculiar glory is not in displays of brute force or cunning. It resides in his moral virtues, his courage and energy, his diplomatic conciliation of the bishops and his conversion to Christianity.[75] It is owing to the fact that "at the age of forty-two, Clovis was willing to accept the office of Consul at the hands of Anastasius;[76] and possibly also because, unlike his descendants, Clovis had made Paris his capital ".[77]

Certainly the Franks' adoption of the Roman language, manners and customs, their imitation of the imperial coinage,[78] their frequent use of Roman law as " more definite, clear, and civilized ",[79] and the absolute legislative and judicial power of their kings[80] go far to make the eighteenth-century Abbé a more fervent admirer of the Franks than the aristocratic Count de Boulainvilliers is of the conquered Gauls. It is the peculiar attractiveness of Dubos' position that he need not hate or vilify the so-called conqueror nation. He accomplishes his ends by merely changing common notions of the Franks' original character, showing the complete fusion of the two races beginning after Charlemagne,[81] and ascribing the nobiliary privileges to a little group of wilful men who, profiting from a weakened royal power, destroyed the fundamental laws of the monarchy and seized the onerous privileges of which they boast today as their racial heritage.

It is from this angle that Dubos is especially significant

[75] *Hist. Crit.*, vol. iii, p. 59.

[76] *Ibid.*, vol. ii, p. 324.

[77] *Ibid.*, vol. iii, p. 22.

[78] *Ibid.*, vol. iii, p. 612.

[79] *Ibid.*, vol. iii, p. 375.

[80] *Ibid.*, vol. iii, pp. 617-23.

[81] *Ibid.*, vol. iii, p. 632.

in the intellectual history of the eighteenth century. His is the first upsetting by historical methods of the apple-cart containing the privileges of the upper orders. His voicing of the bourgeois point of view differs notably from all previous attacks on "despotism". It is truly the Gallo-Roman communal rights, vainly invoked by the "Councillor of Rouen", now finding orderly and would-be scientific expression.

CHAPTER X

D'Argenson—Foncemagne—The Academy

THE provocative ideas of Boulainvilliers did not arouse discussion only in the breasts of the Third Estate. As early as 1737, the well-born Marquis, René Louis de Voyer, better known as d'Argenson, had indited and circulated a short work of *Considérations sur le Gouvernement, ancien et présent de la France.*[1] One of the manuscript copies at the Bibliothèque de l'Arsenal bears this remark: " This treatise upon politics was composed upon the occasion of those of M. de Boulainvilliers regarding the old feudal government of France." [2] The treatise is not only brief, but sententious in the manner — and without the virtuosity — that Montesquieu had already made noticeable in his own *Considérations on the Romans,* in 1734.

From the beginnings of the Monarchy in France, d'Argenson recognizes the impossibility of drawing valid inferences. " Neither advancement nor decadence can be attributed to the internal workings of a barbarous Nation." [3] The second " race " is characterized by the same disorders as troubled the peace of the *"Gaulois et nos premiers Français"*, but with its decline arose the feudal system—a usurpation by the nobles who made " everything that was not the nobility into slaves ".[4] In this belief d'Argenson coin-

[1] Amsterdam (Paris), 1765.

[2] No. 2334 of the Bibliothèque. References are to the 1765 ed., Amsterdam (Paris).

[3] d'Argenson, *Consid.,* ch. v, art. i, p. 131.

[4] *Ibid.,* p. 132.

cides exactly with Dubos, though he recognizes that possibly even in the ninth and tenth centuries there was more liberty than in the eighteenth century " among the people ".[5] For d'Argenson, unlike Dubos, pursues the tradition of anti-absolutism. But as some authors have boasted of the feudal organization as precisely militating against absolutism, d'Argenson examines it. Feudal Right is only itself a usurpation against royalty, though d'Argenson admits that " in the origin of things almost every power is usurpation. . . ." [6] " The feudal government so much vaunted by M. de Boulainvilliers, and to which he ascribes all the greatness of Charlemagne was . . . only the right of the strongest . . . nothing limited, never uniform. . . ." [7] The highest authority in the nation was " in the hands of a number of chief usurpers who had under them other subaltern usurpers." [8] But despite this fact, " let not the origin of the fiefs be found in the first conquests of our Franks over the Gauls; History presents many other invasions more brilliant than this, and it is far from proved that the conquerors bethought themselves of the Feudal Laws." [9]

D'Argenson does not believe that the Gauls were " sufficiently vanquished " to be enslaved like negroes, or even like Roman slaves. In fact, reverting to the patriotic theory of the seventeenth century, he asserts as common knowledge the fact that " the Romans were driven out of Gaul rather than the Gauls conquered by the Franks." [10] Thus an examination of early origins is unfruitful if one wishes to

[5] *Consid.*, p. 132.

[6] *Ibid.*, p. 119.

[7] *Ibid.*, p. 122.

[8] *Ibid.*, ch. iv, p. 121.

[9] *Ibid.*, p. 117.

[10] *Ibid.*, pp. 118-9.

understand the present constitution. Time and precedent create the establishments that uphold sovereignty. The monarchical authority, d'Argenson decides, " can be useful to men if it is counter-balanced." [11]   The Contract theory which he expands [12] is " conditional and requires the observance of the fundamental laws." [13]

With these axioms, d'Argenson has a very clear notion of the growth of the communal liberties in France, as well as of the concomitant culture, both of which developments he traces under the name of " Progress of Democracy in France, according to our History." [14]   In so doing, d'Argenson reveals himself not only a capable social historian, answering to Voltaire's requirements,[15] but also an early apostle of local self-government in the tradition of French Federalism.[16]   The proposed reforms of d'Argenson, outlined in his seventh chapter,[17] tend to the establishment of Communal and Inter-communal elective bodies.   " This democracy once established, royal authority, far from being impaired, will be able to grow in force and solidity." [18] That this " democracy " is not anything else than a counterweight to the nobility, is seen in the same author's *Pensées pour la réformation de l'Etat*.   The nobility is a nefarious race that should be rooted out of France.   Its privileges are onerous, and weigh upon the tillers of the soil, whose misery

[11] *Consid.*, p. 120.

[12] *Ibid.*, pp. 119, 127.

[13] *Ibid.*, p. 119.

[14] *Ibid.*, ch. v, arts. i-x, pp. 131-179.

[15] See Voltaire's *Nouvelles considérations sur l'histoire*, 1744.

[16] *Cf.* Paul-Boncour, *Le Fédéralisme Economique*, Paris, 1900; and *La République et la Décentralisation*, Paris, 1923.

[17] *Consid.*, pp. 207-50.

[18] *Ibid.*, p. 210.

d'Argenson movingly depicts in numerous places of his Journal and Memoirs.[19]

D'Argenson also combats the notion that the privileged class is the mainstay of the State, and his connexion with the *Journal Oeconomique*[20] probably accounts for his wish that " all the domains in the country should be possessed by those who can cultivate them in person . . . the whole kingdom should be a ' *franc-aleu roturier* '." [21] This economic conviction extends as far as explicit egalitarianism: " I ask only that the stupidest prejudice be put aside to agree that two things are principally to be wished for the good of the State, one that all citizens be equal to one another . . . the other that each one be [only] the son of his works and of his merit: justice would be served and the State would be better served." [22]

No plainer proof of the logical tie between the historical minutiae of Frankish origins and the live issue of reform and revolution in France exists than the reform ideas of d'Argenson. One logical step further, and in him, too, the concept of nationhood, which has pierced through almost every investigation into origins and every cry for reform, appears with keen insight into the contemporary atmosphere:

National opinions prevail and can carry us far. It is observed that never have the names *Nation* and *State* been so [often] repeated as today. These two words were never pronounced under Louis XIV, and the idea itself did not even exist.[23]

[19] Ed. A. Brette, Paris, 1898. Besides the *Consid. passim*, see Oct. 4-5, 1749, p. 71; Sept. 3, 1751, p. 133; Dec. 18-22, 1751, pp. 145-6; Mar. 15, 1753, p. 204.

[20] See his articles from 1751 to 1755. " Political science . . . is today in its infancy . . . ". *Consid.*, ch. viii, art. i, p. 252.

[21] I. e. land held in fee simple by commoners, *Consid.*, ch. viii, art. i, p. 267 *et seq.*

[22] *Consid.*, ch. viii, art. li, p. 294.

[23] He is not aware of or forgets the testimony of Fénelon and others.

Never has there been so much instruction as today concerning the rights of the nation and liberty . . . this comes from the Parlement and the English.[24]

What d'Argenson says of the Parlement and the English is both true and significant. The connection between the two as an influence toward national reforms is even as close as the common confusion between *Parlement* and *Parliament* which Voltaire notices to refute it in his *L'Equivoque*.[25]

The Parlement, as the majority of writers before Boulainvilliers believed, was taken to be an outgrowth of the Estates-General—inoperative since 1614—and as the remaining guarantee of public liberty. A newspaper article in the *Journal Historique de la République des Lettres* for September–October 1732 [26] throws light upon the controversy in a way curiously allied to previous objects of this study. The editor is reviewing an anonymous *Memoir concerning the origin and Authority of the Parlement of France* printed after page 114 of the second volume of Mézeray's posthumous *Mémoires Historiques et Critiques*.[27] The memorialist is anxious to decide the question which " has latterly made so much noise in France," and which, according to the reviewer, " it would have been more prudent not to lead persons to instruct themselves upon." [28] The principal point of the essay is that the Parlement represents the General Assembly of the Franks, and that it is an abridgment of the Three Estates. The critic points out, however, that this is by no means a new theory, but one published eighty years before under the title of *Maximes du Gouvernement de la*

[24] *Journal*, June 26, 1754, p. 262.

[25] In 1759; *Oeuvres*, vol. xxxix, p. 391.

[26] P. 300 *et seq.*

[27] Amsterdam, 1732, 2 vols.

[28] *Journal Hist.*, p. 300.

France [29] and more recently ordered " lacerated and burned by the Paris Parlement itself," as " subversive of the king's sovereignty and contrary to the fundamental laws of the kingdom . . . which was done that same day [August 13 1732] below the grand staircase of the Palace." [30]

The opposition to the conception of an apostolic succession from the Frankish assemblies through the Estates-General to the Parlement found opponents outside the political arena where Boulainvilliers and Dubos had principally placed it. Indeed, the most amiable of disputants that the century ever saw,[31] Etienne de Foncemagne, took up before the exclusive *Académie des Inscriptions* the refutation of Hotman and Boulainvilliers on the hereditary character of the kingship under the Merovingians.[32]

De Foncemagne necessarily has to disprove the thesis that " the sovereignty resided less in the king's person than in the national assembly . . . which possessed legislative power, that of war and peace, and of appointing generals." [33]   The academician would scruple to refute Hotman had not his forgotten point of view been revived by a contemporary " whose name and reputation can give great weight to the opinions he emits".[34]   He means, of course, Boulainvilliers.

From the standpoint of history, de Foncemagne's refutation is interesting because, by adopting tacitly the conclusion made by Fréret in regard to the Franks, he establishes a

[29] In Lelong, *Bibl. Hist. de la France*, No. 9476.

[30] *Journal Hist.*, p. 301.

[31] *Cf.* his courteous quarrel with Voltaire over the authenticity of Richelieu's *Testament Politique*.

[32] *Acad. des Inscr. et Belles Lettres*, vol. x; Leber, *op. cit.*, vol. v, p. 14 *et seq.*

[33] *Ibid.*, p. 15.

[34] *Ibid.*

vital distinction: if the Franks were a league of peoples inhabiting Germany, then they constituted, upon assuming the name, a *new* group with a *new* government. Therefore, all the remarks of Tacitus concerning the Germans, and especially his endlessly quoted "*reges ex nobilitate sumunt, duces ex virtute,*" [35] cannot be applied to the Franks whom Tacitus never mentions. It is gratuitous.[36] From Gregory of Tours, on the contrary, de Foncemagne shows that *reges* was used interchangeably with *duces*; as indeed it is reasonable that " a people concentrated in one camp needed but one chief." [37] The famous letter of Saint-Rémi, already used by Boulainvilliers and Dubos to prove divergent conclusions, is ruled out by de Foncemagne as irrelevant; since, obviously addressed to a Christian king, it cannot apply to Clovis' right of accession which antedates his conversion.[38]

As for the general assemblies of the French people, it is certain that they met in March and played some part in the election of Mayors.[39] But what was the Mayor? The *Major domus regiae,* corresponding to the present Grand Master of the Household. That the Mayors ultimately became kings was due to the infancy or imbecility of the Merovingians, and by the time of Charles Martel and Charlemagne these officers commonly receive the title due their masters.[40] In any case, at the assemblies of the first race the king played a major part and had decisive choice; while it is clear that the usurpation of the Mayors of the Palace under the second race does not constitute a right. On

[35] See above p. 22. De Foncemagne slightly alters the word order.

[36] Leber, *op. cit.,* vol. v, p. 17.

[37] *Ibid.,* p. 19.

[38] *Ibid.,* p. 23.

[39] *Ibid.,* p. 26.

[40] *Ibid.,* pp. 32-4.

neither ground, then, is the right of the Estates-General established.[41]

De Foncemagne, outside the strict limits of his essay, also confronts Boulainvilliers with one of his frequent inconsistencies and by destroying the validity of the allegations, puts in doubt the Count's theory of a Frankish nobility reducing to tribute and servitude the native inhabitants.[42] The academician is, however, too good a critic to systematize his findings into a theory. He gives an excellent idea of himself, as well as the first of several judgments of Boulainvilliers to be quoted in this study, when he concludes:

Besides, I know very well that it would be unjust to wish to judge the historical works of M. de Boulainvilliers according to the rules of severe criticism. Born less for compilation than for reflection, his reflections were no doubt the result of his reading; but these having been drawn up for his own use . . . we must not exact from him the exactness and accuracy that we have a right to expect from ordinary writers. . . .[43]

If the *Académie des Inscriptions* was thus contributing its share to the widening discussion of French origins viewed as a guide to contemporary national affairs, the Academicians nevertheless did not constitute the whole of the scholarly world, nor the whole of public opinion. Within the first category must be placed those indefatigable researchers into history, the Benedictine monks, who boasted of such names as Montfaucon, Denis de Sainte-Marthe,[44] Martene, and Bouquet to compare with the academicians Fréret, de Foncemagne, Bréquigny, d'Anville, and de Vertot. While the

[41] Leber, *op. cit.*, vol. v, pp. 26-29.

[42] *Ibid.*, pp. 35-6.

[43] *Ibid.*, p. 39.

[44] Related to the industrious brother-scholars of the same name and order, mentioned above under the seventeenth century.

latter produced memoirs, the monks prepared vast collections of documents continuing in the tradition of the Duchesne's and Mabillon's, to furnish solid bases to early and medieval French history.

The *Recueil des Historiens des Gaules et de la France* [45] by Dom Bouquet is a monumental work which resulted in a continuing collection that now amounts to twenty folio volumes. It is interesting to note in passing that Dom Bouquet follows Dubos in one of his most novel ideas regarding the Frankish conquest, and credits him in his notes with an unfailing *doctissimus abbas Dubos*.[46] Certainly the Benedictine Order, more independent of the court, was more likely than the Academy to accept so anti-aristocratic a doctrine as that of Dubos. Another Benedictine, Dom Rivet, must also be mentioned in this place as rendering a complementary service to French literature in his *Histoire Littéraire de la France* (1733), while another group was pursuing the collection of the *Ordonnances des rois* begun in 1723.

With such a wealth of documentation being made available, with other similar tasks undertaken and to be mentioned, with less specialized writers like Dubos, Montesquieu, and Mably producing notable works, it may be said that historical interest in the eighteenth century did not sink to a lower level than in the previous period, despite a frequent allegation to the contrary on the part of those who forget the first three quarters of the epoch in question.

Keeping in mind the close interdependence of "pure" history and polemics, it remains now to examine the spread in the public opinion of the two rival theories previously

[45] Eight volumes published from 1738 to 1752.

[46] Thierry has already made this remark, and, according to him, a number of the other Benedictines were very much struck with the Abbé's system. *Récits*, p. 68.

outlined. For the eighteenth century, with its cafés and its clubs, its academies, its "religion of reason" and its advocacy of the experimental method, was eminently a century of truly public opinion and not more remarkably so on any subject than on history.[47]

In 1736 the Academy of Soissons listened to a memoir by one Biet, abbé of St. Léger and Soissons, upon the "*Truth or falsity of the expulsion of Childeric . . . the extent of the authority of Egidius and Siagrius, his son, over the Soissonnais . . . and the spot where the famous battle of Soissons took place.*"[48]

Although the latter part of the essay is of little moment here, the first section presents an able description of the state of Gaul in the fifth and sixth centuries, to disprove Daniel's assertion that French history begins with Clovis. The abbé does not advance any theory of his own regarding the character of the Frankish establishment, but as he indicates the various items of testimony that lead him to believe that Clovis and his predecessors were already in Gaul before his taking of Soissons in 486, it is clear that he visualizes the process as one of conquest, on the part of " barbarians who abandoned their woods and marshes to seek their fortune".[49] And yet he indicates explicitly that " when the barbarians seized a part of Roman territory, they did not drive out the inhabitants, but divided the lands among victors and vanquished, and the two peoples lived as friends and compatriots." [50] But he speaks also of seizing, possessing, conquering,[51] and there is no doubt that Dubos' softer picture

[47] See Flint, p. 243 *et seq.* And below, Montesquieu's work at the Academy of Bordeaux.

[48] Printed in the same year with two other essays, one by a competitor, Abbé Leboeuf, Paris, 1736.

[49] Leber, *Collection de Pièces*, vol. i, pp. 437-8.

[50] *Ibid.*, p. 444.   [51] *Ibid.*, pp. 436, 438-9.

of invited rulers legally acquiring title to land and crown
finds no place in the mind of Biet. He cites and follows
Dubos frequently [52] but refutes him in a long note on that
very point of " legitimate authority ", based by Dubos on
the famous letter of St. Rémi, once more parsed and shred-
ded by Biet.[53]

Biet won the prize which his disappointed competitor
Leboeuf had won a year previously, the latter having written
upon the *State of the inhabitants of Soissonnais before the
conquest of Gaul by the Franks.*[54] This piece, together with
the unsuccessful memoir of 1736, place its superficial author
in a middle position between Dubos and Boulainvilliers on
the question of the Frankish conquest.

A stronger opponent of Dubos was found in the academician Gibert who, four years before the appearance of
Montesquieu's *Esprit des Lois,* takes the abbé to task for his
theories concerning the name of Frank. Gibert is persuaded
that " from the time that the Franks began to appear in history, authors give them indiscriminately the name of Franks
and of Germans." [55] Therefore, he concludes that the modern opinion which would make of the Franks merely a
League name covering various German tribes is false. From
this conclusion he deduces that the Franks, far from forming a league, were rather barbarous tribes fighting among
themselves, and by no means united against the Romans who
always tried to keep on friendly terms with them. The
name of Frank he sees as a military nickname given them
for their use of the *fram,* their principal spear-like weapon,
the name of which they shouted as they went into battle.

[52] Notably on the Thuringian question in Gregory. Biet, *op. cit.,* p. 471.

[53] *Ibid.,* p. 449.

[54] Paris, 1735. Note again the *conquest.*

[55] Leber, *op. cit.,* vol. i, pp. 303, 304. He cites Vopiscus, Trebellius
Pollio, Procopius and St. Jerome.

Foreign nations, hearing the cry, came to call them *Framsi*, or *Fransi* and *Franci* by syncope.[56]

An attorney of Lassay, M. Bottu, undertook the following year to raise doubts on Gibert's point in a letter addressed to the *Journal de Verdun*.[57] And those doubts, perspicacious in themselves, led to the revival in at least one mind [58] of the old Frank-meaning-free theory, which had been definitely exploded by Fréret. In turn, the last-named was once more drawn from his " general observations on the study of ancient philosophy " to refute Gibert on the field of early French history. Not only had Gibert's memoir on the name Frank combated Fréret's opinion, but a second paper on the Merovingians that Gibert read in April 1746, had drawn from the elder academician some written remarks which clearly assume that the Franks reigned with *éclat* in Gaul by means of conquest.[59]

The marshaling of facts is brilliantly imposing — philology, exact citations, chronology and coins are combined in an interpretation remarkable for its common sense. Its chief point is here subsidiary to the important one that the Franks were a league and always opposed to the rival league of the Alamanni, which division was, as Tacitus tells us, " a godsend to the Romans ". [60]

Fréret is consequently opposed to Dubos on the *nature* of the Frankish invasion, but supports his own contention, made thirty years before and adopted by Dubos, of a Frankish League. Noting, however, the facility with which the Romans ceded land to the barbarians, Fréret had admitted in his earlier paper the treaty concluded between the Franks

[56] Leber, *op. cit.*, vol. i, pp. 313-15.

[57] April, 1754, p. 253.

[58] La Tour d'Auvergne-Corret, Leber, *op. cit.*, vol. i, p. 317.

[59] *Ibid.*, pp. 180-1 ; 198.

[60] *Ibid.*, p. 197.

and Aetius against Attila.[61] The final estimate of Fréret must necessarily be that, unlike almost every other historian of his age, he belongs to neither of the rival schools. His thought goes as far as the facts take him, and his feelings add no coda.

Gibert, after Fréret's observations, was given an opportunity to recast his ideas in an answer published in 1759, which adds greater detail but little more persuasiveness, to a point of view intended to give an antiquity [62] to the Frankish royal line, which had lost it since the discarding of the Trojan myth. ". . . I combat . . . an opinion which rules since 1200 years . . . only to propose another, at once more probable and more honorable for our first kings. . . ." [63] That substitute is the notion that the Frankish kings are descended from *Maroboduus*, name akin to *Mérovée*, borne by an ancient king of the Marcomirs, a people forming a part of the Sicambrians, contemporaries of Caesar.[64] If such is the case, the Frankish League is a myth,[65] and all the desiderata of early French history—the sojourn in Pannonia, the appellation of Sicambers, the antiquity and glory of the royal line—are fulfilled. Strangely enough, Gibert makes use of the anonymous geographer of Ravenna—so useful to Leibnitz—for proving a French national thesis noticeably inconsistent with that of the German philosopher.

But while the academicians and others [66] were painstak-

---

[61] Leber, *op. cit.*, vol. ii, p. 94.

[62] Implicitly indicated in the first and last pages of his essay.

[63] Leber, *op. cit.*, vol. i, p. 260.

[64] *Ibid.*, p. 241 *et seq.*

[65] *Ibid.*, p. 243.

[66] *Cf.* Ribaut de Rochefort, *Dissert. sur l'Origine des Francs, Receuil*, Paris, 1748; also Gouye de Longuemare, *Dissert. sur la chronologie des rois Mérovingiens*, prize winning essay in 1746 at the Academy of Soissons, published, Paris, 1748.

ingly disputing these ultimate grounds of inference, a more synthetic mind, already planning a vast work upon the nature and forces of governments, was arrested by these patently confused points in the history of his nation, and devoted to their elucidation the benefit of his penetrating thought during twenty-four years of his life as well as his remarkable gift of concise expression.

That synthetic mind was Montesquieu.

CHAPTER XI

MONTESQUIEU

BORN exactly one hundred years before the French Revolution, Charles-Louis de Secondat, baron de Montesquieu, belonged to that nobility of the robe which, while preserving and profiting from many of the excessive privileges of the old regime, contributed so much by its legalistic spirit and historical-mindedness to clearing the ground for reform.

Although Montesquieu affected to deprecate genealogy as " a very stupid thing ", it was in the course of putting in order the family archives following his father's sudden death that he became, like Boulainvilliers before him, a keen student of early and medieval French history. A legal education at Bordeaux and Paris, the contact of a devoted uncle who was *président à mortier* of the Parlement of the former city, and lastly the position inherited from that uncle in 1715, first predisposed then furthered the young man's interest in law. At the same time, science, history, and literature beckoned and were given ready outlet in the meetings of the recently founded Bordeaux Academy, of which Montesquieu was a member as early as 1712.

To these qualities and talents Montesquieu added a legitimate ambition and the gift of seeing things as they were. It was no doubt a combination of all these which prompted his first unavowed but immensely successful work, *The Persian Letters* (1721). Ten years later he was returning from a three years' tour of Europe, of which the last two years had been spent in England, at the invitation of Lord Chesterfield. The harvest of impressions was not immediately put to use,

198

though Montesquieu's sojourn in Rome had spurred on his ambition to write a truly original and scientific work upon the Romans. This appeared as the famous *Considérations* in 1734, a book so different from all preceding ones upon the same subject that it may be said to be a part detached from the greater masterpiece of the *Spirit of the Laws,* begun more or less consciously that same year.

The " principle " arising from the *Considérations* is that of political realism producing a history in terms of a nation's own self-interest, by reaction to environing circumstances.[1] Since Jean Bodin's theoretical statement of it in the *Method,*[2] such a system had never been thoroughly or scientifically applied to history. Tested in the *Considérations,* it reaches its perfection, with all the limitations of time, temperament, and available data, in the *Spirit of the Laws* (1748). It is in the last part of that stupendous book [3] that Montesquieu applied to the " Origin and revolutions of civil law among the French " [4] the principles and propositions concerning the science of government which he had elaborated in the first part.

Conscious of the two theories of Boulainvilliers and Dubos, current in public opinion and given added sanctity in the minds of their followers by the death of the proponents, Montesquieu determined to steer a middle course :

M. le Comte de Boulainvilliers and M. l'Abbé Dubos have both made systems, of which the first seems to be a conspiracy against the Third Estate and the second a conspiracy against the nobility. When the Sun gave Phaeton his chariot to drive, he

---

[1] *Cf. Considérations,* ch. iv, p. 31 ; ch. v, p. 47.

[2] Montesquieu was also indebted variously to Hotman, Languet, Charron, Machiavelli, de Valois, Baluze and Du Cange.

[3] Bks. xxviii-xxx.

[4] Title of book xxviii which bears the epigraph : " *In nova fert animus mutatus dicere formas* || *Corpora . . .* ", Ovid, *Metam.,* bk. i, l. i.

said: ' If you ascend too high, you will burn the heavenly home; if you descend too low, you will reduce the earth to ashes. Do not go too far to the right, you will fall into the constellation of the Serpent; do not go too far to the left, you would run into that of the Altar. Keep to the middle.' [5]

No doubt Montesquieu's intention was sincere, but his ancestry, his legal mind which rebelled against the supposititious habit of Dubos, and finally Montesquieu's own proudly aristocratic nature [6] conspired to make him much less just to Dubos' ideas than to Boulainvilliers'. Montesquieu is conscious of a mission. As an apology for the number of his own citations, he points to the bulk of Dubos' work. " Nothing retards the progress of science more than a bad work by a famous author, because before instructing one must begin by undeceiving." [7] But he grows more and more merciless to his dead opponent. His work

. . . has charmed many people because it is written with much art; because in it is perpetually supposed that which is in question; because the greater the lack of proofs, the more probabilities are multiplied; because an infinity of conjectures are set up as principles, from which other conjectures are derived as consequences . . . and because a limitless erudition is put, not into the system, but beside it, the mind is distracted by accessories and forgets the principal. Moreover, so much research forbids the thought that nothing new has been found; the length of the voyage makes one believe that he has finally arrived.

But when one examines closely, one finds an immense colossus with feet of clay; and it is because the feet are of clay that the colossus is immense. If the system of M. l'Abbé Dubos had

[5] L'Esprit des Lois, ed. Garnier, Paris, 1921, vol. ii, pp. 257-8.

[6] See, in addition to his Correspondance, ed. Gebelin et Morize, passim, the epigraph above quoted; the Prolem sine matre creatam on the title page of l'Esprit, the concluding remark of bk. xxxi quoted below and numerous instances of patronizing, as e. g., vol. ii, pp. 256, 177.

[7] Ibid., vol. ii, p. 267.

had a good foundation, he would not have been obliged to make three deadly volumes to prove it. . . . History and our laws would have said: ' Don't be at such pains; we will bear witness to your words.' [8]

The *Histoire Critique* of the Abbé, says the baron, " founds a system of the establishment of the Franks in Gaul on the presupposition that they were the best friends of the Romans . . . they who suffered as well as inflicted on them the worst ills. The Franks, friends of the Romans, whom, after they had conquered them by force of arms, they oppressed in cold blood by their laws! They were friends of the Romans just as the Tartars who conquered China were friends of the Chinese." [9]

On the contrary, Montesquieu, by his use of the words " our kings ", " our fathers ", proclaims his feeling of kinship with the Franks who, he insists with Boulainvilliers, conquered Gaul. There is patronizing partiality for that author in these words:

As his work is written without art, and he speaks with that frankness, that ingenuousness of the old nobility from which he was sprung, everyone is able to judge both of the beautiful things he says and of the errors into which he falls. Therefore I shall not examine it. I shall only say that he had more wit than enlightenment, more enlightenment than knowledge. But that knowledge was not contemptible, for of our history and our laws he thoroughly knew the main facts.[10]

Yet, Montesquieu does not subscribe to Boulainvilliers' chief contention that the Franks enslaved the formerly free Gallo-Romans: " M. le Comte de Boulainvilliers has missed the capital point of his system; he has not proved that the

[8] *Esprit*, vol. ii, pp. 282-3.
[9] *Ibid.*, p. 174.
[10] *Ibid.*, p. 256.

Franks made a general rule which put the Romans in a kind
of servitude." [11]   Montesquieu, on the contrary, places the
general spread of serfdom under the third race.   The
Franks, in his eyes, were valiant raiders, who carried off the
women and children and portable booty, and left the Gallo-
Romans their political and civil rights, sometimes against a
ransom.[12]   Likewise, in seizing lands the Franks did not
wholly despoil the Romans of their property; they only took
what suited them best,[13] but when they took, they took outright: " The Burgundians and Visigoths, whose provinces
were greatly exposed, sought to conciliate the former inhabitants, and to give them most impartial civil laws; but the
Frankish kings, sure of their power, had no such care." [14]

This remark indicates at once Montesquieu's sense of
political realities, keener than that of Dubos whom he
reproaches unjustly with having used as sources " only poets
and orators ";[15] and his undisguised admiration for the
conquerors of Gaul.   " Admirable simplicity in the laws of
barbarians! " he exclaims, and exalts their individualism,
freedom and independence as expressed in their customs.[16]
The Franks having left their country, they had the wise men
of their nation draft the Salic Laws, which were " personal
and not territorial " [17] and, when applied to Romans, distinctly not impartial.[18]   Montesquieu makes much of the
difference in composition or *wergeld* which was required of

[11] *Esprit*, vol. ii, p. 256. *Cf.* the point already made in the *Considérations sur les Romains*, ch. xviii, p. 196.

[12] *Ibid.*, p. 257.

[13] *Ibid.*, pp. 254-5.

[14] *Ibid.*, p. 171.

[15] *Ibid.*, p. 174.

[16] *Ibid.*, pp. 172-3. He is thinking in terms of Tacitus' *Germania*.

[17] *Ibid.*, p. 172.

[18] *Ibid.*, p. 173.

Franks and Romans, rank for rank; but leaves a loophole for the partisans of the egalitarian theory by admitting that a Gallo-Roman could, if he wished, live under the Salic Law to take advantage of its provisions. Thus he explains why Roman Law disappeared in the Frankish parts of France while it persisted in the territories of the Goths and Lombards.[19] "Everything," he cannot refrain from concluding, "bends of its own accord to my principles," although more recent investigators have found two misreadings of early documents as the uncertain basis of Montesquieu's belief that Gallo-Romans could become Frankish citizens.[20]

The Frankish conquest, however realistically seen by Montesquieu, appears to have been a source of benefits to the nation: "This event which occurred once in the world and will perhaps never happen again: the appearance suddenly in all Europe of laws which bore no relation to those known previously" has caused "infinite good as well as evil,"[21] of which the "beautiful spectacle of the feudal laws" is obviously one of the good results, bearing comparison to a tall oak with its manifold roots.[22] These were planted on French soil by the peoples who conquered the Roman Empire and who came out of Germany, but it is not true that the Franks on entering Gaul occupied all the lands to make fiefs of them. Had that been fact, the king would have had supreme power, which was not the case.[23]

Montesquieu, asserting that the Franks whom he has identified with the Germans, kept their native tastes and customs, then draws upon Tacitus for a description of their govern-

[19] *Esprit*, vol. ii, pp. 174-7.

[20] See, Thierry, *Considérations sur l'Histoire de France*, 1846, pp. 74-5.

[21] *Esprit des Lois*, bk. xxx, ch. i, p. 249. My transposition of his nouns I believe conveys his emphasis more accurately.

[22] *Ibid.*

[23] *Ibid.*, pp. 250-3.

ment, the one which, for him, ultimately evolved into the parliamentary government of Great Britain, "that beautiful system having been devised in the woods." [24]

After his somewhat self-directed praise of Tacitus, to the effect that he "abridged everything because he saw everything," Montesquieu tackles the matter of serfdom and the fiefs. He decides that ". . . among the Germans, there were vassals but no fiefs . . . because the princes had no lands to give . . ." but the vassals, bound by their words, gave approximately the same services as those since rendered for fiefs. [25]

Now, when the Frankish kings distributed conquered lands to their followers, many freemen remained, both among the Franks and the Gallo-Romans. To Montesquieu serfdom therefore was not the general application of a law, but a progressive process that reached its height during the disorders of the late Carolingian period. [26] Thus in an extremely vigorous manner is exploded Dubos' theory that the fiefs had their beginning in military benefices continued from Imperial times. Roman origins give way to Frank. Dubos, according to Montesquieu, misuses texts. "There is no grammarian who does not turn pale" on seeing how, in a passage from Gregory, *ingenui* is construed as free of tribute. The fact is that *ingenui* means simply freemen and indicates, in the particular passage, that "the Franks, who were free, did not pay tribute." [27]

The point is capital, and Montesquieu hammers it in by repeated citations of law and history, because upon it rests his conviction that the French nobility did not usurp the privilege

---

[24] *Esprit*, bk. xi, ch. vi, p. 162. See above Thoyras. Gibbon repeats the phrase in his 38th chapter, vol. iii, p. 611 of Milman's edition.

[25] *Ibid.*, vol. ii, p. 251.

[26] *Ibid.*, pp. 257 *et seq.*, 231.

[27] *Ibid.*, p. 260.

of being exempt from taxes. No survival of Roman taxation [28] was ever imposed upon any of the Franks. Since there was no general taxation in the monarchy, therefore the rights of the lords were not usurpations. In a word, Montesquieu tries to prove that the nobles' privileges grew up with the establishment of fiefs, themselves established for defense: the freemen fought; the serfs paid.[29] Nowhere is there usurpation. Throughout this delicate concatenation of facts and propositions,[30] Montesquieu bases himself on laws and capitularies rather than the descriptive testimony used by Dubos. In the same way, he proves that the lord's justice was not usurped.

According to German custom, civil jurisdiction went hand in hand with military leadership.[31] The obligations of any vassal (originally a faithful companion of the king) were to bear arms for his lord and judge his peers in the lord's court. Despite this fact, the Frankish government was not despotic. The dukes or counts did not judge like Turkish pashas but called assizes of notables. "This usage of never judging alone had its origins in the German forests." [32] That is why in France justice is patrimonial.[33] Again, therefore, there was no usurpation by the nobles of the rights of either king or people.[34]

On the allied subject of general assizes, Montesquieu allows that under the first two races the "nation" was often assembled; but he means by it an assembly of bishops and lords exclusively, who made the laws known as capitularies.

[28] *Esprit*, vol. ii, pp. 254, 267.

[29] *Ibid.*, p. 267.

[30] *Ibid.*, p. 262 *et seq.*

[31] *Ibid.*, pp. 270-1. Tacitus is, of course, his authority.

[32] *Ibid.*, p. 272.

[33] *Ibid.*, p. 282.

[34] *Ibid.*, p. 278.

After the reign of Charlemagne " whose genius ", incidentally, " balanced all the orders of the state," [35] the Norman
invasions and the weak rulers " set back the victorious
nations into the obscurity whence they had come." Roman
law and the capitularies were forgotten and " customs " grew
up instead. Customs are not, then, to be thought of as barbarian laws, since Pippin gave precedence to law over custom
and Roman law never had precedence over barbarian law.[36]

Thus deductively does Montesquieu create a coherent
system that seems supported in all its parts. The mainspring
of the French monarchy he sees in the " manner of thinking
of our fathers . . ." [37] that is to say the Germans, who being
independent and warlike, " were extremely susceptible to
affronts," and came to adopt combat as a legal regulation of
natural exuberance. Chivalry and the code of honor were
developed as a result, which fit in with the somewhat wider
concept, elaborated in the theoretical part of the work, of
honor as the moving force of a monarchy.[38]

Montesquieu does not scruple, with all his assumed impartiality, to uncover the political prejudice that occasionally
animates him. In the chapters devoted to the destruction
of Dubos' edifice, Montesquieu affirms that the former's
leveling of the Franks to only one order, " a pretension injurious to the blood of our first families, would be no less
so to the three great families which have reigned over us.
. . . In order that Clovis, Pippin, and Hugh Capet be gentlemen, it would be necessary to seek their origins among the
Romans or the Saxons, that is to say among conquered
nations?" [39]

[35] *Esprit*, vol. ii, p. 317.
[36] *Ibid.*, pp. 181-3.
[37] *Ibid.*, p. 187.
[38] *Ibid.*, vol. i, pp. 24-5. See above Loyseau.
[39] *Ibid.*, vol. ii, p. 287.

As Dubos might have retorted that he did not consider the Romans a conquered nation, Montesquieu ironically saps the foundations of that belief. Where are the treaties between the Gallo-Romans and the Franks? Where are the proofs of the existence of the Armorican Republic and its treaties? " If a conqueror enters into a State, dominates most of it by force, and one finds some time later the entire state subjected without history's telling us how it happened, there is very good reason to believe the business ended as it began." [40]

Dubos' main point blasted, the whole system crumbles. Every time he draws a consequence from the principle that Gaul was not conquered by Franks, it can be denied. And indeed, Montesquieu offers to prove in the same manner that Alexander the Great and his Greeks did not conquer Persia.[41] To Dubos' explanation of a passage difficult to conciliate with his theory that *free* and *noble* were in Frankish times synonymous terms, Montesquieu impatiently retorts, " What! because in modern times, a few bourgeois have taken on the quality of noblemen, a passage from the life of Louis le Débonnaire is to apply to such persons!"[42] Summarily dismissing his antagonist, Montesquieu concludes, " M. l'Abbé Dubos has fallen into great errors because he has had M. de Boulainvilliers' work more constantly before him than his own subject." [43]

It will have been noticed by the reader that Montesquieu's own fault is the disregard of chronology in its application to the development of the feudal system out of the Frankish conquest. Laws and accounts of various epochs are made to bear on the same points, and these are seldom grouped into

---

[40] *Esprit*, vol. ii, pp. 283-4.

[41] *Ibid.*

[42] *Ibid.*, p. 290.

[43] *Ibid.*, p. 292.

any historical succession.   It would be unfair, however, to say that Montesquieu was not aware of the progressive changes, for in his very last Book, he attempts the explanation " of the feudal laws among the Franks in their relation to the revolutions of their monarchy." [44]

The first revolution he places at the time of Brunehilde (died 613), when fiefs became irrevocable.   The second dates from the time of Dagobert (died 638), when the nation, reverting to an old German custom,[45] thought it safer to place the power in the hands of a Mayor whom it elected and on whom it could impose stricter terms than on a king whose power was hereditary.[46]   But Montesquieu must safeguard the monarchical principle: " Though the person of the king was unknown, and the mayors had placed whomever they wished on the throne, hereditary royalty was not effaced from the heart of the Franks . . .," [47] and while Pippin, Charles and Carloman were anointed and blessed, the French lords swore under pain of interdict and excommunication not to elect anyone of another race.[48]

As Boulainvilliers before him and Mably after, Montesquieu finds a hero in Charlemagne, no longer the white-bearded Emperor—eight feet tall and two hundred years old —of the French saga, but no less a " prodigious prince," who " eluding all perils with ease, . . . supported by his own hand his vast empire," which,

being great, was maintained by the greatness of its chief.   He made admirable laws.   He did more: he had them enforced. . . .

---

[44] Title of book xxxi.

[45] The familiar " *Reges ex nobilitate, duces ex virtute sumunt* " Tacitus, *Germ.*, ch. vii, p. 315.

[46] *Esprit des Lois*, vol. ii, p. 300.

[47] *Ibid.*, p. 314.

[48] *Ibid.*, p. 316.

One sees in the laws of this prince a foresight which carries everything before it.[49]

Under his successors occurred a third revolution. By the treaty of Verdun in 843, any freeman could choose his lord and change his allodial holding into a fief. When Capet mounted the throne in 987 an even greater change, though not strictly a revolution, took place; a change from anarchy to government, the title of king being united to the greatest fief in the land.[50] He alone could defend the kingdom from the Normans, a task in which he was helped by the change from "political government" to "feudal government".[51] At the same time the irrevocability of fiefs in France led to primogeniture which applied to the Crown as the largest fief. Daughters could inherit fiefs if there were no sons, by a redemption payment to the overlord, but as the Crown was vassal to no lord, daughters were excluded from the succession.[52]

Montesquieu ends his rapid though circuitous voyage with a consciousness of having reached his goal; the attainment of truth by steering a middle course between Boulainvilliers and Dubos. Like Aeneas he exclaims, " *Italiam, Italiam* . . ."[53] I have ended the treatise on fiefs where most authors have begun it." [54]

Still, Montesquieu's account of French origins was by no means definitive, neither in itself, historically, nor in relation to an age seething with partisanships working for reform or revolution. Montesquieu's allowance of the privilege

[49] *Esprit*, vol. ii, pp. 317-8.

[50] *Ibid.*, p. 315.

[51] *Ibid.*, p. 333.

[52] *Ibid.*, p. 336.

[53] *Aeneid*, bk. iii, l. 523.

[54] *Esprit*, vol. ii, p. 339.

enjoyed by the Gallo-Romans to live under Frankish law, was
to engender yet another system in the head of another abbé,
Gabriel Bonnot de Mably, whose influence stretched from the
publication of his work in 1765 into the revolutionary period,
when the form and content of his ideas peculiarly fitted the
common temper.

Before we examine his famous *Observations sur l'Histoire
de France,* however, a passing glance must be cast at several
works, more or less scholarly, which occupied the reading
public in the interim.

CHAPTER XII

Hénault—Voltaire—The Encyclopedists

It will be remembered that in the second decade of Montesquieu's century, a learned Jesuit, Gabriel Daniel, had begun the publication of a new history to supplant Mézeray's and had preceded it by some dissertations discussed above,[1] of which the most radical point was to assail the antiquity of many French institutions by making Clovis the first founder of the French monarchy. For having "cut off" four kings of the first race, Daniel received much more criticism than he did praise for trying to restore to French history local color and that historical accuracy by which "the aspect and the language of each period are scrupulously rendered".[2]

Besides incurring the refutations of such writers as Le Gendre de Saint-Aubin,[3] Dubos, Dom Bernard de Montfaucon, and others, Father Daniel had to refute the charge of lèse-majesté which Abbé de Camps preferred against him.[4] In the re-edition of Daniel's history in 1755, Father Griffet in a dissertation preceding the second volume, undertook to defend him on the interesting ground of an historical calculus of probabilities: since there are such divergences of opinion on the authenticity and power of the first four kings, and

---

[1] See ch. vi.

[2] Thierry, *Lettres sur l'Histoire de France*, ch. iv, p. 45.

[3] In *Antiquités de la nation et de la monarchie française*, Paris, 1741; St.-Aubin believed that Pharamond was the first king; Dubos, Chlodio; Dom Liron, Mérovée.

[4] Cf. *Le Mercure François*, June and Nov., 1720.

since everyone agrees on the facts of Clovis' reign, is not that
a justification of Father Daniel's stand? [5]

This attitude of reasonable skepticism regarding early
French history, notable as being that of Voltaire, as we shall
see in the *Dictionnaire Philosophique* of 1764, was not
wholly new in French history. As Father Griffet points
out, Rubis, early in the seventeenth century, had come to the
same conclusion as Daniel.[6] Before him, La Boétie had
called the history of Clovis fable. Nearer to Daniel, Jean
Hardouin (1646-1729) in a bewildering succession of
memoirs had propounded the theory that the majority of
extant documents upon the Franks were forgeries; [7] and his
friend Jacob Vernot, in inditing Hardouin's Epitaph, was
careful to write " *natione Gallus, religione jesuita; . . . hic
jacet Hardouinus.*" [8]

The posthumous republication of Daniel coincided with
another ambitious attempt to rewrite the history of France
on the part of the Abbé Velly, a man as little fitted for the
task of historian as he was eminently qualified for the post
of historiographer. Imbued with the ideas promulgated by
Voltaire and Montesquieu [9] regarding history, he believed
himself an innovator in wishing to " intermingle the narrative of our victories and our conquests with interesting researches upon our manners, our laws, and our customs." [10]
Velly was keen enough to discover doubt and obscurity in the

[5] Leber, *Collection de Pièces*, vol. i, pp. 425-7; Daniel, *op. cit.*, vol. ii,
p. 121.

[6] *Conférence des Prérogatives . . . de France*, p. 444.

[7] In the *Mémoires de Trévoux* and his own *Chronologiae ex nummis
antiquis restitutae specimen primum*, 1697, 2 vols.

[8] Flint, *Philosophy of History*, p. 253, attributes it wrongly to De Boze.

[9] Voltaire's *Nouvelles Consid. sur l'Hist.*, date from 1744; Montesquieu's
L'Esprit des Lois, from 1748.

[10] Velly, *Hist. de France*, 1755, vol. i, Preface, p. 13.

first years of the French monarchy, and after reviewing the Trojan and Gallic opinions seems to side with Fréret in making " the French " represent a league of German peoples.[11] For him, too, " the French or Germans " is a current expression and Tacitus furnishes the needed description of their manners.[12]

Velly nevertheless deals out glory impartially between the French and the Gauls, the latter being " famous for their antiquity, courage and happy genius." [13]   With such comfortable eclecticism, Velly skims the surface of the debated questions of scholarship to present a rippling, urbane, and satisfactory fairy-tale of French history.   With Velly's continuator, Villaret, the same theory of history [14] serves to entertain and ignores the rival opinions; it is only with Abbé Garnier, the continuator of them both, that something like original investigation and thinking was introduced into the lengthy compilation.

Garnier was Royal Professor of Hebrew, member of the Academy of Inscriptions, and a conscientious if uninspired scholar whose *Traité de l'origine du Gouvernement Français* makes an interesting application of the deductive method frequently employed by Montesquieu as an objective test of his conclusions.   The treatise opens with a comparison of the historian to a physicist dealing with the collision of two bodies.   Garnier distinguishes, however.   In history or politics physical laws do not hold true, owing to the varying degrees and kinds of human emotions.   What he has in mind, of course, is the collision of two races; and he posits likely axioms regarding such a conflict.[15]

[11] Velly, *op. cit.*, p. 2.

[12] *Ibid.*, p. 3 *et seq.*

[13] *Ibid.*, p. 17.

[14] *Cf.* Velley, ed. 1770, *Continuation par Villaret*, vol. vi, ch. vi.

[15] *Traité de l'origine*, in Leber, *Collection de Pièces*, vol. v, pp. 136-7.

I. It is natural that a victorious people should esteem itself more than the people it has conquered. . . .

II. If this victorious people is more numerous, more enlightened . . . than the conquered people . . . it will communicate . . . its administration and borrow almost nothing. . . .

III. If on the contrary . . . the conquered people is more enlightened and civilized, it will communicate much more . . . than it will borrow. . . .[16]

With these *a priori* principles concerning the relations of victor and vanquished he confronts the facts elicited by his study:

I. The Franks, redoubtable in battle, were kind and sociable.

II. The Franks were not a numerous people, owing to which cause they took, from 253 A.D. until after all other barbarians had shared, the finest portions of the empire before they settled in Gaul.[17]

III. The Franks were long familiar with Roman laws and customs; were indeed in close association in every phase of defence and administration of the empire.

IV. The Franks had respect and admiration for the empire, eagerness for its titles.[18]

The conclusion seems ineluctable: " the union between the two peoples, Frank and Roman, must be regarded rather as an association than as a conquest properly so called." [19]

Garnier is obviously a follower of Dubos, with less appearance of forcing documentary evidence and greater concision in his exposé. He cites the Abbé with reservations concerning specific points. He believes that it was the cowardice of

[16] Leber, vol. v, pp. 136-7.

[17] *Ibid.*, p. 140; but patriotism will squeeze through any contradiction: " Not that the Franks were less brave [than other barbarians] assuredly; all records show none were braver," *ibid.*

[18] *Ibid.*, pp. 142-4.

[19] *Ibid.*, p. 147.

Rome's last emperors which delivered Gaul into the power of the barbarians, by giving them concessions in Gaul to save Rome itself and Italy.[20]

Clovis, to this second continuator of Velly, was a suave politician who, though he killed Syagrius at Soissons, conferred the first dukedom in " our " history upon the Roman Aurelian, and gave a proof of the " honorability of his intentions " [21] by renouncing his former superstitions to adopt, with his followers, the religion established in Gaul.

All the offices of the first race, from that of Mayor of the Palace to the dignity of " king's friends," were Roman customs followed by the Franks.[22] He must admit that *vassal* and *leudes* are German terms, but he assails Boulainvilliers and Montesquieu on the nature and extent of the Frankish possessions in Gaul.[23] His is another " middle course ", for in interpreting the feudal administration of war, government and justice as Roman institutions,[24] he finds that Dubos has fallen into the opposite error of maintaining that military lands were subject to the same taxes as other lands.[25] Yet Garnier " cannot refuse the glory which this learned man deserves for the great light he has thrown on the origins and foundations of our monarchy." [26]

Two other followers of Dubos, whose works belong to the decade 1755-65 are the Comte du Buat and the President Charles Hénault. The former, son of an impoverished gentleman of Normandy, first obtained a reputation in Ger-

[20] Leber, vol. v, p. 148.

[21] *Ibid.*, p. 151.

[22] *Ibid.*, pp. 187-8.

[23] *Ibid.*, p. 196.

[24] *Ibid.*, pp. 203-263.

[25] *Ibid.*, p. 202.

[26] *Ibid.*, p. 203.

many,[27] by his publication of a treatise on the origins of the Bavarian nation. But study in retirement led him to alter his views radically and in his best known production, *Les Origines*,[28] of 1757, he supports Dubos on the question of Roman origin and influence, although diverging from him on many points. His is a massive but disorderly treatise, where German sources abound, to the visible neglect of French national prejudices.

According to du Buat, the name of Frank applied not to a single nation, but to a mixture of Germans and revolted Bretons, whose confederation, having taken the name *fraien* were called *Franci* by the Romans.[29] The revolt having taken place in the time of Nero, du Buat asserts and proves to his own satisfaction that the Franks accepted from the Romans governors bearing Roman titles.[30] The " conquest " thus disappears under a maze of ancient and peaceful precedents.

The work, owing to the previous pro-German viewpoint of the author and to its own diffuseness and magnitude, had no popular success in France,[31] though its pro-Roman tone, which in the meanwhile had disappointed the German public, led to a reprinting in 1789 [32] when classical-Republican sentiments enjoyed greater favor in France.

Contrariwise, the second-mentioned historian, Charles Jean François de Hénault, president of the Paris Parlement, found as general a welcome for his work as for his agreeable person. The *Abrégé Chronologique de l'Histoire de*

27 *Cf.* the Count de Gobineau, Introd. to this essay.

28 *Les Origines ou l'Ancien Gouvernement de la France, de l'Italie, de L'Allemagne*; La Haye, 1757, 4 vols.

29 *Les Origines*, ed. 1789, vol. i, ch. i, p. 2.

30 *Ibid.*, p. 5.

31 *Cf.* Michaud, *Biog. univ.*

32 La Haye (Paris), 3 vols.

France first appeared in 1744 but was endlessly corrected by its author until 1768 when a definitive version was given to the public. During the President's lifetime no less than eight editions appeared in France, to which must be added divers translations into English, Italian, and German, and the posthumous printing of 1788.

With perfect modesty, its author always maintained that the work was the result of lectures given at his home by such recognized scholars as de Foncemagne, Secousse, Dom Bouquet, d'Aguesseau and Abbé Boudot, although in tendency, Hénault is a partisan of both Daniel and Dubos. Like the Jesuit Father, Hénault begins with Clovis as the founder of the monarchy on the ground that we know so few events of the reigns preceding that of Clovis;[33] and like Dubos, he believes that Clovis extended his authority by the use of titles and offices conferred by the Roman empire.[34]

The president is naturally in overt opposition to Boulain-villiers on the question of the kingship. Clovis is to him a "veritable king" and not the "leader of mere adventurers".[35] The conquest of Gaul was not "a sudden irruption" but the consequence of "long settlements of the Franks in Gaul".[36] Clovis profited from the people's "hatred of tyrants" i. e. the Romans, and the fear of their neighbors. He was, on the whole, more of a conqueror than a statesman, though the Abbé Dubos emphasizes the reverse.[37]

Despite Hénault's insistence on the word conquest, he shows that it was one almost voluntarily endured by the Gauls, and one which gave Clovis "the glorious title of liberator of Gaul," rather than "the odious one of con-

[33] *Abrégé*, ed. 1788, ch. i, p. 1.
[34] *Ibid. Remarques Particulières*, p. 46.
[35] *Ibid.*
[36] *Ibid.*
[37] *Ibid.*, p. 47.

queror ".[38]   He maintained the laws and customs of his
predecessors, and having " acquired subjects by force,"
Clovis " kept them by mildness."   At the same time Hénault
does not concede to Dubos the existence and power of the
Armorican republic.[39]   Lastly, Hénault thinks it useful in his
Remarks to indicate that some authors deny the disinheriting
of daughters under the first race by the Salic Law, but he
inclines to the opinion of " M. de F." [40] whose memoir [41] on
the subject contains good and sufficient reasons for the
contrary opinion.

That the influence of Dubos on the president was more
than casual may be shown from a manuscript *Histoire Critique de l'Etablissement des Français dans les Gaules* which
is an extract from Dubos' three-volume history, not in the
hand of Hénault, but annotated by him as early as 1738.[42]

It was towards the end of that decade, thirty years after
Dubos' book, that the encyclopedic mind of the century, Voltaire, launched his portable dictionary [43]—" to make one
think ",—into the arena of learned disputation and popular
wrangling.   The book was burned in Geneva, condemned in
Paris and in Rome, but very likely not because it contained
scoffings at Clovis and the Franks, and was later to contain
an article on *Franc ou Franq, France, François, Français*.

In that article, Voltaire gives expression to the spirit of

[38] *Abrégé*, p. 47.

[39] *Ibid.*, p. 48.

[40] I. e. M. de Foncemagne, *ibid.*, p. 49.

[41] *Acad. des Inscr. et Belles Lettres*, vol. viii.

[42] Its publication in 1801, Paris, 2 vols. presents it as Hénault's work
entirely.

[43] *Dictionnaire Philosophique Portatif*, Londres (Geneva), 1764. See
arts. " Lois (Des) " and " Préjugés," sec. " Préjugés Historiques," *passim*.
Seven augmented editions appeared by 1776, but the present 7-vol. *Dictionnaire* dates from the Kehl ed., 1784-7.

historical skepticism [44] which Bayle had inaugurated in his own dictionary, and which has been illustrated in this essay by the example of several specialists in French history. Voltaire, after opening his article with the remark that the Gauls were practically the only western people who lost their names to a conqueror nation, proceeds with a characteristic sally in the first person. " I have but lately read a book," he writes, " beginning: ' The Franks, from whom we are descended ' . . . Halloo, my friend, who told you that you were descended in a straight line from a Frank? " [45]

To Voltaire, Clovis was " the leader of possibly 20,000 ill-dressed and ill-armed barbarians, when he conquered eight or ten million Gauls held in servitude by three or four Roman legions." [46] The skeptic therefore believes in the conquest—the double conquest of Gaul—by the Romans and by the Franks. But he does not believe in any subsequent racial division. " Not a family in France could show, I do not say the least proof, but even the least likelihood of having had a Frank as its founder." [47] And what of the Norman conquests? he asks to show the absurdity of the claim. Did the seven or eight thousand raiders leave proofs?

Reviewing the Trojan origin and Leibnitz' theory of the surviving Cimbrians, he adds, " Nothing is certain except the brigandage of the Franks beyond the Rhine at the time of Constantine." The original Salic Law is " an absurd chimera ": the Franks cannot have had a written law in their marshes; and the French had no written customs before the end of the reign of Charles VII (1461). [48] As for the ques-

---

[44] *Cf.* his own pamphlet, *Le Pyrrhonisme de l'Histoire, par un Bachelier en Théologie*, 1768; *Oeuvres*, vol. xliv, p. 414 *et seq.*

[45] Voltaire, *Dict. Phil.* In *Oeuvres*, ed. Beuchot, vol. xxix, p. 471.

[46] *Ibid.*

[47] *Ibid.*

[48] *Ibid.*, p. 473.

tion " what does *Frank* mean? " the historical philosopher
answers, " the proof that we know nothing about it is that
a hundred authors have tried to guess. . . . What did Hun,
Goth, Welch mean—and what matters it? " [49]

Voltaire sees Clovis' expedition as non-national, violent
and intermittent. " Every vagabond must have joined it." [50]
Then the Franks divided among themselves the conquered
lands and the Welch (Gauls) cultivated them. Thus, and
thus only, did *Franq* come to mean free-owner. But when
these settled in Gaul there were in it Gauls, Romans, Germans, and also Franks who became such under the leadership
of Clovis.[51] The name clung to the country, although
Charlemagne, who spoke German, did not regard himself as a
Frank.[52] After 843 (Treaty of Verdun dividing Charlemagne's Empire) *Frank* and *France* remained as names only
for the western portion of the empire; and in spite of these
invasions foreign to the " Welch ", the French character is
at bottom what it was when Caesar, and Agathias, and
others described it.[53]

Elsewhere in the *Dictionnaire,* Voltaire enters the controversy raised by Montesquieu in *L'Esprit des Lois* regarding
the work of Dubos. In siding with the latter, it is only
superficially that Voltaire seems to contradict himself. To
be sure, he believes in a violent conquest, as does Montesquieu. But Dubos seems to the lexicographer " very learned
and very circumspect ".[54] He has convinced Voltaire of the
existence of the Armorican Republic, as well as of the desire

[49] *Ibid.,* p. 474.

[50] *Ibid.,* p. 475.

[51] *Ibid.,* p. 477.

[52] *Ibid.,* p. 476.

[53] That is to say impetuous, valiant, fickle, etc., *ibid.,* pp. 478-9. *Cf.*
Napoleon on this topic.

[54] *Oeuvres,* vol. xxxi, p. 104.

of a part of Gaul for Frankish domination.[55]   But what especially angers Voltaire is that Montesquieu in his work has made a great deal of fun of the " worthy Perpetual Secretary " of the French Academy.   Montesquieu makes him say things that he never wrote, and in addition utters a good deal of nonsense himself.   In derision of Montesquieu's deriving the English government from the German forests, Voltaire exclaims: " The House of Lords, the House of Commons, the Court of Equity, found in the woods!   Who would have thought it!   No doubt the English likewise owe their fleet and their commerce to the customs of the Germans! " [56]

Again, Voltaire refuses to enter into discussions of the former government of the Franks, of the conquest of Gaul,

into that chaos of bizarre customs and contradictions, . . . barbarism and anarchy, which lasted so long and upon which there are as many different sentiments as we have in theology. Too much time has been wasted delving into this abyss of ruins, and the author of *L'Esprit des Lois* can only have lost himself in it like the rest.[57]

Substantially the same views are reiterated at greater length in the *Commentaire de L'Esprit des Lois* published in Geneva (1777(?)-1778).[58]

Already in the famous essay on the *Customs and Manners of Nations* of 1756, Voltaire had indicated his double viewpoint of the *original* confusion of the two races and the willingness of the Gauls to receive the Franks.[59]   With convic-

[55] Voltaire, *loc. cit.*, p. 105.

[56] *Ibid.*, p. 93.

[57] *Ibid.*, pp. 103-4.

[58] *Cf. Oeuvres*, vol. 1, on the English government found in Germany, pp. 50, 98; on refusal to examine embroiled past history, p. 108; and on approval of Dubos, p. 124.

[59] *Oeuvres*, vol. xv, pp. 417-9.

tion went justice, however, for in *The Age of Louis XIV*
(1752) Voltaire had included in his list of notable writers
the Count of Boulainvilliers, on whom he passes judgment
in this manner:

The gentleman of the realm most learned in history, and the
best able to write that of France, had he not been too systematic. . . . He calls our feudal government the masterpiece of
the human mind. It could be so called in Germany, but in
France it was only anarchistic. . . . His writings, though profound and useful, are to be read with caution.[60]

Shortly after the middle of the century, then, a view had
been developed, combining certain features of both systems,[61]
yet involving a detergent skepticism likely to be spread far
on the reputation of its author and the felicity of its expression. Yet it cannot have been palatable to everyone to be
told that

we are all descended from obscure savages . . . though every
people in Europe wants to cover with some *éclat* the turpitude
of its origins. . . . And who were those Franks Montesquieu
calls 'our fathers'? They were like all the other barbarians
of the North, ferocious beasts who sought food, lodging, and a
few rags against the snow.[62]

It was rational humanitarianism, not lack of patriotism,
that made Voltaire utter these historical and national here-
sies. In spite of them, he insists, " one must especially attach
oneself to the history of one's country [*patrie*], study it,
possess it, deal in detail chiefly with it, and throw a more
general view on other nations. . . ."[63]

[60] *Oeuvres*, vol. xix, p. 67 *et seq.*

[61] *Cf.* the historical note to his tragedy, *Le Triumvirat*, Speech of
Aufide, Act I, Scene II, *Oeuvres*, vol. viii, p. 93.

[62] *Oeuvres*, vol. l, p. 118.

[63] *Ibid.*, vol. xliv, p. 413.

The essence of Voltaire's ideas was given even greater influence by the inclusion in the *Encyclopédie* of his article on *Frank* and *France*.[64] It suffered but few, and those unimportant emendations. One addition, however, is of great interest, namely the assertion that " the government of the French, like those of all northern peoples at first, was [carried on] by means of a general assembly of which the kings were the leaders." [65] The contributor adds that it remained so through the first two races, until the time of Charles the Simple.

A few pages earlier two small articles deserve partial reproduction as possibly indicative of the Encyclopedists' views:

FRANC—sometimes means a free person, one who is not a slave. . . . A noble is, by his rank, frank and exempt from the *taille*. . . .[66]

Franc, or *Frent*—means a Frenchman, and by extension a European, or rather a Latin, because . . . the French nation distinguished itself above all others in the crusades. . . .[67]

The rival publication, the so-called *Dictionnaire de Trévoux,* takes the stand exactly opposite to that of Voltaire by following Boulainvilliers implicitly. " *Franc* . . . in our history, sometimes means noble as opposed to commoner, because the French became the lords after their conquests. . . ." [68] The lexicographer, taking cognizance of the contrary view, that the name of Franc was also given to the

[64] *Encyclopédie, ou Dictionnaire Raisonné des Sciences, des Arts, et des Métiers,* Livourne (Paris), 1772, vol. vii, p. 301 *et seq.*

[65] *Ibid.,* p. 302.

[66] *Ibid.,* p. 296.

[67] *Ibid.*

[68] *Dictionnaire Universel Français,* Paris, 1771, Art. *Franc,* vol. iv, p. 291.

Gallic nobles, concludes that the proof is not very convincing. " It appears much more evident that those so called are the great French lords, and not the Gauls." [69]

Furthermore, A. de Valois and Fréret are the authorities followed by the Jesuits of Trévoux regarding the race of the French. The *Francs* were a German people who formed a league against the Romans. As their name implies, they were " peoples united by love of liberty," who in 420 " resolved on new efforts to conquer Gaul, made Pharam, son of Marcomir, their king . . ." and thus began with him " the monarchy of France, the most ancient and noblest in the world. . . ." [70]

While this well entrenched racial and national viewpoint was still confronting the contradicting " Roman " view shared by Dubos, Hénault and to a certain extent Voltaire, a new subject for inquiry was being brought into existence at the Academy of Inscriptions by Gautier de Sibert. This mild-mannered and meditative aristocrat, whose book on the *Variations de la Monarchie Française*,[71] published in 1765, furnishes his personal viewpoint in its historical setting, was interested in finding out " whether there was under the first two races of kings an order of citizens to whom might be given the name of Third Estate." [72]

From the outset de Sibert's sympathy is discerned to be with the lower order. " . . . how many times have violence and ambition put too much disproportion between man and man! " He knows there was no order called the Third Estate in the period he has chosen, but did the *thing* exist?

[69] *Dict. Univ.*, p. 293.

[70] *Ibid.*, Art. *Francs*, p. 291.

[71] *Variations de la Monarchie française, dans son gouvernement civil, politique, et militaire*, 1765, 4 vols.

[72] Title of his *Mémoire*, in *Collection de Pièces*, vol. v, p. 113.

Familiar with the work of those who have preceded him, Gautier de Sibert aims his critique particularly at Boulain-villiers, putting certain questions to be resolved. Where did the Franks, who were all free, get their notions of slavery? And how do we account for the Roman names of so many admitted by the Franks to the highest functions? Further-more, only a nation held in contempt can be reduced to servi-tude. But Clovis became Christian. Does one, then, adopt the religion of a nation one contemns?[73]

Taking advantage of the loophole left for the conquered Romans by Montesquieu's account, de Sibert argues that if these could choose to live under the Salic Law, the difference in *wergeld* or composition did not work such a disadvantage as Montesquieu thought. The vanquished could overcome the single distinction between him and the victor.[74] The academician is thus led to adopt Dubos' view that the differ-ence in price was designed to protect the Frankish minority. There were, to be sure, slaves in the monarchy, but slavery was not the distinguishing mark of race. And as the Gauls were citizens of the Empire, the Franks' respect for that dignity prohibited the harshness of enslavement.[75] " Let us pay homage," says Gautier, " to the enlightened policy of the founder of the Monarchy. Let us not see in it, as does . . . Boulainvilliers . . ., the origin of the fact that the greater part of the citizens are sullied by the stain of servitude."[76]

Basing himself on Mézeray and Montesquieu, who assert that of the freemen in the early monarchy some were noble and some were not, Gautier comes to the conclusion that, since the Gauls " could become naturalized Frenchmen,"[77]

[73] Leber, vol. v, p. 114.
[74] *Ibid.*, pp. 115-7.
[75] *Ibid.*, p. 117 *et seq.*
[76] *Ibid.*, p. 119.
[77] *Ibid.*, p. 124.

the *antrustions,* or faithful, were the Frankish nobles; and
the *convivi,* or king's friends, were the Gallic nobles.   Now,
as " the existence of a Third Estate would be a chimera without the existence of a body of nobility . . .," [78] and since
documents refer to *ingenui* who were neither slaves nor freed
slaves, it follows that there was a class of men who were free
but neither nobles nor clergy.[79]

De Sibert concludes with a definite statement that although
these freemen could not obtain fiefs, they " always shared the
glory of bearing arms for the defense of their country
[*patrie*]." [80]   In addition, in the *placitum,* the freemen assembled, elected their judges, and took a part in public administration "more extensive, fixed, and definite than the
bourgeois in the cities of the kingdom do today." [81]   The
assemblies, moreover, were not merely expected to hear new
laws read, but "to be consulted and to give their seal and
consent individually to the new capitularies." [82]

Having gone thus far on the road already trod in his
Variations,[83] Gautier de Sibert closes but does not conclude.
He admits that by the end of the tenth century there were
generally in the kingdom only serfs and nobles, and this
division was not as old as the monarchy; but whether before
the tenth century there was a Third Estate in France, he
leaves to " sane criticism . . . and the man without prejudice." [84]

It is indisputable that this preoccupation with the Third
Estate, closely allied to the desire to establish a continuity

[78] Leber, vol. v, p. 125.
[79] *Ibid.,* p. 128.
[80] *Ibid.,* p. 131.
[81] *Ibid.,* p. 133.
[82] *Ibid.,* p. 134.
[83] *Ibid.,* vol. i, p. 13 *et seq.*
[84] Leber, vol. v, p. 135.

for Roman customs and bourgeois privileges from the Empire to the eighteenth century, had acquired in the thirty-five years since Dubos' *Histoire Critique* a maturity and prestige further enhanced by the currents of liberal and democratic doctrine emanating from the Encyclopedists, from Diderot [85] especially. Outside their group, Jean-Jacques Rousseau of course discarded historical investigation or justification as irrelevant,[86] but the temper of his thought influenced a man endowed with native gifts for scholarship, possessed of wide-reading, a logic learned from the Jesuits, and an acquaintance with the classics which Rollin himself would not have disowned.[87] Yet by a tour-de-force he rejected the notion of Roman survival while upholding bourgeois liberalism, in a book that was to influence directly the men who made the Revolution.[88]

[85] *Cf.* in the *Encyclopédie* the articles *Autorité, Liberté, Représentants* and the work of 1775 entitled *Principes de Politique des Souverains.*

[86] *Discours sur l'Inégalité*, p. 4.

[87] Mably "knew almost by heart Plato, Thucydides, Xenophon, Plutarch, and the philosophical works of Cicero." Brizard, *Eloge*, p. 128.

[88] *Cf.* H. Sée, *Les Idées Politiques en France au 18ème Siècle*, p. 179.

CHAPTER XIII

Mably—The Third Estate

GABRIEL BONNOT DE MABLY, born in that province of France where revolution first broke out, the Dauphiné, is distinguished chiefly for his writings rather than for an active participation in affairs. Dedicated to the Church, he never rose above the position of sub-deacon, preferring leisure and independence of thought to worldly fortune. His first publication was a *Parallel between the Romans and the French* (1740), the hasty conclusions of which he later recanted.[1]

It was in the fruitful year 1765 that the first part of Mably's *Observations sur l'Histoire de France*[2] appeared and set forth the clichés which were to appeal so generally to the men of the Revolution by their classical flavor, liberal tendency, and democratic tone. It is interesting to remember that Mably was associated in more than one way with Rousseau. The latter not only acted for a time as tutor to Mably's nephews, but was one of the first to recognize him as one among " good Frenchmen and enlightened citizens." [3] The two men later traveled together and worked independently to fashion a constitution for Poland at the request of Count Wilhorski. The very year that the observations on French history appeared, another volume on the *Study of History* was published by Mably, having been originally

---

[1] *Avertissement* to 1st ed. of *Observations*, p. 162.

[2] *Observations sur l'Histoire de France*, Genève, 1765, 2 vols. References are to the 3-vol. ed. Kehll (*sic*), 1788.

[3] Quoted from Rousseau's *Lettre à d'Alembert sur les spectacles, suite*, in Brizard, *op. cit.*, p. 149.

228

written and printed for the Dauphin, father of Louis XVI.
In that work, Mably openly preaches liberty, equality and
fraternity to the heir-apparent,[4] but with those purely verbal
limitations, that lack of realism, and that taste for compro-
mises between opposite principles which also characterize the
Observations.

In that matured production, Mably ostensibly and by turns
refutes Dubos and Boulainvilliers, Bodin and Montesquieu,
but in reality he is merely recasting into a linguistic mould
taken from the classical historians parts of the theories
evolved by past French scholarship, regardless of point of
view.

Thus it is that like Voltaire he admits ignorance regarding
the origin of the Franks;[5] like most of his contemporaries
he considers them Germans and repeats Tacitus to qualify
them;[6] like Boulainvilliers, he asserts that the French considered Gaul an enemy country to be pillaged;[7] but unlike
him, sees the Frankish government as a democracy:
"whether or not the general assembly and representative
council are established as facts for early times, the French
were sovereignly free, as their manners and way of life
imply."[8] Following Father Daniel,[9] Mably rejects the first
four kings and begins with Clovis, whose "enlightenment,
talents and virtues would have honored the imperial throne
of the Romans."[10] Yet he calls Dubos unscholarly and his
work a "romance".[11] "If the Gauls were not reduced to

[4] *De l'Etude de l'Histoire*, bk. iii, ch. v, *passim*.

[5] *Observations*, vol. i, p. 171.

[6] *Ibid.*, p. 172.

[7] *Ibid.*, p. 173.

[8] *Ibid.*, pp. 176-7.

[9] *Ibid.*, pp. 182, 405, 410.

[10] *Ibid.*, p. 184.

[11] *Ibid.*, p. 187.

servitude it is because the Franks knew only liberty and
treated their own slaves as men." The difference in price of
composition was indeed a humiliation to the Gauls, for the
French were brutal and victory made them insolent, but the
French "knew no system or policy to establish tyranny.
They merely took lands everywhere indiscriminately." [12]

The synthesis of all these remarks is that "the French
maintained their old customs and were in Gaul a free nation
constituting a true republic . . . whose prince was only the
first magistrate." [13] To make the passage from bourgeois
liberties under the Roman Empire to the French domination
seem palatable, Mably explains that the cities of Gaul were
ruled as the German villages had been, by *grafions,* now called
dukes and counts. After the first shock of terror, the
Gauls must have been even better off under the French than
under the avarice of imperial officers. "The French forgot
many of the old taxes . . . some Gauls escaped being
despoiled." [14] Since Gauls could become "friends of the
king" they were obviously not reduced to servitude.[15]

On this point, Mably turns about face to refute Dubos, as
well as Loyseau, Boulainvilliers, and Montesquieu. According to Mably, the Gauls did not retain under French law
their right to bear arms, nor does he believe that they enjoyed freedom under the Romans or had local senates to
judge them instead of "French" magistrates.[16] The Gallic
influence made itself felt chiefly through the ecclesiastics,
who occupied the first place in their assembly, and for whom
the French had great respect.[17] At first despised and humili-

---

[12] *Observations,* vol. i, pp. 190-1.

[13] *Ibid.,* p. 192.

[14] *Ibid.,* pp. 193-4.

[15] *Ibid.,* p. 409.

[16] *Ibid.,* p. 435 *et seq.*

[17] *Ibid.,* pp. 198-9, 448-9.

ated, treated as a conquered race, the Gauls later obtained
" the right to become naturalized Frenchmen." [18]   This is
Montesquieu's famous loophole, through which Gautier de
Sibert also slipped the whole body of the aboriginal Third
Estate.   But in order to suit his ulterior propositions, Mably
asserts that "most Gauls did not avail themselves of the
opportunity and remained subjects." [19]

That ulterior purpose is to account for the persistence of
the legal distinctions between Franks and Gauls [20] until the
tenth century.   It was the habit of slavery inculcated by the
Empire which prevented the Gauls from becoming free even
when they could.[21]   Moreover, owing to the usurpation by
Clovis of greater authority than was allowed by law, the
" democratic government of the French " soon underwent a
rapid change, marked by the " establishment of lordships ",
the " tyranny of the great "; and corresponding to the de-
creased love of liberty shown by the French in their settled
state.[22]

In the period of greed and anarchy which followed, the
Field of March ceased to be attended or convoked, an event
which constitutes for Mably the first " revolution ".[23]   The
benefices were one of its results.   These were not prolonga-
tions of Roman military benefices at all, but gifts from the
king's domains to the *leudes,* or faithful, whom Tacitus called
companions.   There was no need for military benefices to be
created, since all the French had to bear arms.   Among

[18] *Observations,* vol. i, pp. 199, 452-3.

[19] *Ibid.,* p. 201.

[20] Note the consistent use of ' *Gaul* ' where most authors use ' *Roman* '
or ' *Gallo-Roman,*' and ' *French* ' where Fréret and the scholars required
' *Frank.*'

[21] *Ibid.,* p. 201.

[22] *Ibid.,* pp. 202-5.

[23] *Ibid.,* pp. 207, 445.

them, distinctions were based on wealth and personal nobility.[24]

As for the taxes and the exemptions that followed, Mably ascribes them to the refined policies of those who were Gallic *leudes*: such inventions required the subtle corruption of Roman habits; for " to usurp other's rights, to believe oneself master of everything because one is stronger and more unjust . . . demands only the insolence and brutality which the French had brought from Germany." [25] Usurpation alone gave rise to fiefs, *corvées,* tolls, dues, and the lord's assumption of the right to judge. This second " revolution ", being an overthrow of the laws, later brought its redress by another coup d'état.[26]

Mably differs markedly from Montesquieu and Boulainvilliers regarding the feudal government, which he finds not only unjust, illegal, but " contrary to the ideas of the French who conquered Gaul." [27] The combination of French brutality and Gallic softness cannot therefore serve as a justification of arbitrary monarchical government. " A relaxing of morals is not a political principle." [28] Likewise, the treaty of Andely (Andelot, 587) which made benefices hereditary, and therefore fiefs, was not a constitutional precedent but the cause of endless division among the French,[29] including of course the very controversy in hand, for *leudes,* now such by birth instead of by merit, began to think themselves superior to the others, whence our nobility. At this juncture, Mably feels free to exclaim: " At last, M. Dubos is

[24] *Observations*, vol. i, pp. 212-4.

[25] *Ibid.*, p. 216.

[26] *Ibid.*, pp. 217-22, 489.

[27] *Ibid.*, pp. 489, 465-6, 472.

[28] *Ibid.*, pp. 221-2.

[29] *Ibid.*, p. 230.

right for once!"[30]   On this issue, neither Boulainvilliers nor Montesquieu was reasonable, according to Mably, in believing that "the honor of our great houses" was vindicated by showing an exclusively French nobility. It were "pure giddiness" to have wanted to be noble when there was no such distinction. Hence there is no insult to the royal houses of France in having once upon a time been commoners.[31]

Mentioning in passing the new custom of elective kingship introduced by Pippin, Mably hastens to describe the "most curious, interesting and instructive reign in modern history" —that of Charlemagne.[32] Like Boulainvilliers', Mably's Charlemagne is at once "philosopher, legislator, patriot, and conqueror"[33] as well as the restorer of the national assemblies—the goal at which all of Mably's system aims from this point on. Mably paints a vigorous fresco of the state of France before the accession of Charlemagne; of the hatred among nobility, clergy, and populace; of the absence of laws and customs; of the disunity of all the classes in the nation, "not suspecting that there was such a thing" as the *patrie* or the public good.[34]   Then came Charlemagne, who "taught the French to obey the laws by making them their own legislators."[35]   Pippin had begun the reform by calling annual Fields of May, purely aristocratic. Charlemagne had the assembly called twice a year and added the commoners, recognizing the "inalienable rights of the people, despite their humiliation at the hands of the lord's justice and fiefs."[36]

[30] *Observations*, vol. i, pp. 240, 495-6.
[31] *Ibid.*, pp. 497-506.
[32] *Ibid.*, p. 291.
[33] *Ibid.*
[34] *Ibid.*, pp. 292-4.
[35] *Ibid.*, p. 296.
[36] *Ibid.*, pp. 296-7.

Mably eloquently compares the people to a prince deprived of his estates, " the object of mingled compassion and respect." The restoration of the " estates " in the double sense, then, was a great revolution on a national, patriotic basis.[37] The *caetera multitudo* of Hincmar's account is " what we have since called the Third Estate," which sat in the assemblies on a footing of parity with the other two, and separately in its own chamber to deliberate on all matters of state.[38]

The revolution-minded abbé sees the French government almost as a two-session Parliament with a Cabinet to lead it. The first meeting of the assembly, held in the Fall, deliberated on the subjects proposed, not by Charlemagne but " through the ministry of a few prelates and nobles." [39] The second assembly, the following May, legislated on the matters discussed. The prince was then called and he either settled conflicts or embodied the results of the deliberations in " Capitularies." [40]

The remainder of Mably's vision of the reign—for it can hardly rank as history—is in keeping with his favorite " republican monarchy ", a formula adopted by many of the would-be constitution-makers of 1789.[41] Mably's Charlemagne is not a despot; he writes in his ordinances " We wish, we ordain, we command " to express the people's will manifested through him.[42] He works to break down " the spirit of slavery and tyranny that had grown up in France." He always " observed the laws as the foundations of his greatness." He reorganized France into new districts to which

37 *Observations*, vol. i, pp. 297, 537.

38 *Ibid.*, pp. 297-300.

39 *Ibid.*, p. 300.

40 *Ibid.*, p. 301.

41 H. Sée, *op. cit.*, p. 180.

42 Mably, *Observations*, vol. i, p. 303.

he sent royal envoys (*missi dominici*) for greater centralization.[43] He established Provincial Estates, and the practices
of self government focussed the attention of the "entire
nation." "Liberty and union", the "love of country and
glory" made a "new nation" of the French, and the glory
of their name "traveled as far as Africa and Asia."[44]

From the surprise of the French nation at discovering that
one class of citizens could be happy without oppressing the
others, to the touching example of governmental economy
furnished by Charlemagne's sale of surplus vegetables from
his household, illustrations could be multiplied to reemphasize
the nature of Mably's work as no history but a manifesto.[45]
Following the breakdown of feudalism after Charlemagne, it
is of course the people or Third Estate which becomes the
hero of his narrative; the Estates-General being his pan-
acea of contemporary national ills. "It is easy to demonstrate," Mably concludes, "that the reestablishment of these
Estates, not such as they were, but such as they should have
been, is the only thing capable of giving us those virtues
foreign to us, without which a kingdom awaits, in eternal
languor, the moment of its destruction."[46]

These ideas struck public sentiment at the right time to
gain very wide acceptance, even in the scholarly milieu of
the Academy of Inscriptions which sealed them with its authority by opening a competition for the best eulogy of Mably
after the latter's death in 1785.

Meanwhile certain members of that academy, Secousse,
Laurière, La Porte du Theil, and Feudrix de Bréquigny in
particular, simultaneously with the Benedictines of St. Maur,
were preparing further collections of sources on the history

---

[43] *Observations*, vol. i, p. 306.

[44] *Ibid.*, pp. 307, 549, 308-9.

[45] *Ibid.*, pp. 324-7.

[46] Mably, *Observations*, vol. iii, pp. 288-9.

of France, but without either group's taking any decided stand on the questions in controversy.

In the quarter century between 1763 and the Revolution, Bréquigny collected thousands of scattered documents with the most intelligent and indefatigable energy; and commented on their authenticity or chronology with unerring sense and science, but in that same period, the erudite nobleman found occasion to organize any conclusions he may have formed in only two memoirs—one on the *Communes* and one on the *Bourgeoisies*,[47] two subjects of the most immediate topicality to his contemporaries. In neither of these essays, however, does Bréquigny rise beyond a legalistic attitude and the prevailing monarchial influence in making his minute historical distinctions.

True, he defines the commune as "the confederation of inhabitants leagued together by oath to defend themselves against the impositions of the lords. . . .," but he hastens to add "this confederation was really only a revolt until properly authorized . . . the suzerain lord had to assist the establishment of the commune . . . the king had to authorize it by a special concession." [48]

A subject even more closely related to the Third Estate was dealt with by de Bréquigny in the Preface to the first volume of documents concerning Merovingian times which he and his friend du Theil edited and ultimately presented to Louis XVI in 1791.[49]   In the course of that essay Bréquigny deals with Roman institutions, Germanic customs, the forms of the first monarchy, but nowhere does he give coherence and meaning to his researches, except in separate and trifling

[47] Prefaces to vols. xi and xii of the Collection of Royal Ordinances begun under Louis XV.

[48] *Ordonnances des Rois de France*, vol. xii, p. 23.

[49] *Diplomata, Chartae, Epistolae, et alia documenta ad res Francicas spectantia, etc.*, 1791, 3 vols.

instances. The one reference to the contemporary revolution is found in his remark that Louis XVI's new title of "King of the French . . . goes back to the origin of our monarchy," was "borne by the kings during many centuries" and "has finally been restored to them by the unanimous voice of the nation, and confirmed by the sanction of the king himself." [50]

And yet the "status of persons in France under the first two races of our kings" was not a subject altogether neglected by scholars. In 1768 the Academy of Inscriptions rewarded by a prize a dissertation upon that subject by the Abbé de Gourcy. Worthy of notice is the fact that like many of his compatriots the Abbé is animated in his researches not by one, but by two motives. The desire to be "useful to science" is only second to "love of country." [51] The subject proposed is the same as Garnier's, but de Gourcy claims to approach it as an historian, rather than as a jurist, politician, or philosopher. [52]

It is clear, however, that de Gourcy starts with the presupposition of a complete racial mixture when he says that "the cradle of our fathers, whether conquerors or conquered" was "Germanic France and Gaul". [53] Likewise he asserts identity of social organization between the Franks and Germans, and similarity between these and the Gauls. [54] The "mildness of Roman rule" changed nothing of this social organization, as indeed his authority, Dubos, asserts. But the Gallo-Romans no more than the Franks knew "the first good of humanity, without which all others lose their value,

[50] Bréquigny, *op. cit.*, vol. i, p. 172.

[51] *De l'Etat des Personnes en France sous la 1ère et la 2ème Race de nos rois*, 1768, in Leber, *Collection*, vol. v, p. 265.

[52] *Ibid.*, p. 267.

[53] *Ibid.*

[54] *Ibid.*, pp. 272-3.

liberty "; consequently there was a multitude of serfs under both Franks and Gauls.[55]   Despite the fact, de Gourcy denies Montesquieu flatly on the " general enslavement of the Gauls by the Franks." [56]

The Gauls were the equals of the Franks, save in the price of composition, a distinction that de Gourcy adroitly mitigates.   A Roman, according to the Salic Law, paid only 100 *sous* if he killed a Frank; the Saxon, Burgundian, Allemanus paid 160; the Riparian, 200.   Equality is restored, exclaims de Gourcy, and endorses Dubos' theory that the Franks being few sought to protect themselves by the differences in *wergeld*.

Montesquieu was therefore wrong; but so is Mably in refusing to see the survival of Roman institutions in Frankish times.[57]   These things being so, Gourcy believes that the Gauls paid taxes to the Frankish state,[58] yet these payments did not prevent the great mass of the Gallo-Frank nation from being free, with serfs by capture, sale or birth, under them.[59]

To prove the confusion of terms and classes in vindication of the Third Estate, de Gourcy tries unconvincingly to show that the establishment of fiefs gave rise to a new kind of serfs, who were granted offices, honors, who bore arms and held benefices.   At the same time, the class of those who were wholly dependent on the lord increased: the villains, described by a contemporary as " *beast en parkes, pissons en servors, ouseaux en cage.*" [60]   As the separate and continued usages of Gallo-Romans and Franks gave rise to these servile

[55] Leber, vol. v, pp. 274, 276-7.

[56] *Ibid.*, p. 281.

[57] *Ibid.*, p. 292.

[58] *Ibid.*, pp. 300-1.

[59] *Ibid.*, pp. 301, 313.

[60] *Ibid.*, p. 339.

classes, so their former customs also included a definite order of the nobility, not characterized by the privileges of the present noble class, but nonetheless distinct, and based entirely on birth.[61]

Pursuing his modification of accepted theories, de Gourcy tries to prove that both the clergy and the nobility were present at the national assemblies held by both races of kings; thus depriving the nobility of their exclusive privileges.[62] But in addition to the parity of the two upper orders, de Gourcy, to be consistent, finds the presence at the assemblies of non-noble freemen, either French or Roman, who in addition might take the oath of allegiance to the king and bear arms. They not only legislated and fought but gave justice, since the judges of the hundred courts (*centeniers et scabins*) were drawn from this order.[63] Thus is the Third Estate provided by de Gourcy with letters-patent.[64] That gentleman's learned but diffuse contribution can thus be reduced to a combination of a)—Garnier's proof that there was a Third Estate before the thirteenth century, b)—Dubos' belief that Roman civilization was adopted by the Franks who treated the Gauls equitably, and c)—Mably's preoccupation with the Estates-General composed of all three orders and legislating for the nation.

A more vivacious personality than that of the last academician was possessed by the scion of Commerce and gentleman of leisure, Damiens de Gomicourt, who published in the year 1768 two volumes of *Mélanges historiques et critiques*

---

[61] He laboriously refutes de Valois, Pasquier, Dubos, etc. on this point (pp. 381-2), while recognizing with Boulainvilliers that in many early documents *Frank, Salian*, and noble are synonymous terms (p. 393).

[62] *Ibid.*, p. 414 *et seq.*

[63] *Ibid.*, p. 421.

[64] *Ibid.*, p. 424 *et seq.*

of which the first contains a dissertation on the early times
of the monarchy,[65] intended as a refutation of Boulainvilliers,
" whose ideas count so many partisans today." [66]   Boulainvilliers' contentions regarding the general assemblies, trial by
peers, and the limitation of the monarchy are all denied in
favor of a monarchial system built upon an adroit mixture
of the notions promulgated by Vertot and Foncemagne, and
more especially by Dubos and Montesquieu! [67]

Clovis, for de Gomicourt, did not usurp, but legitimately
acquired, absolute authority.[68]   It is monarchy—but monarchy tempered for the late eighteenth century by means of
verbal limitations : " True liberty is at its fullest when a man
can do all that is permitted by law, when he enjoys property
and the freedom to work for his happiness under the protection of the law." [69]

Now, these principles " do not conflict with, but rather pre-
suppose the authority of a sovereign power to which obedience
is due.   Then follow Montesquieu's analyses of democracy,
aristocracy, and monarchy that Gomicourt reproduces to
arrive at the principle of two fundamental laws by which
the king's authority is limited in France.   These are the law
of succession and the right to be tried by several persons,
originally the principle of trial by peers, which changed when
" the victors and the vanquished became indistinguishable." [70]

But as the nation made the fundamental laws, so the nation
alone can repeal them; and as a citizen, the king must obey

[65] *Dissertation pour servir à l'histoire des 1ers temps de la Monarchie,*
in Leber, vol. v, p. 40.

[66] *Ibid.,* p. 50.

[67] *Ibid.,* pp. 61, 98, 112.

[68] *Ibid.,* p. 112.

[69] *Ibid.,* p. 40.

[70] *Ibid.,* pp. 41-5.

the laws of which he is the legislator." [71]   With these axioms, de Gomicourt might be expected to follow in the footsteps of the " monarchical republican " Mably.   Instead he attaches himself to Dubos in showing that the Franks conquered Gaul for dynastic reasons and that " the farther they went away from the Rhine, the farther away they grew from German customs." [72]

The decline of the Field of March—that is of the assembly —was due to a stroke of genius on the part of Clovis who bound the Franks to the soil as cultivators,[73] while his permission to the victors and vanquished to intermingle no longer made it necessary for his entire nation to go to war or to attend the assembly.[74] " Force and policy had built the foundations of the French monarchy, disorder and civil war . . . could not destroy it." [75]   The national assembly became a king's council, composed of a few great lords and a few bishops, with or without whom the king could decide on war and peace, legislate, levy taxes.[76]   As the kings sometimes communicated their motives, so the descendants of Hugh Capet (i. e. the present Bourbons) do likewise in communicating their laws to the Parlement, but as the laws are also communicated to other courts, it proves that the Parlement does not register them as the representative of the nation, which it is not.[77]

Similarly, as the Franks, cultivators in Gaul, must not be confused with the Franks in Germany, so the limited and elective kingship of the latter must not form a precedent for

[71] Leber, vol. v, p. 49.

[72] *Ibid.*, p. 57.

[73] *Ibid.*, p. 74.

[74] *Ibid.*, p. 73.

[75] *Ibid.*, p. 78.

[76] *Ibid.*, pp. 84-7.

[77] *Ibid.*, p. 92.

the absolute authority Clovis acquired by policy and as successor to the Romans.[78]   Such is the ultimate conclusion de Gomicourt would have us apply to understand the French monarchy of his day, free alike from encroachments by the nobles and from all limitations by the nation assembled, "except through the ancient fundamental laws not now revocable." [79]

De Gomicourt's is perhaps the last ambitious attempt to go against the current of bourgeois liberalism set in motion by Mably's volume and bolster up the "rights" of the assailed monarchy.   The next work to be examined, far greater in plan and proportion, though absolutely without influence in its day, is far more indicative of the prevailing "winds of doctrine" even though we learn that it was written in a retired castle in the provinces, towards the end of Louis XV's reign, and by a young woman.

[78] Leber, vol. v, p. 98.

[79] *Ibid.*, pp. 49, 73, 95-8.

CHAPTER XIV

MLLE. DE LÉZARDIÈRE—SIEYÈS—CONCLUSION

MARIE CHARLOTTE PAULINE DE LÉZARDIÈRE was originally inspired to apply her taste for historical research by an omission she discovered in *L'Esprit des Lois*. "M. de Montesquieu," she writes in the foreword to her work, published anonymously in 1792, " after having given the title of theory to his work on our former civil laws, regrets his inability to supplement it by the theory of our political laws. Such is the authority who first gave me the idea of this work and of its title." [1]

Her family had at first objected to what it considered a bizarre pursuit for a young woman, but she persisted and finally won the approval and encouragement of such men as de Malesherbes, Dom Poirier, the Duc de Nivernais, and F. de Bréquigny, who is also said to have suggested the plan of the work. This plan is no less comprehensive than scholarly. It consists of three parts; the first, called Discourse, being expository; the second, or Summary, adduces the nature of the proofs; and the last, entitled Proofs, gives extracts and translations of the documents themselves. This formidable framework is devised to insure impartiality and carry conviction.

That the work, embodying the labor of twenty-five years of its author's life, did not have the results such application might deserve is perhaps chiefly due to circumstance. It was

---

[1] *Théorie des lois politiques de la Monarchie française*, Paris, 1792, 8 vols., vol. i, *avertissement*. *Cf.* also her imitation of his brief sententious chapters.

printing in 1791, Malesherbes himself supervising the work
and correcting the proofs, and was on the point of publication when the monarchy fell. Swept away by sequestration
during the succeeding period, the copies scattered, parts of
the manuscript lost and its author sent on the road to exile,
it was not until 1801 that it reached the light of day, but
with the " Proofs " of the last book missing.[2]

As her purpose and plan might suggest, Mlle. de Lézardière is " systematic ". Although she keeps a strict silence
upon the works of Mably, she is clearly thinking of him, as
well as of Dubos and his absurd continuator, Moreau, whom
she refutes in special chapters. Like Mably, she establishes
the complete break with Roman institutions under Frankish
rule and the conquest of Gaul as a war between Germanic
democracy and Roman imperialism. The cycle opened by
Hotman in the sixteenth century may be considered closed,
for, once more, by a different approach, Mlle. de Lézardière
sees the Gauls liberated from the Romans by the Frankish
troops of Clovis.

Unlike Mably, she does not find in the sources sufficient
warrant for the privilege of naturalization accorded to the
Gallo-Romans. But if these are excluded from the Frankish privileges, then the war of liberation is reduced to a
mere usurpation of power by one despot at the expense of
another. The authoress avoids the dilemma by " proving "
that the Gauls, made socially inferior, were nevertheless
given full political rights by the Franks. Their constitution
is an ideally drawn model of monarchical liberty, which en-
dures until the time of Charles the Bald without modifica-
tions. Charlemagne has therefore no place in her work as
the restorer of national liberties. These were re-acquired
by the Third Estate in the communal charters granted by

[2] For this account see the *Avertissement* to the edition of 1844, written
by the Vicomte de Lézardière, Paris, 4 vols. References are to this edition.

the generous desire of the kings, nobles and bishops, to re-unite the essential " co-legislative power of the French people " after the " division of its exercise ". [3]

Originally all liberty had been wholly lost by the Gauls, first under the Druids and later under the Romans.[4] When the barbarian invasions swept over Gaul, the " Gauls remained cowed spectators of the conflict between Rome and the Barbarians." [5] Of these, the Franks, to Mlle. de Lézardière, are the same as the Germans, " whose truly original character deposited there the precious germ that was to reproduce liberty on earth." [6] " Hatred of luxury, a passion for war, liberty and equality " are the characteristics of these communistic " citizens " from beyond the Rhine.[7]

The division between freemen and slaves among the Germans corresponded to that between fighters and farmers, of whom the first deliberated in the public assemblies, held once a month.[8] At the head of affairs were elective princes; " thus the government was essentially democratic." [9]

After the absolute conquest of Gaul by the Franks, their laws took precedence over the opposed principles of Roman law, with the exception that the clergy, regardless of race, were subjected to the Roman code.[10] But

the Franks associated all the subject nations to the government which they had adopted, leaving no difference subsisting between the political fate of the victor and vanquished. . . . The deepest

[3] *Théorie*, vol. iv, pp. 125-6.

[4] *Ibid.*, vol. i, p. 1.

[5] *Ibid.*, p. 54.

[6] *Ibid.*, p. 57.

[7] *Ibid.*, p. 60.

[8] *Ibid.*, pp. 60-1.

[9] *Ibid.*, p. 61.

[10] *Ibid.*, pp. 78-9.

self-interest had determined this sharing of national political rights with the subject nations and even with the unfortunate Gauls.

Had they not done so, asserts the author, the monarchy would have perished from despotism.[11]

The Franks, exercising to the full the rights of conquest, took all the lands they could seize in the Gallic provinces,[12] and reduced in every possible way in their civil code the status of the conquered Gaul or Roman.[13] The Gauls were everywhere in the minority among the free inhabitants of the Frankish empire;[14] yet in spite of these two facts they took part in the general assembly of the nation, where the presence of "the people" means the totality of citizens. There the preponderance of the Franks soon changed the national meaning of that word into that of freemen.[15]

In this "union of the king and the people in legislative functions which so closely embraced political and military affairs . . . ," the authoress concludes, "one notices an equal intent of the laws to prevent the enterprises of the kings against the people's liberty, and the enterprises of the people against the prerogatives of royalty, and this balance is truly the distinctive character of the monarchical government."[16]

The documentation of Pauline de Lézardière is altogether thorough, as indeed it must have been to arrest and hold the attention of the able critics about her. The flaw in her system is therefore not that of arbitrary selection, which has

11 *Théorie*, vol. i, pp. 87-8.

12 *Ibid.*, p. 87.

13 *Ibid.*, p. 88 *et seq.*

14 *Ibid.*, p. 102.

15 *Ibid.*, p. 103.

16 *Ibid.*, p. 125.

indeed discredited most if not all the systems expounded in this essay. The young noblewoman is in fact a capable critic of the methodology of Dubos and Moreau whom she particularly refutes,[17] but she allows her attitude to suggest inferences from and references to ancient laws and customs that, by a slight shading away from the written text, fit her preconception. Despite the flaw, her work might have earned her greater fame than she possesses had it not come forth when the régime which she had so carefully elaborated out of documents into a past where it did not exist, had already run through its life in a present in which she scarcely lived.

Had she published five years earlier, she might still have ranked with Mably; only three years earlier, and she would have found one of the main propositions of her work and that of her predecessors, not refuted, but swept out of court by a man whose voice was to be one of the most oracular in the new National Assembly—Sieyès.

It was during the months of indecision regarding the representation of the Third Estate in the Estates-General convoked for 1789, that Emmanuel Joseph Sieyès, a middle-aged abbé from Brittany, published his electrifying pamphlet, *Qu'Est-ce que le Tiers-Etat?* [18] Sieyès has but little to say upon history; most of his principles are arrived at by reason, as his *Essay on Privileges* [19] of the year before demonstrates. Yet Sieyès had to confront the historical cohorts because of his belief in liberty and equality as the only livable states of society, and because of his passion for the Third Estate as the embodiment of the nation.[20] The

[17] *Théorie*, vol. i, bks. ii and v.

[18] Paris, 1789. There were four editions that year, augmented each time.

[19] Paris, 1788. *Cf.* the two essays in ed. Champion, Paris, 1888.

[20] " *Le Tiers Etat est une Nation complète* ", ch. i, p. 2. References are to the 2nd ed. of 1789.

privileged order is not only a financial burden on the nation, he argues, but it cannot be a part of the nation as it consumes without producing, and is assuredly foreign to the nation by its idleness.[21]

It is in the second chapter of his famous query-pamphlet that Sieyès brushes aside the controversies of seven hundred years and the rights supposedly conferred by history:

If the Aristocrats undertake, at the price of liberty itself, of which they will be found unworthy, to maintain the People in oppression, the People will dare to ask by what right. If it is answered, by right of conquest, it will be admittedly going back rather far. But the Third must not fear to go back into past times. It will go back to the year before the conquest, and since it is today strong enough not to let itself be conquered, its resistance will no doubt be more efficacious. Why should it not drive back into Franconia all those families who maintain the absurd pretension of being issued from the race of the conquerors, and of having succeeded to their rights?

The Nation, thus purified, will not regret being reduced to believing itself composed exclusively of descendants of Gauls and Romans. In truth, if one insists upon distinguishing between race and race, could not one reveal to our poor fellow-citizens the fact that being descended from the Gauls and Romans is worth at least as much as being descended from Sicambrians, Welch, and other savages out of the woods and marshes of old Germany? Yes, it will be said, but conquest has upset all relations, and the Nobility by birth has gone to the side of the Conquerors. Very well then, it must be made to come back to the other side; the Third will once again become Noble by conquering in its turn.[22]

This argument, suggesting acquaintance with Voltaire's view, is in itself so definitive and expressive of the senti-

[21] Sieyès, *op. cit.*, p. 8.

[22] *Ibid.*, pp. 10-11.

ments to which it appealed that further investigation among the voluminous pamphlet literature of that year would be worse than profitless, so far as obtaining more original or representative views is concerned. The re-publication of Mably's work in 1788; the re-printing of Du Buat's treatise, the next; the expansion of Gautier de Sibert's view in a new essay on the *Antiquity of the existence of the Third Estate and . . . the causes of the suspension of its rights for a time,* add but slight confirmation for our purposes to the documented assertion that " all the pamphlets of 1789 are equally unanimous in demanding guarantees in favor of natural liberty and the right of property for citizens, unanimous in wishing the abolition of all the privileges which infringe civil and legal liberty." [23]

Destruction and re-construction engage the best minds, to the exclusion of problems requiring long years of thoughtful investigation into the past. In 1792, when the eight books of Mlle. de Lézardière were ready for the public,[24] far greater practical and national questions were at issue than the exact nature of the *placitum* among the early Franks. The fate of the limited monarchy, the stabilization of finances, the emigrés, civil war in the Vendée, and plans for foreign war against Prussia and Austria—these affected private interests and focused public attention.[25]

[23] H. Sée, *Idées Politiques au 18ème Siècle*, Conclusion, p. 225. That these demands were purely rationalistic is shown by the words of Cerutti quoted by Sée, *loc. cit.*: " It is the salvation of France and not our archives that we must consult . . . let us not go back to past centuries but to eternal principles." *Mém. pour le peuple français*, p. 37.

[24] The confiscated edition was very likely burned by the authorities, as were so many other works dealing with the history, rights, or origins of the upper orders. *Cf.* Condorcet's speech before the National Assembly, June 19, 1792; the decree of February 22, 1793 ordering a holocaust for 347 volumes and 39 boxes; and the communications of Roland, that same year, to the curators of the *Bibliothèque*.

[25] *Cf.* Gottschalk, *Era of the French Revolution*, New York, 1929, p. 197 *et seq.*

In the absence of a receptive public and of scholars willing to pursue a polemic [26] which seemed to have been settled
along the lines suggested by Sieyès, it happened to be a very
practical lawyer, Thouret, deputy of the Third Estate from
Rouen, who for the better education of his son in anti-
monarchical French history compiled a little volume of extracts and comments.

The *Abrégé des révolutions de l'ancien gouvernement
françois* is composed of two précis from the great works of
Dubos and Mably, incompatible opponents now conciliated
by the pen of a legislator awaiting his death in the Luxem-
bourg prison.[27]

Thouret, possibly influenced by the classical spirit which
was to make the oratory of the Legislative Assembly so
floridly allusive, abstracts from Dubos all the enthusiasm for
the Roman institutions, which Mably and his followers had
denied for more than fifty years.   What Thouret derives
from Mably is the essence of German democracy,[28] degen-
erating under the later Merovingians and restored for a time
by Charlemagne.[29]

The immediate pedagogical application is visible in such
statements as that concerning historiography in France,
which is said to have always concealed " the usurpation of
kings, nobles and priests, ever leagued together to despoil
the people of its rights. . . ." [30]   The Revolution " has shed

[26] *Cf.* the prefaces of the continuator of Dom Bouquet, Dom Brial
(1781-6) ; Du Theil and Bréquigny's Ordinances have been dealt with
above.

[27] *Abrégé des Révolutions*, Paris, an IX, G. F. A. Thouret, ed., Discours,
p. 9.

[28] *Ibid.*, p. 60 *et seq.*

[29] *Ibid.*, p. 89 *et seq.*

[30] *Ibid.*, p. 57.

a new light on our history," formerly perverted because " slavery is the father of lies." [31]

In conclusion the author asserted,

. . . the Nation avenges itself by a revolution forever memorable . . . of the ills she has suffered during twelve centuries and of the crimes committed against her during so long an oppression. She is giving a great example to the universe.[32]

By its revolutionary ardor, by the authority of its sources, and perhaps mainly by the touching history of its author who teaches his child with tender thee's and thou's, the little work, published in 1801, enjoyed widespread success, prolonged by several editions until 1821. By that time, however, the French nation had undergone a rapid succession of experiences that had greatly altered in the space of twenty-five years the preoccupations and prejudices of its writers and reading public. With the compromise settlement and ultimate reopening of the issue of Frank *versus* Gaul, this essay does not concern itself in detail. It is another and even more complex story.

Conclusion

Though the goal has been reached, it may not be amiss to complete the cycle of this investigation by recapitulating briefly its significant results. It has been shown that the very roots of French history since the sixteenth century have been buried deep under and around the issue of race; that in determining whether the France of their day was chiefly German or Roman or Gallic, the respected historians of each century, as well as the obscure pamphleteers of each party, have touched on every important national question. Many of their works now lie forgotten and unread, but their

[31] Thouret, *op. cit.*, p. 59.
[32] *Ibid.*, p. 348.

thoughts at the time conditioned action and reflected the belief of the public opinion. The fate of the Paris Parlement, the pride of the bourgeoisie, the antiquity of the *noblesse,* the power of the Estates-General, the authority of the king—all these historical entities which are still objects of modern study, were in their day encrusted with multiple Nordic-Latin race-theories.

The germ of these theories is found in the fruitful ideas of Tacitus regarding the Germans he so admired; while the no less prevalent opposition of German to Gaul has both its source and refutation in the earlier historian Caesar, upon whom the pro-Gallic view which assumes an origin common to both races rests its claim. If the actual invasions of Gaul by the Germans are examined in the light of modern scholarship, it is discovered that the process of racial mixture was in fact thorough and its effects reciprocal. Contrary to a long-established belief, the fusion of the two races—Romanized Gauls and Germans—was accomplished by the seventh century, rather than the tenth; and a right understanding of Gregory of Tours' testimony supports that conclusion at the same time as it sheds valuable light upon early Frankish institutions.

The period from Gregory to the end of the Middle Ages, in contrast, definitely shows the absence in medieval France— notwithstanding one or two exceptions — of any rancor against the old Frankish invaders, of any feeling of opposition between Gallo-Romans and Germans, as representatives of different social classes. Indeed the tenacious theory of Trojan descent strikingly demonstrates how lacking the period was in sound historical-mindedness though not in speculation regarding national origins.

With the emergence of the Estates-General, especially in the fifteenth century, a class consciousness groping for historical justifications makes its appearance. By the middle of the sixteenth century, in the person of Etienne Pasquier, a critical spirit is at work rejecting the Trojan myth, seeking reliable origins, and launching the theory that it was the Roman masters of the Gauls who suffered conquest at the hands of the Franks, rather than the Gauls themselves. In consequence, Pasquier thinks the French nobility of his day is truly descended from both races.

In the same century, Hotman gave vogue by his *Franco-Gallia* to an even more palatable theory of national origins which had been hinted at by Bodin in a less popular work. That theory rests upon the belief that the Frankish conquerors were descendants of Gallic tribes that had previously emigrated to the other side of the Rhine. Hotman went further than Bodin in drawing extremely democratic principles from the organization of the German state; while a score of prolific historians were compounding these and other elements in highly individual doses that reflect their political bias.

When the movements of revolt and reformation had run their course in France, historiography naturally began to betray the presence of an absolute king. Legitimate origins for the monarchy are assumed by visualizing it as complete in the early Frankish state; or else the historian takes refuge from the live issues in pure erudition. One jurist, Loyseau, does not blink the fact of a Frankish conquest, but his sympathies are with the nobility, not the king. Loyseau is the first modern writer to state baldly the thesis that the Franks furnished the body of the nobility, and the Gauls that of the serfs and commoners.

Simultaneously, in Loyseau's day, the rivalry for power between the Third Estate and the nobles is apparent on more than one occasion, culminating in an alliance of the former with the king and against the aristocracy.

This joining of forces in turn affected historical writing,

and in the most celebrated History of France produced in the seventeenth century, that of Mézeray, a patriotic attitude was revealed, which assumed the original unity of the two races. In addition, Mézeray contributed the notion that Clovis, the " founder of the Monarchy ", like Louis XIII his " descendant," had the support of the Church and the Roman Empire in establishing his kingship. Despite the pressure of royal centralization and the disorders of the Fronde, much solid historical research was going on in France. Adrien de Valois, lacking in influence though not in merit, realized the value of Gregory of Tours and with the aid of other medieval chronicles established the original race struggle upon solid bases. Building on the same foundations at the end of the century, the Count of Boulainvilliers erected a complex and antagonistic system, whereby the Nordic nobility is the only legitimate power in France, as well as the true mainstay of " free ", that is to say, regulated government. At the same time, in England, Rapin-Thoyras exalted the Anglo-Saxon origins of the British government as providing freedom under a monarchy; while Leibnitz similarly defended the claims of the Nordic governmental genius against a vindication of the Gauls by the Jesuit Tournemine. The battle was now fully engaged between Gallo-Romans and Nordics over every question of government, politics, and nationality.

For a time the " Latins " triumphed with the help of Abbé Dubos' three massive tomes and such unexpected support as the Marquis d'Argenson's; but the tide soon turned under the impact of Montesquieu's reputation and devastating judgments. The idea that the Germans were the " fathers " of the French and of their government gained favor even in academic circles until Voltaire's skepticism, propagated partly through the *Encyclopédie*, partly through his own *Philosophical Dictionary*, made the Nordic descent seem an absurdity. The rival *Dictionnaire de Trévoux* hung on to the older prejudice, but the era for compromising had arrived with the wave of reform.

To both, Mably devoted his lucid mind and generous feelings, producing a new concept of Franco-Roman origin, and reviving in a sense Hotman's justification of constitutional monarchy. Mably influenced the theorists of the Revolution, just as Sieyès by his appeal to force on behalf of the downtrodden " Gauls ", influenced the doers. By 1801, the issue of historical rights *seemed* settled and the belief in racial unity prevailed.

The basing of any general conclusions upon so wide and diverse testimony as three centuries' controversial writings should at least be preceded by an assurance that the conflict of ideas is at an end. Unfortunately no such guarantee can be given. The French Revolution and its concomitant wave of patriotism appeared to give the race issue its quietus. The record certainly shows a willingness to regard modern France as a complete fusion of the Nordic and Latin and Gallic (Celtic) elements. The *Mémoires de l'Académie Celtique* (Paris, 1807), dedicated to the Empress Josephine, unmistakably reveal the spirit of union, while their editor spurns the adoption of any system, save that of bringing together the " titles to glory of all Frenchmen " in their Gallic, Celtic, or Frankish past.[33]

In his magnificent historical epic of the nation, Michelet presents in all its perfection the theory of the " happy blending " of both racial elements that have produced the well-balanced culture and outlook of the modern Frenchman. Augustin Thierry, often cited in these pages, adopted the same idea [34] and contributed many fresh facts and views to

[33] *Mémoires, Préface*, p. i.

[34] Flint, it seems (p. 354) mistook his valuation for a vindication of the Frankish institutions.

a knowledge of the melting-pot period of French history. Mutually inspired by one another, Thierry and the Romantic prose-poet Chateaubriand emphasized the free and valorous character of the Frankish people, the impetuosity and mysticism of the Gauls, the practicality and organizing genius of the Romans. In *Les Martyrs*, that admirably documented epic, Chateaubriand is careful to stress the " double origin " of the French,[35] leaving the way open to a renewal of the old issue; for, as historical knowledge of the invasions grew, the conquest of Gaul by the Franks could no longer be glossed over. In fact, admiration for the Nordic genius and its works was manifested in more than one way. Beginning in 1810 with the publication of Mme. de Stael's *L'Allemagne*, the spirit of recognition can be variously seen in the influence of Herder on Edgar Quinet who translated him in 1823, in that of Hegel on Victor Cousin (1824-7) and in Guizot's adoption and re-edition of Mably; it is visible in Gérard de Nerval's translation of Goethe's *Faust* (1828), Hector Berlioz' setting of it to music (1829),[36] his passionate defense of Weber's and Beethoven's then despised compositions; and not less significantly perhaps in young Renan's discovery of Kant and hope for intellectual salvation from Germany (1845).[37]

The ready welcome, however, of the Nordic elements from within and without France carried the seeds of subsequent strife, indicated in a strong mid-century reaction towards Gallic and Roman origins. This reaction coincided rather naturally with the establishment of the Second Empire and culminated physically in the Franco-Prussian War.

[35] *Les Martyrs*, Paris, 1852, *Notes sur le Livre X*, p. 472.

[36] *Huit Scènes de Faust*, Paris, 1829. *La Damnation de Faust*, Paris, 1846. *Cf.* also his *pièce d'occasion* " *La Menace des Francs*" the words of which, written by Berlioz, imply the democratic and national character of the Frankish nation in opposition to an absolute king.

[37] *Cf.* P. Lasserre, *Renan et Nous*, 1923, p. 207.

The swing of the pendulum can be discerned in the changed ideas of the same Edgar Quinet, liberal-republican historian and lecturer at the Collège de France, who as a young man had translated Herder and made himself an interpreter of Germany re-discovered. By 1857, in his *Philosophie de l'Histoire de France*,[38] he violently combats the " prevalent " notion that the Franks so thoroughly conquered the Romanized Gauls that modern French institutions have Germanic origins.[39] On those grounds he attacks the " historical fatalism " of Thierry, Lavallée,[40] Guizot, and Buchez and Roux;[41] as well as the anti-Gallic bias of the pro-German historians.[42]

Guizot, of course, persisted in his " legitimist " view that whatever powers were historically acquired by any race or class in France have concurred in the making of the nation. With certain reservations he admitted the diverse claims of Boulainvilliers, Dubos, and Mably. His contemporary, Mignet, best known for his history of the French Revolution, seems to have followed the more conventional theory of the complete conquest of the Gauls by the invading Franks,[43] who then absorbed Roman culture. This dogma, accepted by such scholars as Gaston Paris, Ozanam, and others, was at the very same time assailed by two opposite movements, the Celtic revival centering around the energetic personality of Ernest Renan,[44] and the Nordic doctrines

[38] *Oeuvres*, vol. iv, p. 357 *et seq.*

[39] *Ibid.*, p. 380.

[40] Theophile Lavallée, *Histoire des Français*, an apology for nobility and monarchy.

[41] Quinet, *op. cit.*, pp. 373, 377, 389, 394, 408, etc.

[42] *Ibid.*, p. 369.

[43] *Cf. Nouveaux Eloges Historiques, Amedée Thierry*, Paris, 1878, p. 331.

[44] *Sur les races celtiques, Journal des Débats* (185-?) *Essais de Morale et de Critique*, Paris, 1860, pp. 103 *et seq.*, 374, 380.

emitted by the Count Arthur de Gobineau.[45]   As in the past, the scholarly issue was inextricably fused with contemporary political problems, and it is not difficult to see how royalist and aristocratic tendencies in France would cluster about the vindication of historical rights of conquest, while the republican elements would prefer to appeal to immemorial rights of Gallic or Roman origin.

As a result the live race-struggle may still be felt in the twentieth century beneath the eloquence of a Jean Jaurès, the poetical logic of Charles Maurras' *Enquête sur la Monarchie*, and the romantic imagination of a nationalist like Maurice Barrès.

The entire generation of the 1870's—as their own writings prove [46]—came under the influence of both the contending forces that have divided contemporary France — the Revolutionary-Romanticist leaders like Michelet, Hugo, Chateaubriand, Quinet, Renan, and their Monarchical-Classicist opponents from Joseph de Maistre on.   In the political division the race issue is embedded.   Midway, outside the political arena, a member of the older generation, Fustel de Coulanges, had taken up the challenge [47] of the pro-Nordics in favor of the Gallo-Romans and embodied it in his monumental *Histoire des Institutions Politiques de l'Ancienne France* (1875-92), but scholarship, as this study has fre-

---

[45] *Essai sur l'inégalité des races humaines*, 1854.   See above Introd.

[46] *Cf.* Pierre Lasserre, *Renan et Nous*, Paris, 1923, p. 207 *et seq.* Maurice Barrès, *Les Maîtres*, 1925, *Renan*, p. 297 *et seq.; Hugo sur le Rhin, ibid.*, pp. 262, 267.   Charles Maurras, *Romantisme et Révolution*, Pref., p. 4; *Trois Idées Politiques, Chateaubriand, Michelet, passim.*

[47] *L'Invasion Germanique au V*[e] *Siècle*, Revue des Deux Mondes, 15 mai, 1872; and besides the six volumes of the *Histoire* cited in the text, a paper on the nobility in *Compte-rendu des séances de l'Académie des sciences morales*, vol. civ, p. 420 *et seq.*   Also his unpublished ' Suis-je romaniste ou germaniste? ' reprinted in Guiraud, *Fustel de Coulanges*, p. 143.

quently shown, is no settler of disputes. Quite the contrary. It may be that in retrospect the War of Nations will appear as a deciding event similar to the French Revolution in its influence on the " race conflict." It is too soon to tell. The future of the Nordic-Latin antagonism is still in the making.

BIBLIOGRAPHY

I. Guides, General Works, and Collections of Sources

Bengesco, Georges, *Voltaire: Bibliographie de ses Oeuvres*, Paris, 1882 et seq. 4 vols.

Bibliothèque de l'Ecole des Chartes, revue d'érudition consacrée spéciale-ment à l'Etude du Moyen-Age, Paris, 1885, vol. 46; 1906, vol. 67.

Bouquet, Dom, *Recueil des Historiens des Gaules et de la France*, 1738-52. 8 vols.

Calmet, Dom A., *Histoire de Lorraine*, vol. 4, Nancy, 1751.

Collection des Documents Inédits sur l'Histoire de France, Paris, 1838 et seq.

Deville, Etienne, *Index du Mercure de France, 1672-1832*, Paris, 1910.

Duruy, V., *Histoire de France*, translated by M. Cary and continued by J. Franklin Jameson, ed., New York, 1929.

Encyclopedia Americana, Boston and New York, 1920.

Franklin, A., *Les Sources de l'Histoire de France*, 1877.

Guizot, F. P. G., *Essais sur l'Histoire de France ... pour servir de com-plément aux Observations sur l'histoire de France de l'Abbé de Mably*, Paris, 1847.

——, *Histoire de France*, Paris, 1875, 5 vols.

Hayes, C. H., *An Introduction to the Sources relating to the Germanic Invasions*, New York, 1909.

Lalourcé et Duval, *Recueil des cahiers généraux des trois ordres aux Etats-Généraux, 1560-1614*, Paris, 1789, 4 vols.

Lavisse, E., ed., *Histoire de France depuis les origines jusqu' à la Révo-lution*, Paris, 1900-1911.

Leber, C., *Collection des Meilleurs Dissertations, Notices et Traités Particuliers relatifs à l'Histoire de France*, Paris, 1838, 20 vols.

Le Blanc, F., *Traité historique des monnaies de France*, Paris, 1690.

Lincy, L. de, *Recueil de Chants historiques français; première série*, Paris, 1842.

——, *Chants historiques et populaires sous Charles VII et Louis XI*, Paris, 1857.

Lot, F., *La Fin du Monde Antique et le Début du Moyen-Age*, Paris, 1927.

Mémoires de l'Académie des Inscriptions, Paris, 1663 et seq., vols. ii, viii, x, xix-xxiii.

Mémoires pour l'Histoire des Sciences et des Beaux-Arts (Journal de Trévoux), vol. 61, January, 1716.

Michaud, MM., *Biographie Universelle ancienne et moderne*, 2ᵉ ed., Paris.

Molinier, A., *Les sources de l'Histoire de France*, Paris, 1901-6, 6 vols.

Monod, G., *Bibliographie de l'Histoire de France*, 1888.

Paris et Langlois, *Chrestomathie du Moyen-Age*, Paris, 1914.

Petitot et Monmerqué, *Collection Complète des Mémoires relatifs à l'histoire de France ... jusqu' à 1763, Paris*, 1819-29, 131 vols.

Picot, G., *Histoire des Etats-Généraux, Paris*, 1888, 5 vols.

Rapine, F. de, *Recueil des Etats-Généraux*, Paris, 1786, 16 vols.

Revue des Questions historiques, Paris, 1866, vol. i; 1894, vol. 55; 1895, vol. 57; 1896, vol. 60.

Saint-Maur, Congrégation de, *Histoire littéraire de la France*, Paris, 1733, 6 vols.

Société de l'Histoire de France, Paris, 1833-75, 130 vols.

Weller, E. O., *Die falschen und fingierten Druckorte*, 1864.

II. Works Relating to Contemporary Race Theories

Barrès, Maurice, *Scènes et Doctrines du Nationalisme*, Paris, 1925, 2 vols.

——, *Les Maîtres*, Paris, 1925.

Bédier, J., *Chanson de Roland*, 73ème ed., Paris.

Belloc, H., *A History of England*, New York and London, 1925.

Berlioz, H., *Vox Populi, No. 1 — La Menace des Francs*, ed. Richault, Paris, 1850.

Boas, Franz, *Anthropology and Modern Life*, New York, 1928.

Brooke, S., *English Literature*, New York, 1894.

Bryce, James, *Race sentiment as a factor in history*, London, 1915.

Chamberlain, H. S., *The Foundations of the Nineteenth Century*, London, 1911.

Clauss, L. F., *Rasse und Seele; eine Einführung in die Gegenwart*, München, 1926.

De Stael, Mme., *De l'Allemagne*, Paris, 1845.

Fox, D. R., *Atlas of American History*, New York and London, 1920.

Gehring, A., *Racial Contrasts: Graeco-Latins and Teutons*, New York, 1908.

Gobineau, A. Comte de, *Essai sur l'Inégalité des Races Humaines*, 2ᵉ ed. Paris, 1884, 2 vols.

Grant, Madison, *The Passing of the Great Race, or the racial basis of European History*, New York, 1916.

Green, J. R., *Short History of the English People*, New York, 1916.

Guérard, A. L., *French civilization from the Origins to the Middle-Ages*, London, 1920.

Hankins, F. H., *The Racial Basis of Civilization*, New York, 1926.

Hardy, Thomas, *Collected Poems*, New York, 1926.

Hauser, Henri, *Principe et origine des nationalités*, Paris, 1916.

Hawkins, D. A., *The Anglo-Saxon Race, its History, Character, and Destiny,* New York, 1875.

Hertz, F., *Race and Civilization,* New York, 1928.

Lea, Homer, *The Valor of Ignorance,* New York, 1909.

——, *The Day of the Saxon,* New York, 1912.

Legouis, E. and Cazamian, L., *A History of English Literature,* New York, 1930.

Neff, E., *Carlyle and Mill,* New York, 1926.

Oakesmith, J., *Race and Nationality,* New York and London, 1919.

Ripley, W. Z., *The Races of Europe,* New York, 1899.

Rivarol, A., *De l'Universalité de la Langue française,* ed. Comfort, New York, 1919.

Roosevelt, T., *The Winning of the West,* New York, 1904.

Taine, H. A., *History of English Literature,* London, 1906, 4 vols.

III. PRIMARY SOURCES—ROMAN TIMES TO THE FIFTEENTH CENTURY

Bordier, Henri, *Histoire Ecclésiastique des Francs par Saint Grégoire, Evêque de Tours,* Paris, 1859, 2 vols.

Brehaut, E., *The History of the Franks,* Selections, trans. with Notes, New York, 1916.

Caesar, Julius, *de Bello Gallico Libri VII,* ed. Towle and Jenks, Boston, 1903.

——, *Commentaries on the Gallic War,* trans. by E. Brooks, Philadelphia, 1895.

Chambers, R. W., *" Widsith ", A Study,* Cambridge, 1912.

Child, C. G., *Beowulf and the Finnesburh Fragment,* trans. ed. in Riverside Literature Series, Boston, 1904.

Grandes Chroniques de France, ed. M. P. Paris, Paris, 1836-8, 6 vols.

Masselin, J., *Journal des Etats-Généraux de France tenus à Tours en 1484(3),* Paris, 1835.

Matthaeus Parisiensis, *Historia Major Angliae seu chronicon,* Rich. Luard, London, 1872-80, 5 vols. in *Script. Rer. Brit.,* No. 57.

Matthaeus Westmonasteriensis, *Flores historiarum,* Francfort, 1601.

Orosius, Paulus, *Historiarum Adversum Paganos Libri VII,* ed Zangemeister, Leipzig, 1889.

Pluquet, F., ed., *Wace, Le Roman de Rou et des ducs de Normandie,* 1827.

Salvian, *On the Government of God,* trans. by Eva M. Sanford, New York, 1930.

Spaeth, J. D., *Old English Poetry,* Princeton, 1921.

Tacitus, C., *Historical Works,* trans. by Arthur Murphy, London, J. M. Dent, 2 vols. Volume II, " Germany, Its geography, manners, customs, and tribes."

——, *Cornelii Taciti, Libri qui supersunt,* ed. Halm, Leipzig, 1907.

IV. Primary Sources — The Sixteenth Century

Anonymous, *Discours non plus mélancolique que divers, de choses mesmement qui appartiennent à notre France,* Poictiers, 1557.

Belleforest, F. de, *Les Grandes Annales et Histoire générale de France, dès la venue des Francs en Gaule . . . contenans la conqueste d'iceux François du pays gaulois . . . etc.,* 1579.

Bodin, J., *De Republica, libri sex,* Francfort, 1583.

——, *Les Six Livres de la République,* Paris, 1599.

——, *Methodus ad facilem historiarum cognitionem,* 1595.

Bouteiller, J., *Somme rurale, ou grand coutumier de pratique civile,* 1603.

d'Aubigné, Th.-A., *Histoire universelle,* 1550-1610; in *Oeuvres Complètes,* Paris, 1873-7, 4 vols.

De Seyssel, Claude, *La Grant Monarchie de France,* Paris, 1557.

du Haillan, B. de G., *Histoire générale des Rois de France, contenant les choses mémorables advenues tant au royaume de France qu'ès provinces estrangères sous la domination des François, depuis Pharamond jusqu'à Charles VII inclusivement, 1576.*

Fauchet, Claude, *Recueil de l'Origine de la langue et poésie françoise,* Paris, 1581.

——, *Antiquitez gauloises et françoises,* Paris, 1610.

Gaguin, R., *Chroniques de France: excellens faicts et vertueux gestes . . . en nostre vulgaire françois,* 1515.

——, *Compendium super Francorum gestis a Pharamundo usque ad annum 1491,* Lyon, 1524.

Gilles, N., *Les Chroniques et Annales de France depuis la destruction de Troye jusques au Roy Louis unziesme.* Paris, 1566.

Goulart, Simon, *Mémoires de l'Estat de France sous Charles IXème.,* 1576, 3 vols.

Guyart, Jean, *Traité de l'origine . . . de la Loy Salique, fondamentale et conservatrice de la Monarchie Française,* Tours, 1590.

Hotman, F., *Franco-Gallia,* in Goulart, *Mémoires de l'Estat de France sous Charles IXème,* t. ii.

——, *Franco-Gallia,* English trans. by R. Molesworth, London, 1711.

La Boétie, E. de., *Oeuvres complètes,* ed. Bonnefon., Bordeaux, 1892.

Languet, H. (Junius Brutus), *Vindiciae contra Tyrannos,* trans. Harold J. Laski, London, 1924.

La Popelinière, L. de, *Histoire de France,* 1581.

Montaigne, M. Eyquem de, *Essais,* ed. Leclerc, Paris, 4 vols., 1925.

Pasquier, E., *Recherches de la France,* Paris, 1633.

Philadelphus, Eusebius, *Réveille-Martin des Français,* 1574.

Pithou, F., *Grandeur, droits, prééminence des rois et royaumes de France,* 1594.

Relations des Ambassadeurs vénitiens, trad. Tommaseo, Paris, 1838, 2 vols. in *Coll. Documents Inédits.*

Satyre Ménippée, ed. Ch. Read, Paris, 1876.

Vignier, *Traité de l'origine, estat et demeure des anciens Français,* preface to: *Sommaire de l'Histoire de France,* 1588.

V. Primary Sources—The Seventeenth Century

Anonymous, *Soupirs de la France Esclave,* 1689-1690 (?).

Audigier, *De l'origine des Français et de leur Empire,* Paris, 1676, 2 vols.

Bayle, Pierre, *Dictionnaire Historique et Critique, Rotterdam,* 1697, 4 vols.

——, *Dictionary, Historical and Critical,* trans. by Des Maizeaux, London, 1734-8, 5 vols.

Bignon, J., *De l'excellence des rois et du royaume de France,* Paris, 1610.

Boulainvilliers, Comte H. de, *Mémoires Historiques sur les anciens gouvernements de la France, avec quatorze lettres historiques sur les parlements ou états-généraux,* La Haye, 1727, 5 vols.

——, *Etat de la France . . . extrait des mémoires dressés par les intendants du royaume par Ordre de Louis XIV pour le duc de Bourgogne, avec des mémoires historiques sur l'ancien gouvernement de cette monarchie jusqu' à Hugues Capet,* Londres, 1737, 6 vols.

——, *Extrait de Mézerai,* MS (Bibl. des Avocats), 4 vols.

——, *Notes et préface critique sur le Journal du règne de Saint-Louis,* MS. (Bibl. de l'Arsenal), 4 vols.

——, *Histoire de l'ancien gouvernement de la France, avec 14 lettres historiques sur les Parlemens ou Etats-Généraux,* La Haye et Amsterdam, 1727, 3 vols.

——, *Dissertation Abregée sur les 1ers Français et sur leur origine, ibid.*

——, *Mémoire pour la Noblesse de France contre les ducs et pairs,* 1717.

——, *Abrégé Chronologique de l'Histoire de France,* La Haye, 1733, 3 vols.

——, *Essais sur la Noblesse de France,* Amsterdam, 1732.

——, *Mémoires présentez à Mgr. le Duc d'Orléans,* La Haye et Amsterdam, 1717.

——, *Lettres sur les anciens Parlemens de France que l'on nomme Etats-Généraux,* Londres, 1753, 3 vols.

Cayet, P. V., *Chronologie Novénaire,* 1608 (1607), 3 vols.

Charron, J., *Histoire Universelle de toutes les nations et spécialement des Gaulois ou François,* 1621.

Chantereau-Lefèvre, L., *Traité des Fiefs et de leur origine,* 1662.

Coquille, Guy, *Institution au droict des Français,* Paris, 1608.

Daniel, le P. G., *Deux dissertations préliminaires pour une nouvelle Histoire de France, etc.,* Paris, 1696.

——, *Histoire de France,* 1755, 17 vols.

de Serres, J., *Inventaire général de l'histoire de France,* 1647.

Ducange, C. du F., *Glossarium ad scriptores mediae et infimae latinitatis,* 1678, 3 vols.

Duchesne, A., *Antiquitez et recherches de la grandeur et majesté des Roys de France*, 1609.

——, *Bibliothèque des auteurs qui ont écrit l'histoire et la topographie de la France*, Paris, 1627.

——, *Historia Francorum scriptores*, 1636-49, 5 vols.

Dupleix, S., *Histoire générale de France avec l'Etat de l'Eglise et de l'empire* et,

——, *Mémoires des Gaulois depuis le déluge jusques à l'establissement de la monarchie françoise*, Paris, 1621.

du Tillet, J., *Recueil des Roys de France*, 1618.

Fénelon, François de, *Ecrits et lettres politiques*, ed. Urbain, Paris, 1920 (1921).

——, *Oeuvres*, ed. Villemain, Paris, 1825.

Hardouin, J., *Chronologiae ex nummis antiquis restitutae specimen primum*, 1697, 2 vols.

Joly, C., *Recueil de Maximes ... pour l'institution du Roy ...* 1652.

——, *Traité des restitutions des Grands*, 1665.

Jurieu, C., *Lettres Pastorales adressées aux fidèles de France, etc.*, Rotterdam, 1688-89.

Lacarry, Æ., *Historia coloniarum tum a Gallis in exteras nationes missarum, etc.*, Paris, 1677.

Loyseau, C., *Oeuvres*, Paris, 1701.

Malingre, C., *Traité de la Loi Salique, armes, blasons, et devises des Français*, Paris, 1614.

Mazarin, J., *Lettres*, ed. Chéruel, in *Coll. Doc. Inédits*, Paris, 1872-1906, 9 vols.

Mézeray, F. E. de, *Histoire de France*, ed. 1685.

——, *Abrégé Chronologique, ou Extraicts de l'Histoire de France*, Paris, 1676, 2 vols.

——, *Mémoires Historiques et Critiques*, Amsterdam, 1732, 2 vols.

Montchrétien, A. de, *Traicté d'oeconomie politique*, 1615, ed. Funck-Brentano, Paris, 1889.

Moreau, C., *Choix de Mazarinades*, in Soc. de l'Hist. de France, Paris, 1853, 2 vols.

——, *Bibliographie des Mazarinades*, Paris, 1850-1.

Paulus Emilius, *De rebus gestis Francorum libri quatuor*, 1601.

Richelieu, Armand Duplessis, Cardinal de, *Testament Politique*, in Petitot, 2ème série, vol. x.

Rubis, Claude de, *Conférence des Prérogatives ... et maisons de France*, 1610 (?).

Ruinart, Dom Thierri, *Opera Gregorii Turonensis*, Paris, 1699, 5 vols.

Saint-Simon, duc de, *Mémoires*, ed. Chéruel, Paris, 1872, 20 vols.

——, *Ecrits Inédits*, ed. P. Faugère, Paris, 1880-93, 8 vols.

——, *Projets de gouvernement*, Paris, 1860.

Valois, A. de, *Gesta veterum Francorum sive rerum Francicarum usque ad Chlotarii senioris mortem, libri VIII*, 1646. 3 vols.

——, *Notitia Galliarum . . . in qua . . . aliaque ad Historiam Franciam pertinentia tractantur*, Paris, 1675.

——, *Valesiana, ou Pensées critiques, historiques et morales*, Paris, 1694.

VI. PRIMARY SOURCES — THE EIGHTEENTH CENTURY

Anonymous, *Lettre d'un conseiller du parlement de Rouen au sujet d'un écrit du Comte de Boulainvilliers*, in Desmolets, *Mém. de litt.* vol. ix.

Anonymous, *Mémoire traitant de l'Origine et l'Autorité du Parlement de France*, etc. in *Mézerai Mémoires Historiques et Critiques*, Amsterdam, 1732, 2 vols., vol. ii, p. 114.

Biet, Abbé de, *Dissertation sur la Véritable Epoque de l'Etablissement Fixe des Francs dans les Gaules*, etc. in Leber, vol. i, p. 432 *et seq.*

Brette, A., *La France au milieu de 18ème Siècle d'après le Journal du Marquis d'Argenson*, Paris, 1898.

Bréquigny, F. de and du Theil, La P., *Diplomata, Chartae, Epistolae, et alia documenta ad res Francicas spectantia, etc.*, 1791, 3 vols.

Brizard, Abbé, *Eloge de Mably* in *Observations sur l'Histoire de France*, ed. Kehll (*sic*), 1788, pp. 5-159.

d'Argens, Marquis, *La Philosophie du Bon Sens*, La Haye, 1740, 2 vols.

d'Argenson, L. de Voyer, *Considérations sur le Gouvernement, ancien et présent de la France*, Amsterdam (Paris), 1765.

——, *Journal et Mémoires* ed. by E. J. B. Rathery, Paris, 1859-67, 9 vols.

De Camps, *Deux Dissertations* in *Le Mercure François*, Ju. and Nov. 1720.

de Foncemagne, E., *Examen Critique d'une Opinion de M. le Comte de Boulainvilliers sur l'ancien gouvernement de la France*, in Leber vol. v, p. 14.

de Gourcy, Abbé, *De l'Etat des Personnes en France sous la 1ère et la 2ème race de nos rois*, 1768, in Leber vol. v, p. 265.

de Sibert, G., *Variations de la monarchie française dans son gouvernement civil, politique, et militaire*, 1765, 4 vols.

Dictionnaire Universel Français (Dict. de Trévoux) ed. Brillaut, Paris, 1771, 8 vols.

Diderot, Denis, *Oeuvres*, ed. Assézat, Paris, 1875-7, 20 vols.

Dubos, J. B., *Histoire Critique de l'Etablissement de la Monarchie française dans les Gaules*, Amsterdam, 1735, 3 vols.

du Buat, Comte, L. G., *Les Origines ou l'Ancien Gouvernement de la France, de l'Italie, de l'Allemagne*, La Haye (Paris), 1789, 3 vols.

Encyclopédie, ou Dictionnaire Raisonné des Sciences, des Arts, et des Métiers. Livourne (Paris), 1772, 21 vols.

Frédéric le Grand, *Oeuvres*, Berlin, 1857, 25 vols.

Fréret, N., *Oeuvres*, Paris, 1798, 20 vols.

——, *Dissertation . . . [sur] la véritable Origine des Français*, in Leber, vol. i, pp. 127 and 178.

Garnier, Abbé, J. J., *Traité de l'origine du Gouvernement Français*, in Leber, vol. v, p. 136.

Gibert, J. B., *Mémoires pour servir à l'histoire des Gaules et de la France*, Paris, 1744.

Gomicourt, Damiens de, *Mélanges historiques et critiques*, Paris, 2 vols., 1768.

——, *Dissertation pour servir à l'histoire des premiers temps de la Monarchie*, in Leber, vol. v, p. 40.

Griffet, P., *Observations sur la Première Race*, in Daniel, *Histoire de France*, vol. ii, p. 121 *et seq.*

Hénault, Ch., *Nouvel Abregé Chronologique de l'Histoire de France*, Paris, 1788, 5 vols.

——, (Abbé Boudot?), *Histoire Critique de l'Etablissement des Français dans les Gaules*, Paris, 1801, 2 vols.

Journal Historique de la République des Lettres, Sept.-Oct., 1732.

Journal des Sçavans, March, 1677, April, 1791.

Leibnitz, G. W., *Oeuvres*, ed. Foucher de Careil, Paris, 1859-65, 6 vols., vol. iv, pt. ii.

——, ed. Thurot et Desrez (*Panthéon Littéraire*), Paris, 1840.

——, *Essai sur l'origine des Français*, in Leber, vol. i, p. 97.

Leboeuf, Abbé, *Etat des habitants du Soissonnais avant la conquête des Gaules par les Francs*, Paris, 1735.

Lelong, J., *Bibliothèque historique de la France... avec des notes critiques et historiques*, Paris, 1719.

Lézardière, Marie-Pauline de, *Théorie des Lois Politiques de la Monarchie Française*, Paris, 1844, 4 vols.

——, *Ecrits inédits, avec introd. et notes par E. Carcassonne*, Paris, 1927.

Liron, Dom Jean, *Singularitez historiques et littéraires*, Paris, 1734-40, 4 vols.

Lombard, A., *La correspondance de l'Abbé Dubos*, Paris, 1913.

Longuemare, G. de, *Dissertation sur la chronologie des rois Mérovingiens*, Paris, 1748.

Longuerue, Abbé de, *Recueil d'Opuscules*, Genève, 1769.

Mably, G. B. de, *Oeuvres Complètes*, Lyon, 1796, 12 vols.

——, *Observations sur l'histoire de France*, Kehll, 1788, 3 vols.

Montesquieu, Ch-L., *Esprit des Lois*, ed. with notes of Voltaire, Mably, etc., Paris, Garnier, 1922, 2 vols.

——, *Lettres Persanes*, ed. Tourneux, Paris, 19—, 2 vols.

——, *Considérations sur les Causes de la Grandeur des Romains et de leur Décadence*, ed. Franceschi, Paris, 19—.

——, *Correspondance*, ed. Gebelin et Morize, Paris, 1914, 2 vols.

Montfaucon, Dom B., *Monumens de la Monarchie française*, 1729-33, 5 vols.

Moreau, F., *Discours de l'Histoire de France*, 1777.

Ordonnances des Rois de France, Paris, 1723 *et seq.*, 20 vols.

Rapin-Thoyras, P. de, *Histoire d'Angleterre*, La Haye, 1724, 8 vols.

——, *Rapin-Thoyras' History of England*, trans. and continued by N. Tindal, London, 1726, 20 vols.

Rochefort, R. de, *Dissertation sur l'Origine des Francs* in *Recueil*, Paris, 1748.

Rousseau, J. J., *Discours sur...l'Inégalité Parmi les Hommes*, ed. Muller et Vaillant, London, 1922.

Sieyès, E. J., *Qu' Est-ce que le Tiers-Etat?* with *Essai sur les Privilèges*, ed. Champion, Paris, 1888.

——, *Qu Est-ce que le Tiers-Etat?*, 2nd ed. (?) 1789.

St. Aubin, Le Gendre de, *Antiquités de la nation et de la Monarchie française*, Paris, 1741.

Thouret, J. G., *Abrégé des Révolutions,* ed. G. F. A. Thouret, Paris, an IX (1801).

Tournemine, P. René, *Réflexions sur la Dissertation de Leibniz touchant l'origine des Français*, in *Mémoires pour l'Histoire des Sciences et des Beaux-Arts*, vol. 61.

Vaissette, Dom Joseph, *Dissertation sur l'origine des Français*, Paris, 1722.

Velly, Abbé, *Histoire de France*, 1755, 4 vols.

Vertot, René A., Abbé de, *Dissertation* [*sur*]...*la veritable origine des Français*, in Leber, vol. i, p. 43.

Voltaire, François, *Oeuvres*, ed. Beuchot, *Paris*, 1829-40, 72 vols.

VII. Secondary Sources

Albert, Paul, *La littérature française au 17ème siècle*, Paris, 1875.

——, *La littérature française au 18ème siècle*, Paris, 1875.

Allen, J. W., *A History of Political Thought in the 16th Century*, New York, 1928.

Aubertin, C., *Histoire de la Langue et de la Littérature françaises au Moyen-âge*, Paris, 1883, 2 vols.

Barckhausen, H. A., *Montesquieu, Ses Idées et ses Oeuvres*, Paris, 1907.

Baudrillart, H., *J. Bodin et son temps. Tableau des Théories Politiques au 16ème siècle*, Paris, 1853.

Boissier, G., *Tacite*, Paris, 1903.

Brissaud, J., *Un Libéral au 17ème siècle: Claude Joly*, Paris, 1898.

Brunner, H., *Deutsche Rechtsgeschichte*, Leipzig, 1887, 2 vols.

——, " Sippe und Wergeld," *Zeitschrift der Savigny-Stiftung*, vol. xvi, 1882.

Carré, Henri, *La Noblesse de France et l'opinion publique au 18ème siècle*, Paris, 1920.

Chateaubriand, F., *Les Martyrs*, Paris, 1852.

——, *Etudes ou Discours historiques*, Paris, 1833.

Cohen, G., *Les Ecrivains français en Hollande dans la première moitié du 17ème siècle*, Paris, 1920.

Dareste, R. de la Chavanne, *François Hotman*, Paris, 1850.

Dezeimeris, *Renaissance des lettres à Bordeaux*, Bordeaux, 1899.

Faguet, Emile, *Dix-Septième Siècle: Etudes Littéraires*, Paris, 1903.

——, *Dix-Huitième Siècle: Etudes Littéraires*, Paris, 19—.

Flint, R., *Historical Philosophy in France and French Belgium and Switzerland*, New York, 1894.

Fournel, V., *La littérature indépendante et les écrivains oubliés du 17ème Siècle*, Paris, 1866.

Franck, A., *Réformateurs et Publicistes de l'Europe, Dix-Septième Siècle*, Paris, 1881.

——, *Réformateurs . . . , Dix-Huitième Siècle*, Paris, 1893.

Fustel de Coulanges, N. D., *Histoire des Institutions Politiques de l'Ancienne France*, Paris, 1888-92, 6 vols.

Gottschalk, L., *Era of the French Revolution*, New York, 1929.

Havet, J., *Questions Mérovingiennes*, 1885.

Hayes, C. J. H., *Essays on Nationalism*, New York, 1926.

Kurth, G., *Histoire Poétique des Mérovingiens*, Paris, 1893.

Larroque, D. de, *Vie de François Eudes de Mézeray*, Amsterdam, 1726.

Levillain, Léon, "Le Baptême de Clovis," *Bibliothèque de l'Ecole des Chartes*, Paris, 1906.

Méaly, P., *Publicistes de la Réforme sous François II et Charles IX*, Paris, 1903.

Michelet, J., *Histoire de France*, Paris, 1879, 19 vols.

Morgan, B. T., *Histoire du Journal des Sçavans*, Paris, 1928.

Paul-Boncour, J., *Le Fédéralisme Economique*, Paris, 1900.

——, *La République et la décentralisation*, Paris, 1923.

Poirson, A., *Histoire du Règne de Henri IV*, Paris, 1865-6, 4 vols.

Quinet, E., *France et Allemagne*, ed. Cestre, Oxford, 1908.

Reynaud, L., *Français et Allemands*, Paris, 1930.

Reynolds, B., *Proponents of Limited Monarchy in 16th Century France: Francis Hotman and Jean Bodin*, New York, 1931.

Savigny, F. C., de, *Histoire du Droit Romain au Moyen-Age*, trans. Guenoux, Paris, 1839.

Sée, Henri, *Les Idées Politiques en France au 17ème Siècle*, Paris, 1923.

——, *Les Idées Politiques en France au 18ème Siècle*, Paris, 1920.

Thierry, Augustin, *Dix Ans d'Etudes Historiques*, 12ème ed., 1874.

——, *Essai sur l'histoire de la formation et des progrès du Tiers-Etat*, 15ème ed., 1880.

——, *Lettres sur l'histoire de France*, 14ème ed., 1874.

——, *Récits des Temps Mérovingiens, précédés de Considérations sur l'Histoire de France*, Paris, 1846.

Urbain, Ch., *Ecrits et Lettres Politiques de Fénelon*, Paris, 1920 (1921).

Wertheimer, M., *The Pan-German League*, New York, 1924.

INDEX

271